Other books in the Nuffield Primary History Project series

Teaching the Life in Tudor Times History Study Unit
    by John Fines, Jon Nichol and Ray Verrier
    (edited by Jacqui Dean)

Teaching the Ancient Greece History Study Unit
    by John Fines, Jon Nichol and Ray Verrier

Teaching Key Stage One History
    by Ray Verrier
    (edited by Jon Nichol)

John Fines Professor Fines is widely recognized as Britain's leading authority on the teaching of history in schools. All of his ideas are firmly based upon a continuing wealth of classroom experience. In particular, he has pioneered the use of drama and storytelling in the teaching of history. Based in West Sussex, he is currently working on approaches to teaching the History National Curriculum.

Jon Nichol Dr Nichol has spent the last twenty-five years trying to put some of the soul back into history teaching. As the author of several series of books for children, throughout his work he has emphasized the teaching and learning of history as an enjoyable and stimulating activity that develops pupil thinking, with such thinking securely based on, and reflecting, the evidence that has survived from the past.

Jacqui Dean Jacqui Dean has taught in schools and university in South Africa, Australia and England. She teaches history extensively at KS1 and KS2 and has based her Nuffield Primary History materials upon this practice. Currently she is a lecturer at the University of Exeter specializing in primary history.

Paul Flux As headteacher of a primary school in Somerset, Paul Flux has been able to develop his school into a recognized centre for excellence in the teaching of history. Currently, these developments include a range of active learning approaches, including the use of CD-ROMs, drama, classroom archaeology and pupils learning through artefacts.

Ray Verrier With John Fines, Ray Verrier has played a major role in the development of drama as a teaching medium in schools. He has been a teacher and a teacher-trainer. Within the Nuffield Project, he has produced a range of stimulating approaches to the teaching and learning of history at Key Stage One, drawing on his extensive work in primary schools. This hands-on approach, in partnership with class teachers, has developed methods that are widely adaptable to any KS1 classroom.

All of the authors are members of the Nuffield Primary History Project Team, which is based at the University of Exeter's School of Education. The NPHP team is building support networks of teachers within LEAs and runs in-service courses nationally.

TEACHING PRIMARY HISTORY

John Fines

Jon Nichol

with
Jacqui Dean
Paul Flux
Ray Verrier

First published in Great Britain by Heinemann Educational Publishers
Halley Court, Jordan Hill, Oxford OX2 8EJ
a division of Reed Educational and Professional Publishing Ltd

MELBOURNE AUCKLAND
FLORENCE PRAGUE MADRID ATHENS
SINGAPORE KUALA LUMPUR TOKYO SÃO PAULO
CHICAGO PORTSMOUTH NH MEXICO CITY
IBADAN GABORONE JOHANNESBURG
KAMPALA NAIROBI

Typeset by Books Unlimited (Nottm) NG19 7QZ
Printed by Ashford Colour Press, Gosport.
Illustrated by Oxford Illustrators, Jon Soffe

00
10 9 8 7 6 5 4 3

ISBN 0 435 32172 2

British Library Cataloguing in Publication Data is available
from the British Library on request.

This book is for Anthony Tomei

Acknowledgements
The Publishers would like to thank the following for permission to reproduce
photographs:

The Bridgeman Art Library p. 133; Belvoir Castle p. 135; Syon House p. 51b; Jacqui
Dean p. 87; Paul Flux p. 62; Michael Holford p. 51t; Chris Honeywell cover, p. 146;
Hulton Getty Picture Collection pp. 126, 143; Topham Picturepoint p. 141.

The authors would like to thank the following: *Jon Nichol* The staff and children of
Lanscore Primary School, Janet Postance, Chris Harris, Jill Peters, Norma Edwards,
Laura Austin, Clive Marriot, Graham Fisher and Carrie Keenan. *John Fines* Ro Linck,
West Wittering School; John Warwick, Michael Ayres School; Anne Farmer and Jenn
Williams, Birdham School; Nina Siddall at North Mundham, Clapton and Patching
Schools; Stevan Radoja, Netley School, Camden; Sue Edwards, Lorne Noble and
Tony Hopkins, Midhurst Intermediate; and all the wonderful children. *Jacqui Dean*
Jane Cross and Tony Winfield, St Peters C. of E. Primary School, Harrogate; and
Andrea Budge, Sheena Berry and Pam Sedge, Central First School, Exeter. *Paul Flux*
Sally Flux and the staff and children of West Huntspill Primary School. *Ray Verrier*
The staff and children of Hartsplain Primary School. Thanks to all the project staff, in
particular Jennie Vass, our much imposed-on secretary.

The personal voice: Throughout this book, members of the Nuffield Primary team
have used the personal voice when describing their part in lessons and lesson
planning. The six different individuals involved have decided not to separately
identify themselves, but to be a personal, but anonymous 'I' in this context.

Contents

Illustrations

Preface
The Nuffield Primary History Project

In 1991 the Nuffield Foundation gave its support to a new primary history project which aimed to examine the National Curriculum and explore its implications for the teaching of primary history. During the past five years John Fines, Jon Nichol, Jacqui Dean and Ray Verrier have worked alongside classroom teachers in a wide range of schools, experiencing the reality of primary history teaching and learning.

What we did was to teach the full range of the National Curriculum in history, at least twice, and in some cases, four times. We did this in a wide variety of settings, from tiny country schools with a total enrolment of 43, to huge triple deckers in London; from schools in the urban North, to schools in the suburban South. We taught good children and wild children, clever children and those called special – we tried the lot.

Part of our aim was to provide narratives of these varied experiences. We felt that at this time of great change, the last thing teachers needed was theoretical statements about how things might happen. What we could best do would be to say, quite simply, here is what happened to *us* teaching the Greeks. It might give you a laugh and stimulate you to think just how *you* want to do it. We list our resources in case you want to take on board any of our practical ideas, and we give examples of children's work so that you can see some comparisons with the children in your own class. In this, as in all things, we have tried to be scrupulously honest, and have not edited the children's work at all.

NPHP's five principles

Throughout, the Project's work has been based on 'doing history', as encapsulated in the five principles below:

1 Questioning History is about asking and answering questions, and above all, getting children to ask questions.

2 Challenges In both our materials and in the questions we ask of children, we challenge them to persist, to speculate, to make connections, to debate issues, to understand the past from the inside.

3 Integrity and economy of sources We teach real history, so that what we use are authentic sources of history. More wide-ranging and useful questions can be asked of a few well chosen sources, than from an unfocused jumble.

4 Depth Real historical knowledge, even at primary level, demands study in depth. Only by getting deeply inside the past can pupils develop expertise and confidence.

5 Accessibility We make history accessible to all children by starting with what the children can do and building on that. This is done by using a wide variety of teaching approaches, including well paced whole-class teaching, co-operative pair work and group work.

At the heart of the curriculum

A good part of the business of teaching history is to recognize the place of history at the heart of the curriculum. History is interesting and there is a lot of it, enough so that at all stages, and in all other parts of the curriculum, learning can take place via history. It doesn't need to be thought of as an item contending with all the subjects in an over-full curriculum – history using the right approach can be the real heart of it all, the centre of the wheel from which all of the spokes radiate.

Reflection Using this book

This book deals with the principles underlying the teaching of history, the planning of a programme of study, schemes of work and individual lessons and the range of teaching strategies and approaches you can adopt.

To support your own study we have included reflections that highlight what we feel are teaching issues. Our first reflection refers to the five principles listed above.

- Think about how you currently teach history.
- How does it reflect the NPHP's five principles?
- If you agree with the principles, how might you change your current practice?

Introduction: Precepts and Practice

History in the context of teaching has two meanings. There are the findings of historians – their histories – and the process of enquiry that led to their conclusions. History as enquiry is based upon the mostly random surviving sources that come to us from the past. At no stage is history a body of definitive knowledge. Historical enquiry results in propositions for debate, and there are as many histories as historians.

Since it is history as a process of enquiry that we teach in schools, it must be done in terms of investigation and debate.

Pupils working like historians Involving children in the process of enquiry means that they engage in genuine historical learning activities from which they construct their own views of the past, that is, their own histories. Children's histories, however, must be rooted in the authentic record of the past, otherwise they are fiction. Here the historian questions rigorously the integrity of sources. Without seeing the source in its own context, the historian cannot evaluate its worth as evidence. Yet to set a source in context, the historian must use imagination and experience of life. Thus in history in the classroom, imagination, questioning, critical awareness and scepticism must work hand in hand, with the teacher supporting the pupil at every stage in making sense of the record of the past. Many children equals many histories, but for each one to be complete it must reach the stage of presentation. This too can take many forms, including poetry, drama or display.

Economy of sources Since knowledge of history is based on sources, it might seem the more sources the merrier. In history we need at times to survey all available sources, but then to focus on a manageable amount of evidence from which we may ask questions about authenticity and use. In classroom terms, this is the function of the teacher through lesson planning and resource provision.

The narrower the focus, the more intensive and rigorous the questioning of a source must be, and it is our experience that an economy in resourcing is also best in the classroom. Often we use only one document, one picture, one object or one story to work on in depth.

Challenge

However, this economy is not advised as a way of making history easy or simplistic. Indeed we have noted throughout that it is only when you use challenging materials that you get a good response. Questioning drives the enquiry process forward. Children must be faced with open, speculative questions, either their own or the teacher's. In pushing forward the enquiry the children must refine and focus the initial questions and develop their own. Within a co-operative pattern of learning involving both the teacher and the children, the pupils must be essentially in charge of their own work.

Study in depth

Our experience on the NPHP has taught us that the more pupils go into depth, the more professional they become, the more confident they grow in their abilities and the more they treasure the knowledge they find. This knowledge, and the experiences, skills and values learned in its accumulation, means that the pupil acquires the expertise to 'do history'.

Within a study in depth, we include the development of an understanding of the concepts, themes, information and chronology needed to make sense of the topic being studied. By the end of their study in depth the pupils will have acquired the outline knowledge and skills the National Curriculum requires. But, it will be real, significant and meaningful knowledge, anchored in a specific context. By definition, any genuine historical knowledge must arise from study in depth.

Accessibility

History, by its very nature, involves pupils in reading and writing. Here we see clearly the divisions between those who can and those who can't easily use written materials. History reveals a hidden past, hard to get at and understand and riddled with value-loaded questions. So, how do we make it accessible to all children?

The teacher is the key, but it must be a teacher working with all the children in a co-ordinated way, making the written sources in particular accessible to all pupils using verbal, visual and enactive media. We see teaching and learning as both a social and an individual activity, with the teacher, crucially, at the centre of the social dimension. The advantages of getting all the children close to you so that you can see their eyes, spin your questions to everybody and judge with care their reactions is clear and obvious to the NPHP team.

Similarly by going through all our materials and questions verbally with the whole class so that everybody has a chance to understand, the least literate children have a chance to show how clever they are and to take courage from their successes. The challenge of having everybody working on the same real question (at their own level of ability) can thus prove viable, and wherever the result is at least partially verbal (as in debate or drama), it is a joy to see how well those children whose written work usually lets them down can do. This does not mean, of course, that we do not at all times stress the importance of reading and writing in our work, and drive all children to attempt to do their best in these fields of learning and expression.

The teacher as expert

The teacher's role is that of an expert who directs, manages and supports the pupils' learning by drawing upon his or her own knowledge of history: both the record of the past and how that is treated to produce history. The teacher transforms such knowledge into teaching strategies that engage pupils using historical sources to create their own, personal views of history.

Teaching strategies, the craft of the history teacher, have been at the heart of the NPHP, ranging from approaches to the use of artefacts, pictures and documents, to storytelling, drama and site visits. The strategies provide teachers with a reservoir of ideas to adopt, adapt and build upon in creating their own teaching programmes tailored to their specific needs.

Managing the classroom

The children's learning needs to be managed and guided throughout. Setting the scene first is vital. A great teacher, Dorothy Heathcote, once said 'Think where you want to start the lesson, and then take five steps back'. The NPHP has helped us understand the central importance of this principle. The first minutes of a lesson are crucial, and if you get it wrong there, it is hard to recoup. We go in as teachers, full of our plans, of the exciting material and questions we are to use, inspired by knowledge itself – indeed we have quite forgotten what it is like to be at the start of the process of learning. So we must restrain our enthusiasm and give time for settling down, for building confidence, for putting the first planks down on which the rest is to be built.

And by planks we don't necessarily mean information. Often we try to make something difficult accessible to children by starting with something they know and can do with confidence. Recently one of the team had set to a class of ten year olds the hard task of reading substantial tracts of Anaximander and Heraclitus in order to think about the Greek view of the world. He knew what he wanted at the end; it was the beginning that would count. Eventually he decided to spend the first half hour (half the lesson) getting the children to list the contents of a modern scientific laboratory. Then he looked at the list and ticked those items the Ancient Greeks might have had. It was, of course, pathetically small, and it gave the children a structure by which they could approach the texts with the question, 'Given how little they had, how well did they do?'

Pacing a lesson

Starting right is vital to success, but the other element that governs the rest of the teaching is pace. The formula for correct pace in teaching is simple to write but complex to achieve: you must make the children feel that they are hurtling ahead whilst really you are going slowly enough for everyone to keep up. This is something we can do, but is hard to describe because it is a function of the teacher's role as an actor. For example, we use the pressure of time a lot – 'Only three minutes to do this, hurry, hurry' – and that hides the fact that we may use the next twelve minutes hearing the responses of every group or indeed of every child in the class. Then more scurry and flurry, but we know where everyone is and have time to devise the next necessary step. Part of this game is for the teacher to give him or herself time to think so that when the next task is set it has a chance of being the right one!

Much of our work necessarily stresses the importance of whole class teaching, but children need sometimes to work on a one-to-one basis, sometimes to work alone and sometimes to work in groups with or without the teacher.

Conclusion

The NPHP's precepts underpin the project's central tenet, that school history is a creative art in which the teacher and pupils construct their own histories on the basis of available sources. Questioning drives the process forward. This results in a piece of history that the pupil or pupils may communicate in a variety of ways. The form of teaching depends largely upon what you believe history to be. What is the nature of history? How do you go about mounting an historical enquiry? How do you reach conclusions and substantiate them? This book will address these and related issues, hopefully presenting history as a discipline accessible from a myriad of starting points, using the full range of teaching methods.

1 Doing History

Of all the historians who have set out to explain in layman's language the nature of history, we are convinced that the most successful has been Jack Hexter. He shows that history is an activity, a process, and that those who make a living from it are members of a profession. It is from him that we have borrowed the idea of 'doing history'. The phrase seems to us to describe effectively the very personal, positive and active approach to the subject which we favour in the school context.

This is not to fall in with the rather twee notion of children being historians, rather we see children as acting like historians, doing their work the historian's way, following the rule book of historians and understanding that what they are doing is historical, and how that differs from doing English or Geography. In our teaching of history pupils interact with the teacher at all stages of the enquiry and its resolution. We present 'doing history' in the classroom as a collaborative activity with the teacher in the driving seat. The idea of pupils being let loose as creative, independent souls, 'doing' their own history while the teacher assiduously studies *Sporting Life* or, more likely, the situations vacant column of the *TES*, is daft. So let us first define what 'doing history' consists of, then describe the elements that are involved, and finally illustrate it with an example from the classroom.

- First, we must be examining a topic from the past and raising questions about it.
- Second, we must search for a wide range of relevant sources to provide evidence to help us answer our questions.
- Third, we must struggle to understand what the sources are saying (and each source-type has a different language) so that we can understand them in their own terms.
- Fourth, we must reason out and argue our answers to the questions and support them with well chosen evidence.
- Finally, we must communicate our answers for the process to be complete.

History as a view of the past is something that KS1 and KS2 pupils construct for themselves from working on sources under the teacher's guidance. The past can be made to make sense from a multitude of perspectives, from a children's cartoon, to a Flashman novel based on the continuing exploits into adult life of the disgraced villain of Tom Brown's schooldays, to the pontifical perspective of *The Times'* leader writer. By definition, any history is an interpretation. The validity of the interpretation rests upon the sources used. Their nature, range, extent and provenance determine how well the account can stand up to a critical buffeting. In being critical we adopt an empirical stance in the collection, marshalling, analysis, ordering and deployment of information.

The first and second records

We create history from processing the available sources – what Jack Hexter calls history's 'first record' (Hexter, 1972). The 'first record' covers both the raw materials of history, the original, firsthand sources, and the later interpretations. We bring to bear upon the 'first record' our own wealth of experience, what Hexter defines as 'the second record'. The 'second record' is individual to each of us. Much of it is wholly personal and private, hidden away from public view until we choose to reveal it. It contains knowledge, expertise, judgements, interests, intuitions and values nurtured through many years, for example, a knowledge of art, economics or anthropology. Hexter argues that in historical thinking you use your 'second record' to create a history from the 'first record'.

While children obviously have their own 'second records', by definition they are relatively unsophisticated, although we must not underestimate the extent and nature of pupils' knowledge and experience. In dealing with sensations of pain, hunger, desire and anger, with experiences of family life and marital conflict, many of our children are only too knowledgeable and experienced. When a pupil 'does history' the teacher plays the crucial role in directly or indirectly extending the pupil's own as yet underdeveloped 'second record', sometimes providing a surrogate 'second record' for the pupil to use to make sense of the 'first record'.

Equally important, the class can pool all of its members' 'second records' through talking in pairs and groups and teacher-led class discussion. Pair, group work and whole class teaching thus become central to the process of developing children's understanding. The collective knowledge and intelligence of a class of children is often far greater than our own.

Doing history in the classroom – Michael Ayres

An example of 'doing history' with children is the work done by the NPHP at Michael Ayres School in Bognor Regis. The big question we had to ask was, 'Who was he?'

In the school were some memorials to this man – a three-in-one stained-glass window rescued from a demolished church remembering him and his wife, two formal photographs of him, one as a young Royal Flying Corps pilot, one as an elderly man, a plaque recording the naming of the school, a box of photographs and newspaper cuttings and a couple of addresses of people who knew him. From these sources it was clear that he had been a distinguished local Medical Officer of Health who had played a significant part in community affairs and had had a particular concern for poor children, running a care fund to relieve want.

The local record office had his annual reports. They gave an interesting picture of a man very concerned with the environment, with improving living conditions and health and, above all, concerned with saving children from unnecessary suffering. John Warwick, the class teacher, also found some newspaper reports at the local library and other documents from a local history collection housed at the Bognor Regis campus of the Chichester Institute.

Next I went to see Mrs. Gray, his former housekeeper, now verging on 80, and Mr. Allatt, only slightly younger, who had been Michael Ayres' secretary and factotum. They spoke of him with such warmth and delight, almost with reverence, so that I began to see that here was someone worth devoting attention to, someone who should be known about.

Yet all we had as resources were some rather dull old snaps, some dreary documents, two elderly people and a decaying grave – could these be the successful ingredients for a half term's work? Could it be fun? Could it be inspirational?

The 33 nine year old children in the Year 4 class were a cheerful crew, full of energy, anxious to please, not very confident in their ability and from a mixed background, including a large council estate with a high level of unemployment. Some of the children knew about trouble, poverty and the difficulties of life already. But they were not downcast. The lessons went as follows:

Lesson 1

In the first lesson I began by asking the children whether they thought it was possible to find out about people by just looking at them. They were a bit dubious when I asked them to look at my colleague Ray Verrier and have a go, but they had a tentative attempt. Then I asked them to look just at Ray and turn their backs on me. How well could they describe me from memory? They began to get more confidence and see that this was a bit like a game, rather than a test, so spoke more readily.

Then I showed them the two portraits of Michael Ayres, one as a young Royal Flying Corps pilot, and one as an old man. We started with the old man, and they observed detail first – spotted tie, suit, hair brushed back, spots on his skin like splodges, round eyes, kind mouth, nose pushed in a little – maybe 84 years old. With the younger man they were more confident – this is to do with the war because he has medals. He's about 29. Big nose – has been broken. Pilot – he has wings, buttoned jacket, white shirt, black tie.

Who is this? Of course they know because they pass one of the pictures every day – he is Dr Michael Ayres. Given some more pictures, could you find out more? In groups of three, they looked at the snaps and tried to write down three things about Dr Ayres.

After about fifteen minutes the children reported back and they had clearly learned a lot. John Warwick, the class teacher, asked them to write up their observations neatly and use the photograph for making careful drawings. This took place in class, after a break, with the children examining the photo closely using magnifying glasses.

Lesson 2

In the second lesson I reviewed the ideas that had been generated from the pictures, and told the children that they had a much harder task now. We would be using documents, which were hard to read. But first I asked them just to glance over the surface of their document and try to find just one word or phrase that could stand as a title for the document, that would say what it was about.

For a group of not specially able nine year olds this was indeed a daunting task, but they very quickly came up with responses, including words I would have thought would baffle them, such as 'nutrition' and 'immunization'. So I put them back to the documents, saying that if they were that good they could do something much harder. Each group of three was to find out three things about Dr Ayres from their document and write them down.

In the last part of this lesson we decided to try out an approach through role play, with a view to thickening the texture of the children's knowledge by personal experience. Ray directed the children's attention to one of the documents, about council house repairs. He then told the children that I would shortly try to 'be' Dr Ayres for them, and would visit a house in the locality. They were to watch and judge whether I got it right.

I arrived in a chauffeured car and addressing four pupils at random, quizzed them about their health and living conditions. After a moment's surprise the children joined in and indicated that things weren't too good in their house, mainly because the roof leaked. I promised to have it repaired and drove off.

Ray now asked the children whether they thought I had got it right. They thought Dr Ayres would have come on a bicycle, that he would have waved cheerily to people on the way, but that at the house he would have been 'stricter'. I replayed the scene with another group who raised a new issue of a child who wouldn't go to school because of bullying. Clearly the children were taking to this mode of work like ducks to water, and we would have to do more.

Lesson 3   At the beginning of this session Ray reviewed their findings with the children in a document he had prepared for them:

THINGS WE HAVE FOUND OUT FROM DOCUMENTS ABOUT MICHAEL AYRES

- some children needed milk but could not get it
- some children were not in school
- he started the Children's Care Fund
- children were short of food
- he provided honey and milk
- poor children would have free milk
- sick children were looked after by his Care Fund
- 1937 – immunization against diphtheria
- bath chairs provided for sick children
- books and clothes provided for poor children
- death of Michael Ayres
- he was chairman of the Boys' Club
- he was famous before he died
- he collected money for children
- free fresh milk for poor children
- immunization
- he was chairman of the Flower Society
- he died on a Wednesday at Bognor Hospital
- he was 85 when he died
- he looked after children whose parents had died
- he was in the Air Force
- he was a doctor
- he helped the sick
- he rescued people in the war
- he was M.O.H. (Medical Officer of Health)
- he saved the injured
- freedom from infectious diseases
- he was a kindly grey-haired man
- he was given the freedom of Michael Ayres School
- he helped raise thousands of pounds
- doctor
- M.O.H.
- helped people in the air raids
- Royal British Legion
- he worked 25 years in Bognor
- he had a three month illness before he died
- the Council named a school after him
- he helped during air raids
- gave people food

He then asked the children whether there was any way in which they could arrange the ideas under headings so that they would become more manageable. The children found this quite a hard idea, but, willing as ever, pitched in and after considerable effort came up with the following headings:

Things he did
People he helped
Raising money
What happened to him

The children discussed where the various findings on their document would fit under these headings, and the hard work they did here validated the effort Ray had put in getting their ideas back to them on a printed sheet.

The children were keen to do more role play work, so in the second part of the lesson I quickly set up five visits Dr Ayres would make:

1   to check on hygiene in an ice-cream factory
2   to ask the Council for funding to do urgent repairs to Council houses
3   to see children who had refused inoculation in school
4   to see a rat-infested house
5   to visit the worst (or as the children said, the worstest) family in Bognor.

The children had only a few minutes to prepare but were, in the event, ready for the occasion. At the factory, Dr Ayres was polite, but firm. With the Council, he was very angry when they tried to tell him there was no money. With the children who refused inoculation, he was tetchy. In the rat-infested house, he was understanding. With the dreadful family, he was very cross – they weren't even trying and refused all help.

Afterwards the children began to revise their list of Dr Ayres' qualities – he could lose his temper, he could be inquisitive, he could be quite bossy.

Lesson 4

In session four we had planned a visit to Dr Ayres' tomb and we already had our plan for eleven groups to operate on the tomb and in the area. The plan for the visit to Michael Ayres' grave cast the children as investigators, with each group set a task.

Michael Ayres' grave : the pupils' eleven tasks

1 Photograph front of tomb
2 Photograph back
3 Record words on front
4 Record words on back
5 Measure height
6 Measure width
7 Measure depth
8 Measure circle and its spars
9 Record texture by rubbing
10 Record colour by note-taking
11 Draw, for the record

Groups finishing their tasks would then go on to try the following questions:

1 Can you find other memorials as good as Michael Ayres's?
2 Can you find some better? Note in what way they are better and whose they are.
3 Is Michael Ayres' tomb like all the rest or different?
4 What is the most common type of memorial?
5 Can you find the person mentioned on the reverse of the Michael Ayres memorial?

In the event it was pouring with rain and we were not able to go as a class, although a substantial number of the children later went on their own or with parents.

We had some blown-up photographs of the tomb, so I began the session by showing these to the children and reading out the inscriptions. The front, recording Dr Ayres and his wife was no problem, but on the back was a rather mysterious inscription:

> 'Also in memory of Catherine Amelia Robins, interred elsewhere in this cemetery, who passed away on 19th June 1933, aged 70 years.'

The children worked hard on the mystery – who could she be – a sister, relative, cousin, housekeeper, mother-in-law? They were most careful and thoughtful in presenting their guesses, and we noted that this would certainly be one question we must ask of our visitors next week.

We then turned to the memorial to Dr Ayres and thought about what words we might use for him. I gave them the beginning of a sentence:

'I remember Dr Ayres, he was …'

The children very quickly produced a whole range of responses: fit, fought in the war for us, fair, friendly, caring, joyful, fantastic, exciting, posh, thoughtful, a gardener. We went on (noting that so many of our words began with the letter 'f') to do an alphabet for Dr Ayres.

Finally we worked on the questions we were going to ask the following week when Dr Ayres' housekeeper and secretary would visit us. Much follow-up work was done by the class in the ensuing week. When the visitors arrived the children were ready with a question each, which they had categorized under four headings: house, family, job, and hobbies and pastimes.

Questions for the visitors

The '**House**' questions were:
What was the inside of his house like?
What was Dr Ayres' favourite food?
What type of flowers did Dr Ayres like the most and why?
What sort of food did Dr Ayres like?
Did he like to go to restaurants?
Who looked after Dr Ayres' dog when he was at work and who took him out for a walk?
Who looked after his dog when he died?
Because he was at work all of the time did he take any notice of his dog?
What was the name of the brown and ginger dog that Michael Ayres owned?
Did Dr Ayres have any animals apart from his dog?

The '**Family**' questions were:
Do you know what his mum and dad's names were?
How long did you know Dr Michael Ayres?
Did you like Dr Ayres and if so in what way and why?
Was Dr Michael Ayres close to you in any way?
Did he have any unusual habits?
Do you know when they got married and where and did you go?
Did you know his wife? What was she like?
Did he have a brother or sister? If he did, what were their names?
How old was Dr Michael Ayres when he died because on the

documents it said 85 and in the school library it said 84?
What did Michael Ayres die of?
Did you go to Dr Ayres' funeral and how many relations went?

The '**Job**' questions were:
How many hours did he work, and what time did he get home in the evening?
How long did you work for Dr Michael Ayres?
Which part of his job did he like the best?
What jobs did he make you do when you worked for him?
How much of his money did Dr Ayres spend helping people?

The '**Hobbies and Pastimes**' questions were:
Was Dr Michael Ayres fit because in the photographs he looked fit?
Did he have any favourite hobbies?
Why did he smoke?
What brand of cigarettes did he smoke?
How many cigarettes did he smoke a day?
Did Dr Ayres collect anything, and what did he collect?

Lesson 5

The final resource we presented to the children was human – two people who had worked closely with Dr Ayres: Mrs Gray, his housekeeper and long-standing friend and Mr Allatt, who had run his office for him for eight years. We had talked with both of these people in advance and it was clear they had a great deal to offer and had no problems communicating – Mrs Gray, despite her eighty years, was lively and well capable of dealing with all situations, and Mr Allatt had considerable experience of addressing troops by the thousand, so he had no fears.

Yet it isn't that easy – just presenting older people to the young doesn't necessarily produce the best results, so we worked quite hard to get it right in advance. The class teacher worked with the children to get them to develop their questions, and we made sure they were really their questions and not adult impositions. One little girl, Rebecca Quinn, badly wanted to know about his dogs, and one boy, James Day, wanted to know the brand of cigarettes he smoked.

To make sure the children understood the answers on the day, I cast myself as secretary. As the children asked their questions and got their answers, I told them that if they heard anything important or useful to put their hands up, and then I would write it down for them on a big white board. But if no one put their hands up I would write nothing. It was their responsibility to listen and find what needed recording. Further, when they told me to write things down, I quizzed them on the best way of putting it and several children showed a good aptitude for writing a formal record. When I wrote up 'wife very pretty' Luke Mines said, 'No, that could be any woman, write "Dr Ayres's wife was very pretty"'. I was, of course, abjectly obedient and the children enjoyed the role reversal and became ever more seriously minded.

Our visitors were good and had lots of interesting things to say, including some 'secrets' that I was not allowed to record. The children sat on a hard floor for an hour and ten minutes and there was only a moment of concentration loss from just two children. At the end they were still full of questions. The children then showed our visitors round the school and they went away delighted, as did the children and our team.

The Presentation to the school

The final activity was a whole school assembly, lasting three-quarters of an hour, when the children showed the results of their work in the presence of all who had contributed. They talked, showed their pictures, repeated their role play activities with me in role as Dr Ayres. They sang and said prayers they had created. It was an inspiring occasion and also one that served a number of important educational objectives. First, in their preparation for the assembly, the pupils had to recall, select and organize from a vast amount of historical information gained over the previous weeks. Second, the assembly called upon the pupils to demonstrate their knowledge and understanding orally, visually and in writing, using a range of techniques including role play, short narratives and the writing of suitable prayers. Third, the pupils were addressing their interpretation of Dr Ayres to an audience of peers, teachers and the two visitors they had interviewed. This required of the pupils a sense of confidence in, and grasp of, the historical material they were handling. Finally, the experience helped the pupils take a further step in making the material their own.

Prior to ending the assembly with the school song, three prayers were said in memory of Dr Ayres. Mrs Gray was very moved by them, so copies were given to her.

Reflection Teaching strategies on Michael Ayres

Consider the techniques used to teach about Michael Ayres. Taking each lesson in turn, work out the teaching approaches and how they linked together.

---

2 Children Learning History

Children live in a world where scale, perception, relationships, proportion and biology are all rather different. Most children are having enough difficulty in coming to grips with their own identity, never mind trying to make some sense of the minds of a Saxon missionary, pagan priests, royalty and thanes, or the thought processes of Queen Victoria. So, caution and consideration are essential when looking at children's learning of history. Crucially, what they bring to bear upon their historical sources, their second records, can be extremely limited, yet lightened often by insight, imagination and perception denied adults. However, we should not be too condescending. Many of our children are exposed to aspects of the adult world that many of us have not experienced and, mercifully, never will.

History is a creative art. As such, history draws upon the whole range of human thinking, from the coldly logical to the wildly speculative and imaginative. What kinds of cognition are involved? How can we, as teachers, develop such mental processes in our pupils, focused on the task in hand? Our teaching of history reflects an understanding, no matter how naive it may be, of how children's thinking develops from the earliest age until they reach adulthood, and the form that such thinking takes. But one must always be cautious, bearing in mind the huge disparity in abilities, aptitudes and performance between children. Some talents will lie in writing and talking, others in art, music and dance. By the age of ten there will be some pupils with mental ages of five year olds and others whose minds are on the same level as sixteen year olds and above. Many ten year olds are demonstrably cleverer than their teachers in certain areas.

The issue of cognition becomes more pointed when we have to deal with assessment schemes which attempt to delineate the thought processes of children in a schematic and hierarchical manner – see Chapter 3. An analysis of children's thinking and learning has to map on to the elements of historical thinking analysed in Chapters 1 and 3. How much of this kind of historical learning are children capable of? When? What are the circumstances in which pupils learn best?

The child's mind   Discussion of children's thinking revolves largely around the work of Jean Piaget. As the great pioneer of developmental psychology, he still provides the focal point for current thinkers and researchers – all paths lead back to him. Piaget analysed man as a developing biological organism. Thinking is linked to the maturation of the organism, from the infant dealing with the immediate, tangible and observable to the adult pondering on the abstract, hypothetical, mystical and philosophical. The mind matures through assimilating new information, either by accommodating, adapting and integrating this with existing patterns of thinking or by using it to develop a new pattern or patterns (schema). Schema are how we store information, concepts and ideas. A sequence of schema provide blueprints for action – memory organization packages (MOPs). In terms of developing teaching strategies, MOPs are central to the transferability of ideas. We can tell what is essentially the same story, but with different characters and situations, for example, Cortes and the Aztecs, the saving of a Victorian chimney sweep and a royal visit to Bognor. How we structure the story is the same, only the context is different. If we analyse the way stories are constructed and told, we can train teachers to create their own stories, such as 'The King's Feather', (see Chapter 13), through creating their own MOPs for story making.

In history how do children make sense of the past? Throughout the process of creating their own histories pupils must have access to knowledge in a form they can understand. Jerome Bruner in his *The Course of Cognitive Growth* argued that we represent knowledge in three basic ways, through visual, pictorial representation (iconic), physical actions (enactive) and written or spoken language (symbolic). Accordingly, we can extend and deepen our understanding of a subject through thinking about it in different ways.

Translation/ transformation   A second, important theory put forward by Bruner is that the teacher and the pupils translate knowledge from a relatively inaccessible medium into a more understandable form. Children can develop their own knowledge and understanding from translating ideas into symbolic-iconic-enactive modes. For example, frequently in our teaching we tell stories or describe a scene in which we ask the children to draw a picture or pictures as we go along. Children respond enthusiastically to producing their own pictures or strip cartoons, with the quicker workers, or more able, adding titles and captions.

The Viking boat enactive learning experience

Reflection Words into pictures, pictures into words

- Study Illustration 1. Copy the picture and complete the activity. Think about the representation of knowledge, iconically, enactively and symbolically.
- Read the source below, The Sparrow in the Hall, one of the most powerful, stirring and compelling pieces ever written.
- Draw the story of the sparrow in cartoon form to represent the Christian view of man's life, including life before and after death.

The Sparrow in the Hall

(Edwin, King of Northumbria, holds a council with his chief men about accepting Christianity in AD 627. Paulinus, a missionary, had addressed the King and his council. The chief priest argues that Christianity seems to have more to offer than the old religion, which 'seems valueless and powerless'.)

Another of the King's chief men signified his agreement with this prudent argument, and went on to say: 'Your Majesty, when we compare the present life of man on earth with that time of which we have no knowledge, it seems to me like the swift flight of a single sparrow through the banqueting-hall where you are sitting at dinner on a winter's day with your thanes [nobles] and counsellors. In the midst there is a comforting fire to warm the hall; outside, the storms of winter rain or snow are raging. This sparrow flies swiftly in through one door of the hall, and out through another. While he is inside, he is safe from the winter storms; but after a few moments of comfort, he vanishes from sight into the wintry world from which he came. Even so, man appears on earth for a little while; but of what went before this life or of what follows, we know nothing. Therefore, if this new teaching has brought any more certain knowledge, it seems only right that we should follow it.' (Bede).

Enactive learning involves the children in many different kinds of role play, placing themselves in the situations of people in the past and facing them with real life choices. The idea of enactive learning underlay our teaching about a Viking boat with a class of

Year 3/4 pupils. We were studying Viking life, including boats and travel, through the medium of pupils creating their own saga. Part of the saga involved the children visiting the shipyard where their boat was being built. The question was, how would the boat builder be able to plan out the boat that they wanted, according to their specification? We were able to work out that the boat would be marked in outline with sticks stuck in the ground and string, as the ground plan.

To help us we had a detailed aerial drawing of a boat. In our teaching we used these resources:

Ball of String.
Chalk.
Playground or hall.
Aerial view, or a plan of a Viking boat.

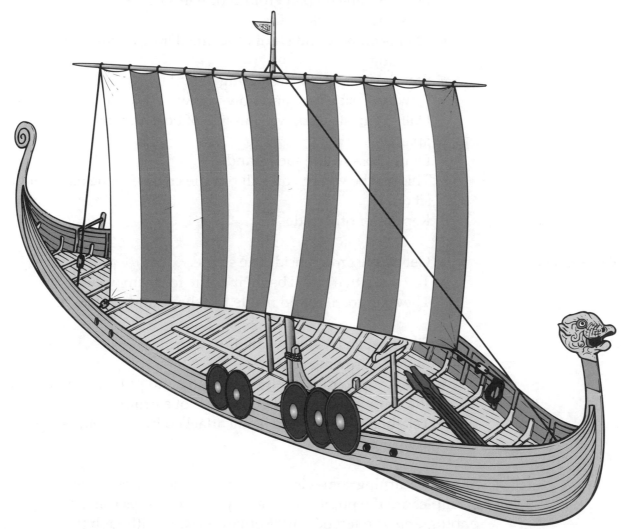

Illustration 1   *A Viking boat*

Our lesson plan **1 Introduction**	We are going to see our boat being built. What might it look like? Look at the boat plan.
2 The Plan – the Boat	Say we are going to plan out our Viking boat in the hall or playground.

Say we are going to plan out our Viking boat in the hall or playground.

- **The keel.** Pace out or measure out length. Put someone at the front and back.
  Stretch string between them, draw in keel.
- **The mast**. Stand person in middle of keel, draw circle around him or her, the mast's position.
- **The sides/width**. Work out how wide the boat will be, put pupil at widest point on each side of the boat.
  Put group in arc from bow to stern, put string around them to measure in outline the shape of one side of boat.
  Draw outline on playground or hall surface.
  Do same for second side.
- **Planks on bow and stern covering**. Draw in bow and stern covering.
- **Steering oar**. Draw in steering oar.
- **Rowing**. Ask where and how you would sit to row.
  Half group stand down one side of boat an arm's length apart.
  Draw cross where each stands.
  This will be where you will put the chests for the oarsmen to sit on.
  Repeat for other side.

3 The Voyage

- Get whole group inside the shape.
- Tell them that it will be their home for many weeks.
  They can roam round inside the shape and explore it.

4 Rowing

- Sit down on crosses, facing the stern.
- Show the rowing action.
- Get group to row together, winging and pulling their oars to the shout of command or the beat of a drum.
- Tell them that they are being attacked by an enemy ship.
  They act the scene.

Enactive learning comes in many shapes and guises. Other examples are the pupils making clay Roman lamps using a photograph as reference and Roman cooking, although the doormice weren't all that popular as a gourmet dish. How would you apply enactive learning in your own teaching?

Children and the iconic medium

Children can understand the same ideas in different media. Like Illustration 1, the artist's reconstructed historical scenes found in many primary history books can represent complex information visually. The Reflection which follows asks you to work back from such a picture as icon to the same information in a different, iconic form or as a piece of symbolic writing.

Logical and imaginative thinking

What kinds of thinking can children engage in within Bruner's iconic, enactive and symbolic forms of representation? Along a spectrum, historical thinking ranges from the formal, coldly logical, with its deductive chains of thinking to the spontaneous, warm, creative, inductive, imaginative, and speculative approach of creative thinkers.

There are three main facets to logical thinking: induction, deduction and analogical thinking. Induction is the step-by-step following of a chain of reasoning. Deductive thinking sees logical connections between separate pieces of information and supports an argument with related evidence. Analogical thinking simply says that something was like something else. Archaeologists use analogical or typological thinking to make sense of finds as follows:

Pot A has some of the features of Pot B.
Pot B in turn has some of the features of Pot C.
Pot C is similarly like Pot D.
Therefore Pot A is similar in kind to Pot D.
Pot D was found on a site where there was other evidence to date it. The evidence also provided a cultural context for Pot D.

Therefore we can make judgements about Pot A and the culture it was from.

Analogical reasoning plays a crucial part in our informed imaginative historical thinking, sparking off connections between different pieces of information.

Children live in a world of myth and fantasy, of make believe, which is peopled with monsters and dragons, good and bad fairies and superheroes. The only constraint on such thinking in history is that it must be rooted in the 'first record' of the past, and thus we must be able to trace back to its source every statement that is made.

Such imaginative thinking is fundamentally associative thinking. In thinking associatively we make links and connections between different and, often, apparently unconnected pieces of evidence. Such thinking is reflected in our pupils' creation of concept webs. To create a web we place the key word or phrase we want to illuminate, such as Queen Elizabeth, at the centre of the page. Along the legs we write a verb or phrase that links the key word or phrase to a statement at the end of the leg. Each pupil, pair or small group can produce an example:

Key Word[s]	verb or phrase along the leg	Balloon words
Queen Elizabeth	had	bad teeth
Queen Elizabeth	was	queen for a long time

You can try the same approach yourself: using the Reflection on page 19.

Looking at the historical imagination

Tied into such associative thinking are our affective, emotional and imaginative selves that help bring the past to life. There are many facets to historical imagination (see *Lee*, 1984; *Little*, 1983). We would like to stress five of these: imaging, sensing, inferring, colligation and getting pupils to share the thoughts and feelings of people in the past – empathy.

Imaging is the ability to form a picture in the mind of what the past physically looked like. Thus imaging can result in the pictorial reconstructions of artists like Alan Sorrell and Peter Connally, and the verbal imagery of novelists such as Rosemary Sutcliff.

Sensing is related to imaging, but involves the smells, tastes, sounds and feel of a bygone age. Sensing plays a major part in our historical teaching, ranging from cooking Roman food, listening to music, poetry and stories of the Dark Ages, pulling sledges of coal in a nineteenth century coalmine or climbing through a space the size of one of the chimneys in Buckingham Palace.

Inferring entails filling in gaps in the historical story through inferring what might have been and checking this against the existing evidence. If we know a King was at two places on different dates we can work out that he marched between them and even his route. A favourite is to tell our children we are going on a pilgrimage to Canterbury. Soon they are busy with atlases working out their routes, bearing in mind that they are travelling on foot and that there are no modern roads, towns, hotels or other amenities.

Colligation is central to 'doing history'. Through this process

The Great Farmhouse Attack

Dear Mum and dad,

In 1642, 31 august we planned an attack at Farmhouse farm.

We marched down a track with heavy armour on and thick clothes. The farmhouse was grand, crops all around it and animals running around. I went to the barn and pulled a cart out, then I quietly in to get the horse, but he went mad so I whipped him, he calmed down. I tied the horse to the cart and tied them to a post so I could get my goods in.

John and Tim shot the farmer + wife while their children ran off and hid.

First I went all round the house to see if any one was in. Only servants and two dogs were there, I killed 1 servant with sword and a dog with a gun. Then I went to the kitchen and got 3 buckets.

Then I went to the well and filled them up, I put them in the cart. Then I got 6 bales of hay to sleep on and put them in the cart. Then I got 6 chickens, oh how the smelled! I killed them instantly. I got 3 sheep, 2 cows and tied them to cart. After every one had got their goods we made a fire and burnt the house. I felt a bit hot and sweaty, a bit sad to. We threw the farmer + his wife the fire and watched it till it died down. Then I got on the horse and drove back.

Love
from
Amelia.
× ×

Illustration 2   *Pupil work*

pupils select separate pieces of information from their sources and see links between them to create an understanding of what occurred. The story forms a coherent, connected pattern that makes sense of the past.

The thoughts and feelings of people in the past : empathy A central aspect of the historical imagination is to try to understand what people in the past were thinking and feeling, to be them. Story telling, drama and simulation are powerful ways for pupils to enter into people's minds and take on their roles, their thoughts and feelings. Storytelling is a wonderful medium of bringing the past to life, presenting information in a coherent, connected form. Written and told stories range from narrative, poetry, fiction and documentary to film script. Role play enables children to enter into the spirit of an age. Such empathetic thinking can be small-scale. Continually we bring the children face to face with the situations that confronted people in the past and the problems they had to grapple with. Almost every lesson has one such problem-solving episode, be it children in the role of marriage guidance counsellors to Henry VIII, to asking Saxon villagers how they would react to the news that a band of Vikings is approaching.

The use of both logical and imaginative thinking was reflected in our Local History study with Year 3 and 4 children working on the Civil War in Crediton. We had visited the local museum in the church and re-created a Civil War trooper from the remains of his armour stored there. After using outlines of troopers to produce a collage of Cromwell's army, basing their dress on the museum remains and book illustrations, we mustered the troops on the local meadow. Next we gave the pupils a poem to work on. Following the poem we created a camp of soldiers, cold, tired and hungry in the early morning. They decided to raid a local farm. The raiding party trudged around the classroom, the farmhouse came in sight, the raid was mounted. That evening the troopers wrote home. Amelia's letter (Illustration 2), tells the tale. Here we see a heady mix of factual information and informed imagination, woven together into a gripping narrative.

Social learning   A central, vital feature in the teaching of history is social learning, that is, children learning from working cooperatively with the teacher and with each other. Here they must work in pairs, small and large groups and as a whole class, sharing ideas, jointly solving problems and reaching conclusions.

Organizing group work

In terms of organizing group work there are important implications:

resources The resources must be appropriate to the task.

skills The children should be skilled enough to undertake the task.

size Groups should be no bigger than four; in a class of 36 children this means there will be at least nine groups.

composition What is the best way of organizing the groups? Do you want mixed ability? Setting according to ability – with different groups having different roles – can be worth considering. Psychological mixing – extrovert in a group of introverts? Mixed gender? Forced mixing of children who do not work together, ever, and even hate each other?

pattern Make sure that the starting, research and presentation phases are properly organized.

noise Children working together make a noise. There is an acceptable, working noise, and there is an unacceptable, non-working row. The first is a beelike hum, the second is a shrill staccato of irregular volume. Riots can usually be recognized immediately!

Learning theory

What are the optimum circumstances in which learning can occur? A powerful argument is that the pupil should only move on to the next part of a task when s/he has mastered what s/he is working on. Learning moves at the speed of the child's achievements. This is a deadly serious point that is overlooked all too often, that is, that children should master a task before moving on to the next one. For example, when we first taught the Tudors, we felt that we had to rush from our half-finished houses, leaving confusion and chaos behind us. The message is clear – teach at the pace of the pupils, working on a few things in depth and detail, using the particular to illuminate the general. This is blindingly obvious, until you realize that much of education is based on a timetable in which many pupils rush to the next task before they have learned anything.

3 History in the Curriculum

Planning for teaching the National Curriculum involves five elements. In this chapter we consider each in turn:

- The requirements of the National Curriculum for history at KS1 and KS2
- Planning history in relation to the rest of the curriculum over the two years of KS1 and the four years of KS2
- Planning a history study unit
- Planning individual lessons
- Planning for assessment.

Post-Dearing we have a framework curriculum: teachers can use their professional judgement in their history teaching. The new history curriculum has three related components: the key elements and concepts, the programme of study and the attainment target.

The key elements and concepts

The five key elements – chronology, range and depth of historical understanding, interpretations of history, historical enquiry and organization and communication of knowledge – are the focus of the new history curriculum. They provide a good description of what doing history entails. If you plan and evaluate your teaching in relation to the key elements, you won't go far wrong.

Underlying concepts

Within the key elements are eight underlying concepts central to history:

1 time
2 historical situations (a sense of period)
3 continuity
4 change
5 cause
6 consequence/result
7 interpretations/points of view
8 historical evidence

Doing history as described in the key elements involves:

- learning and understanding historical vocabulary, including that of time

- understanding historical situations, their diversity and the people living in them
- identifying reasons, results and changes
- asking and answering questions
- using sources
- making connections
- selecting, recording, organizing and recalling information
- giving reasons for different points of view
- communicating knowledge and understanding gained

Questions

Questioning is the wind that moves the sailing ship of historical study along. We can help children to develop their understanding of history's underlying concepts by asking questions that stimulate investigation and discussion, for example:

Time When did it happen? How long did it take?
Historical situations What happened? Who was involved? What was it like?Where did it happen?
Continuity How long did it last? Is it still like that today?
Change What changed? How did it change?
Cause Why did that happen? Why did people think like that?
Consequence/result What happened as a result?
Points of view How did it seem to this person? Why does that person see it differently?
Historical evidence What can this source tell me? Can I trust it? Where can I check this information?

Organizing concepts

A second set of concepts are those which help us make sense of institutions or ideas – organizing concepts. Without them we can't fully understand historical situations. Organizing concepts include words such as parliament, monarchy, the Church. Find out what understandings your pupils have about these words, as their historical (or modern) meaning may be very different from the mental pictures children have of them. Children may well believe parliament to be a place where members roar rudely at each other, without any idea that it is a law-making body.

Specific concepts

Third are concepts specific to a particular period in history, such as the Reformation (HSU 2), the Blitz and the Home Front (HSU 3b).

The programme of study

In history, the National Curriculum now has six History Study Units at KS2, and within each HSU the content is described in broad topic headings, ranging from two to six. You now have real choices: the programme of study tells you what to teach only in the most general way. You can select your own areas of investigation under such general headings as 'the lives of ordinary men and women'. Even where a specific event is mentioned, for example 'Elizabeth I and the Armada', you are free to tackle it as you wish – you choose the details, the issues, the perspective, the teaching method.

For anyone who still feels overburdened, the wording of the programme of study brings succour. Each HSU is introduced with the words 'Pupils should …', note, not 'Pupils must'. The word 'should' is a conditional imperative: you do something if you can. Given your circumstances, could anyone else do better?

The programme of study's focus statement for KS2 is simply a summary of the six HSUs' content. The two most important bits come at the end:
- Children should be able to learn about the past using a range of sources of information.
- The HSUs and the key elements should be taught together.

Good and simple, they form the core of planning.

Organizing the programme of study

How do you fit the six HSUs happily into the four years of KS2? You could do one history topic a year for two years, and two a year for the other two years. Alternatively, you could combine some units to give a total of four, that is, one a year – see below.

HSUs 1-4:	Can combine with:
Romans, Anglo-Saxons & Vikings in Britain	local history
Life in Tudor Times	Aztecs, local history
Victorian Britain *or*	Benin, local history
Britain since 1930	local history
Ancient Greece	Egypt (at a pinch)

The attainment target

Assessment emerged from the Dearing slimming treatment reduced from three ATs containing 44 statements of attainment to one AT containing eight level descriptions. But in the post-1995 curriculum, SCAA has decreed that the AT be used only for summative assessment, that is, at the end of a year or key stage. On-going, formative assessment is to be done in relation to the key elements. A fuller discussion of assessment follows on pages 37-40.

Planning history in relation to the rest of the curriculum

There are six main options open to the teacher, some overlapping:

- integrated topics
- joint topics (usually history and geography)
- history as part of another subject topic
- history-led topics
- straight history topics
- history through English

At KS1 history commonly forms part of integrated topics such as My Family, Flight, Toys and Games. As long as you address the key elements, and give children a chance to develop a sense of period, you can in this way deliver children's entitlement to history. At KS2, OFSTED's 1995 report on history in the National Curriculum noted that history-led topics were often the most successful in terms of children's learning. However, there are no right answers. Your planning will be constrained by the situation in your school – its philosophy, size, development plan, etc. The NPHP advocates history-led topics and history through English.

History and other subjects

Traditionally history has been linked with geography: all history is concerned with place as well as time. Maps and plans and patterns of human settlement, like timelines, are an intrinsic part of history. History in the primary school combines equally well with subjects such as art, technology, religious studies, music, drama and science. For example, in our Year 3 teaching, the creation of a Roman market involved mathematics (market goods priced realistically, trading with 'real' Roman money) and art/craft, as the children spent a week making Roman pottery and mosaics, knives and jewellery, and drawing signs to advertise their stalls. A Year 4 class movingly interpreted a Victorian coal-mining disaster through music and dance. A group of Year 4/5 children built working models of ancient boats: a design and technology project as much as a history one.

History and language

We are all language teachers, and history provides the perfect vehicle for teaching English. They are totally compatible, fitting together like hand and glove. Language is at the heart of both English and history: both are reading subjects. Discussion and debate is central to both. Both explore people's feelings, conditions, motives, relationships. Both are concerned with the selection, questioning and interpretation of evidence. Historical knowledge is overwhelmingly organized and communicated through language. Every English attainment target can be reached through historical activities.

How much time is there for history?	The post-Dearing primary curriculum allows history a notional 45 hours per year of teaching time, which averages out at just over an hour a week. That reduces to barely one hour a week once bank holidays, sports days, trips, floods and snowstorms have taken their toll. But if you teach most of your English through history, you gain more time for both subjects.

Reflection The history programme of study

- Review the current programme of study for history in your school in relation to the overall curriculum plan.
- Take each of the elements discussed above, and in the light of them, recommend changes to the existing programme of study.

Planning a history study unit	The requirements for the six HSUs vary. For example, HSU 2 asks that children be taught about six areas of Tudor life, whereas the past non-European society HSU lists only two areas. The important point is that you are free to choose how to teach each HSU, and how much time to spend on the aspects you select. There is nothing to stop you investigating only one event or situation in detail, and teaching others through, say, a story.
	So, which aspects of the HSU will you choose to teach in detail? How will you satisfy the requirement that 'across the key stage, pupils should be given opportunities to study:'

- in outline and in depth
- aspects of English, Welsh, Scottish and Irish history; also Europe and the world where appropriate
- history from various perspectives

Outline and depth	Since the arrival of the National Curriculum, many teachers have felt they should 'cover' all possible subject matter. So they rush children through the programme of study, giving them no time to learn anything. Real knowledge, expert knowledge, is knowledge in depth, and if children are to have time to acquire it, they can't investigate in detail more than one or two aspects of an HSU. In the words of Marjorie Reeves, creator of the wonderful 'Then and There' series, 'I want children to sit down in a good rich patch of history and stay there for a satisfying amount of time' (*Reeves*, 1981, p. 53).
Study in detail	As an example, in a Leeds multi-racial school our Year 6 children investigated the circumstances surrounding the death, allegedly

through his mother Hannah's cruelty, of Patrick Collins, a crippled Irish child. Working from newspaper reports of Hannah's arrest and the inquest into Patrick's death, and from census returns, the children climbed imaginatively inside the situation faced by Patrick's family. Through reading documents, debate and drama, they came to understand the harshness of life for destitute immigrants, the attitudes of 'respectable' society to them and Victorian notions of justice. They confronted issues such as justice, racism and the lost people in society. They gained a real knowledge of the reality of Victorian England from working from the sources. As immigrant children, many of them also identified with the Irish family's situation, and at the end understood better both the past and their own situation in the present.

Study in outline

There are many ways of building up an overview, none of which need take up much time. Again in the words of Marjorie Reeves, the rich patches of in-depth history can be seen as fat beads, which can then be linked by the string of outline history to form a necklace. It follows that you can only string the necklace once the fat beads exist. The children can place their in-depth knowledge in a wider context through creating concept webs or timelines – the necklace's string.

Windows on the past

A Somerset teacher's class developed in-depth knowledge of the Britain since 1930 unit through creating for each decade a pictorial view through the same window. Each picture included items on the window sill (ornament, newspaper), curtains and part of the room's wall-covering. The children spent a whole term researching the details of their pictures, deciding what was the headline of their decade (the 1960s group chose 'President Kennedy shot'), writing to Sandersons for wallpaper samples for each decade, and so on. At the end, the pictures, viewed together, were a splendid overview of the HSU. The children who had made them had a coherent understanding of key features of each decade. If you feel your pupils need a context for their historical study first, another way you can provide it is through story (see Chapter 13).

Topic book blitz

A fun way to build up an overview in one session is the topic book blitz. For this you need cards for the children and a box of books related to the HSU being studied, for example, Life in Tudor Times:
- Put the HSU heading on the board.
- Divide the children into pairs.
- Let each pair choose a topic book.

- From their book each pair finds two to five pieces of information which interest them.
- Pool and list them on the board.
- The pairs can also write questions on their cards; the other children find the answers in their books. One Leeds teacher who tried this couldn't stop the class asking and answering questions – they were only stopped two hours later by the end of the school day.

Beyond England

This is a difficult area to deal with, probably one of the most ignored sections of the history order. It's partly to do with where in Britain you're teaching, partly with availability of sources, and partly with time. But if you look creatively at the HSUs, there are opportunities to bring in aspects of British, European and world history. The Irish famine and its effects, for example, fits very well in Victorian Britain, where the huge influx of impoverished Irish into the cities of the industrial revolution offers opportunities to investigate patterns of Irish settlement (census records), the workings of the poor law, the conditions of life of the poorest in Victorian society.

Political, Economic, Religious, Social, Cultural

If you're worried about looking at history from various perspectives, first decide what topics you're going to teach during an HSU, then draw up a table like the one below. Fill in your topics under the matching heading. If a form is filled in for each HSU, the history co-ordinator can easily see if there are any glaring omissions over the four years of the key stage. You don't have to teach from every perspective in every study unit.

Example: Ancient Greece				
Political	**Economic technical scientific**	**Religious**	**Social**	**Cultural**
Democracy City States Athens v Sparta	Archimedes pottery inventions maths	myths The Parthenon power of gods	women's role education	plays sculpture pottery

When planning a unit, first decide which aspects of the programme of study to investigate, then decide on a series of key historical questions to focus the teaching and learning. We strongly advise against trying to plan and resource a whole HSU in advance. Know overall where you're going, and plan the first few lessons in detail. A rolling programme of weekly review and further planning is more flexible, and makes it possible to adapt to new developments and changing interests. Revise ideas and fill in your developing programme a couple of steps ahead.

Reflection **Planning a History Study Unit**

We only plan the first couple of lessons, using the following template.

- Take your next HSU. Work out the focus of your teaching, and plan the first two weeks of its teaching.
- Put in the key question, the learning activities to answer it and the resources needed.

Planning individual lessons We have developed a simple template for our lesson planning: introduction, key question[s], learning objectives, resources, the learning activities and assessment.

Introduction This sets the scene telling the reader the point the teaching has reached.

Key question Again, the idea of key questions is central. We focus and drive each investigation with a key question which gives the lesson focus and purpose. For example, in the case of Patrick Collins (see above), our starting key question was: 'Was Hannah Collins a bad mother?' With a Year 2 class our key question was, 'Why did Amundsen survive when Scott didn't?'

Learning objectives We state clearly both the specific and general learning objectives, that is, the intended learning outcomes of the lessson.

Resourcing The important thing is not how many resources you have, but how you use them in the classroom. Key questions in resource selection are:

- How is this resource furthering the children's learning?
- Are we asking historical questions of the resource?
- Is it being used to engage the children actively with the past?

Resourcing an HSU need not be an expensive business. For local resources, try your local history society, local record office or reference library, LEA or local newspaper. Newspapers have extensive collections of past local photographs and articles, and many are now happy to collaborate with schools to produce local history supplements.

Become a collector and hoarder: attics, junkshops, relatives, and older friends, are fair game in your hunt for artefacts, documents and oral evidence. People are a rich and underused resource. At a Sussex school John Fines had a Year 4/5 class writing a history of South Africa in one morning, their only resources being ten South African visitors.

Finding documents Resources in the form of documents often need a little hunting out, so here are five possible sources.

1   Documents are often hidden inside the topic books you have on the subject.
2   Teaching materials, that is, textbooks and history 'boxes' for KS2 and KS3 are now littered with documentary extracts you can use with your own class.
3   Teacher guides and local authority materials for teaching history nearly always have a mound of documents attached to them.
4   A brief visit to the local records office will give you instant access to census, trade directory and newspaper materials. For under a pound spent on photocopying you can have your own, rich local resource material.
5   Your class can also provide a plethora of documents, both written and printed for example parents' and grandparents' memories in letter, memoir or diary form.

Learning Activities We devise learning activities to answer the key question. The learning activities form the central element of lesson planning; they are how the children will 'do history.' The learning activities should challenge, excite and interest the children and they should result in learning. A learning activity requires that children come to grips with people in the past, and their circumstances. They can only do this if we can give them ways into the past. For example, before we ask children to try to make sense of a handwritten Victorian census return, they have to understand what a census is, so we ask them to make a census return for their own family, or for the class.

The learning activities must be anchored in the 'first record' of the past, or they will not be valid. They should result in historical understanding, in the children's construction of their own version of an historical situation, one that has been tested against the evidence and in debate. And the children must communicate their knowledge, enactively (drama, expressive movement, dance), iconically (pictures, cartoons, plans) or symbolically (written reports, narratives, oral presentations). For example, the activity devised to answer the key question about Scott and Amundsen was an investigation of the differences between the two expeditions. We told the children the story, then they examined pictures showing both parties' clothing, food and transport arrangements. The children compared these, looking at how much each man in Scott's party had to eat daily, working out what he would have eaten for breakfast, lunch and dinner. They then drew and wrote their reasons for Scott's failure.

Differentiation

How will you provide learning activities accessible to all the children? We adopt four main strategies:

- All the children in the class engage in a common activity, and achieve according to their abilities. For example, they can describe scenes, argue in a debate, enact situations, do detective work, analyse a picture. The activity is carefully structured to support all the children's learning.
- Giving slower, less confident learners more time (see Chapter 6).
- Scaffolding. The teacher and/or more able peers support the needs of individual children.
- Extension materials of greater difficulty for the more able, combined with extension activities to engage them fully.

In planning learning activities the teacher's role and teaching style are central to the children's learning. The teacher structures and manages the learning activities, making sources accessible to the children and devising tasks that challenge, excite and engage the whole ability range. Many examples are given in the book covering the range of teaching activities that you migh wish to adapt in your teaching of history.

The teaching – learning activities

The example below outlines how the NPHP put theory into practice. The lesson described was taught to a Year 3 group of 44 children. The topic was local history and we were looking at the Great Exeter Fish War of 1309.

The key questions we asked were:
- What was the quarrel between Hugh, Earl of Devon and the City of Exeter about?
- Can we believe John Hooker's story? (Illustration 4)
- Did the jurors' document, fit in with what we learned from John Hooker's story?
- What could the Exeter Chamber do about the quarrel between the Earl and the town?

The story of the quarrel

We sat the children round us on the floor, and told them John Hooker's story about Hugh Courtenay, the Earl of Devon and his 1309 quarrel with the mayor and citizens of Exeter. To a child, the class condemned Earl Hugh as a bully.

We broke the news that although the events described happened about 700 years ago, they were written down by John Hooker, a man who lived in Exeter about 400 years ago. He was writing 300 years after the event – was his story likely to be reliable? How would he have known what happened? The children's ideas were spot-on:

Tom : 'From his ancestors.'

Sam : 'He could have got it from a book.'

Checking the evidence

The only contemporary evidence that exists for the dispute between the city of Exeter and the Courtenays is a 1290 jurors' statement about the Countess of Devon's weir, Illustration 3. We felt it was probably too difficult for Year 3 children to tackle, but

> ... the water of the Exe belongs to the said city, and of old used to belong, as far as the port of Exmewt; and the great fishery was common to all who wished there, Isabella Countess of Devon, six years ago, raised a certain weir across the water of the Exe at Topsham, and so built it, that the catching of salmon and other fish which used to be caught in the said water this side of the weir was completely stopped, to the grave damage of the city and others in the neighbourhood; and also whereas all kinds of boats used to come up towards the city as far as the bridge of the city with wine and other merchandise, to the great benefit of all the countryside, now no boat can ascend on account of the impediment of the weir to the greatest damage of the said city and all the neighbourhood.

Illustration 3 *Jurors' statement*

The 3rd year of King Edward the 2nd, 1309

Roger Beynym mayor

This year there was a great controversy which caused great trouble between Hugh Courtenay, 3rd Earl of Devon, and the mayor and common people of Exeter. What happened was this:

One market day the Earl sent his servant to the city to buy fish. That day there were only three baskets of fish in the market. The bishop of Exeter's servant also came to buy fish. Both servants wanted the whole supply of fish and they argued about who was to have it. The mayor, for his part, said that the common people should also be served and have the benefit of the market. So he decided the argument by delivering one basket to the Earl's servant, one to the Bishops servant, and reserving the third basket for the people at the market. When the Earl heard this, he considered himself insulted by the mayor, in that he had not been given all the fish, and threatened that he would be revenged. Not long after this Earl Hugh came to the city, staying in his lodgings in the Black friars' house. He immediately sent for the mayor to come to speak with him. The mayor, who was a retainer of the Earl's hearing of the Earl's displeasure and knowing his temper, feared the worst. So he called all his friends and the common people to the Guildhall. He told them how the Earl was offended with him and why, that the Earl had sent for him, and that he was afraid to go unless they would accompany his and help him if need be. This they promised to do. Then the mayor said: 'Masters, I knew the Earl will fall out with me, and as he has threatened will take his revenge on me.. As he is angry with me because I did my job by favouring the city people, I pray you to accompany me and stand by me. And when I am with the Earl, if you see that I am kept there for a long time, then break open the doors by force and search me out. Otherwise I shall be in great peril and danger'. After this, and several similar speeches, they all went together to the house of the Black friars. When they arrived the mayor was received into the Earls lodgings, but the door was locked behind him. As soon as the mayor entered, the Earl began to rage stormily, and would not be pacified. The mayor, seeing that none of his excuses or answers would be listened to, suddenly took off his coat, which bore the Earl's coat of arms. He handed it to the Earl (indicating that he would no longer be the Earl's man). At this the Earl was so furious that he became choleric, and the mayor feared what would become of him. The common people were outside, wondering what had become of him, because he was so long with Earl. They knocked at the door and demanded the mayor. After a long time and many demands their wish was still not granted, so they got ladders and other stuff to rip open the house and break open the doors. The Earl, taking his friends' advice and fearing what might happen if the commoners didn't get their way, then begged the mayor to pacify them. The mayor did this, and the commoners went quietly. The Earl had to put a good face on it at the time to avoid peoples fury, but he hated the city of Exeter and its citizens ever after.

Illustration 4   *Exeter Fish War document*

not daunted, gave out one copy per pair of children. We stressed that this was a very, very difficult piece of writing from 700 years ago, then read it aloud while the children followed on their copies.

Who could tell us more or less what it was about? The children struggled, and after several tentative tries, came up with a pretty competent summary of what the document meant. 'Weir' was one word they didn't understand – weirs were to loom large as the topic progressed – every child in the class ended with an expert knowledge of the structure and purpose of weirs.

Next key question: Did this document fit in with what we learned from John Hooker's story? The children decided that yes, it did, although they would have preferred Isabella to have been Hugh (instead of his aunt), so that the finger of blame could fall entirely on him.

Role play/ decision-making

We now divided the class up into groups of 2-4 children, telling them they were the members of Exeter's Chamber 700 years ago. Their problem was Earl Hugh's blocking of the river and exaction of tolls and dues. What could the Exeter Chamber do about the quarrel between the Earl and the town?

Acting it out

The members of the Chamber discussed possible solutions for three or four minutes. Each group then reported its favoured solution to the whole Chamber. We wrote their proposals on the board. Most groups preferred to go for the jugular and kill Hugh. Their suggestions were:

1 Break the weir.
2 Kill Hugh.
3 Put a magic spell on him.
4 Refuse to pay dues for landing goods at his Topsham quay.
5 Be kind to him.

We added a sixth option, to vote for none of the above. Before we voted, we and the children argued each option long and passionately, with us asking people to volunteer any objections they had. The objections to, and feasibility of, each proposal were thoroughly discussed. When the vote was taken, the rather surprising result was:

Option 1 – 3 votes   Option 4 – 12 votes
Option 2 – Nil votes   Option 5 – Nil votes
Option 3 – 4 votes   Option 6 – 25 votes

By testing their ideas against each other and the teacher in debate, the class had moved from an unrealistic view of the possibilities open to them as the city chamber, to a position of uncertainty, needing new thinking.

What new option would the chamber now choose? To direct their thinking, we posed several questions about power, such as, 'Who could make Hugh take away his weir?' 'Who was more powerful than him?' It didn't take the children long to arrive at the king. They decided to petition him, and duly did so.

We moved the scene on to Tudor Exeter by continuing the story of the city's tribulations with the Earls of Devon – their petitions were unsuccessful for 250 years because the Courtenays were favourites of the monarchy. Only when a later Earl of Devon proved traitorous to Henry VIII did the city finally win through and gain permission to remove the Courtenays' weir, tolls and dues.

Assessment

History SATs have been banished: primary school children are now to be assessed in history by their teachers alone. The only statutory requirement is that teachers report each year on children's progress. The form the reporting takes is up to the teacher and the school. The important thing about reporting is that it should make perfect sense to the children, their parents and other staff. Also, if our aim is to help children to learn and to improve (and what else is it?), we should assess their work against their own previous efforts. 'Have you done better than last time?' is infinitely preferable to making children feel stupid compared to their peers.

Progression

The AT is there primarily to measure progression. The AT's level descriptions are based implicitly on Bruner's idea of the spiral curriculum, where children are introduced at an early age to a subject's core concepts (Bruner, 1960 and 1966). These are then revisited regularly over time, at ever-increasing levels of sophistication and complexity, enabling pupils to deepen their understanding incrementally. Thus concepts such as time, cause and consequence, change and continuity, are described in ever more complex ways as we move through the AT's levels. For example, for cause and consequence, at Level 2 we have: 'They are beginning to recognize that there are reasons why people in the past acted as they did', and at Level 5: 'They describe and make links between relevant reasons for, and results of, events and changes.' This theory of progression makes sense, but is largely untested. We argue that deep and sophisticated thinking about historical questions is possible by children of all ages.

When should the AT's level descriptions be used?

According to SCAA's history officers, the level descriptions are not meant to be used for formative assessment but for summative judgements, usually at the end of a key stage. Formative evaluation should be done in terms of the key elements.

How easy is it to place each child at a specific level? The level descriptions don't specify any particular knowledge. So, you have to use your own judgement far more than in subjects with specific level descriptions (for example, from English AT3: Writing. 'Punctuation to mark sentences – full stops, capital letters and question marks – is used accurately. Handwriting is joined and legible.') Does the history AT seem at once too vague and too complex and demanding to come to grips with?

Best fit

When the time comes for summative judgement at the end of the key stage, we are asked to turn to the National Curriculum Attainment Target and its eight level descriptions. SCAA advocates that you use a 'best fit' philosophy, that the level description that is most characteristic or typical of a child's work is the one to choose.

What does 'best fit' mean in practice? First, it means there's no such thing as an exact fit. When you start looking in detail at the level descriptions they are unsatisfactory in that they are rarely if ever applicable to a particular piece of work produced by a child. To be able to assign a child to a level, you will have had to compile a portfolio of that child's work over the key stage.

A working group in Leeds has devised another way of doing it: the teacher constantly monitors the children's learning and selects pieces of work or makes notes as evidence. She underlines the sentence in a level which best describes each child's work. At the end of the key stage, the level which has most underlined sentences for the child is deemed the 'best fit'. It's a vast improvement on ticking boxes and it also allows you to see at a glance which aspects are not underlined – for example, the child may not have identified reasons for the actions of people in the past. Teachers have found this useful for highlighting gaps in their teaching strategies. This underlining method hasn't yet been tested over the whole four years of KS2. Does it leave enough room for teachers' professional judgement? And does progression as envisaged in the history order actually happen? History assessment in the national curriculum is still a flawed instrument, and, certainly from level 3 upwards, favours 'outline' knowledge rather than in-depth study.

Annotating assessed work On in-service courses, we often ask teachers to bring in their children's work for joint attempts at assessment. What is striking on these occasions is the impossibility of assessing the work out of context. Without knowing what the class had experienced beforehand, the circumstances in which the work had been undertaken, what resources the children were using, and without the class teacher's insights and assessment notes, parents and other staff can't make a fair judgement of its worth. The answer is to annotate each piece of work selected for a portfolio. Annotation is particularly important if you are trying to build up portfolios for use by all teachers in the school. These benchmark portfolios can help maintain consistency of assessment across the school.

Reflection Assessing pupils' work
- Choose a piece of work recently done by your class in history. Chose two or three examples, and annotate them, noting the key elements addressed and assigning them a level.

Analysis of the children's work: an example at KS1 Both children have understood the task set and their accounts relate to events or features of 50 years ago. Their information is relevant. They have constructed personal understandings about the past from the various sources encountered over four teaching sessions. They have understood that statements about the past must be backed up and sources of evidence acknowledged, thus

Nicola Mrs Dolbear told us about the war. And I learnt that old shops have long windows. And new shops have wide windows. And Mrs Dolbear told us that there were bombs dropping down from aeroplanes. And they dropped a bomb on my shop. Because my shop wasn't there 50 years ago. because Mrs Dolbear told us and I drew my shop the spar and when Mrs Dolbear showed us little tearsheet stamps [ration book] she told us people in the war could have a little bit of each. And she told us a story about her self and her husband and fifty years ago they had to take a gas mask nearly all the time in case a bomb could drop and spread poisonous gas. And they had a box to carry them about. and you could breathe through the holes which was on the gas mask. and you could have childrens gas masks. Mrs Dolbear told us that there was a bomb dropped on her house.

Emma In the war every one had to take a gas mask round with them. In case a bomb fell which had poisonous gas in. a lot of shops in Magdalen Road got bombed in the war. after the war a lot of the shops got built again. Mrs Dolbear told us her house got burnt down and she had to live in a chicken house and it was a very big chicken house though and they went to live in her sisters house before she lived in the chicken house I know this because Mrs Dolbear came in and she was around then.

Illustration 5 *Pupil work*

taking the first steps towards recognizing the role of sources and how we find out about the past.

Nicola Nicola's six statements contain information selected from at least four sources (shop window shapes from class discussion, comparing buildings built since Blitz with older structures plus observation; ration stamps, gas masks, bombing raids from Mrs Dolbear plus posters and books; gas masks carried in boxes from boxed gas mask in classroom; one breathes through holes in the mask from her own observation plus questioning class teacher). Her account is full and varied. She has clearly constructed a complex personal picture of the past. Her first two statements also show an appreciation of change over time.

Emma Like Nicola, her account includes six statements, three sets of additional details and two explanations. In the first two categories, however, her account is far less precise and detailed than Nicola's. Emma has made deductions from the street directory ('a lot of shops in Magdalen Road got bombed in the war'). She shows that she is beginning to evaluate evidence with her reason for believing Mrs Dolbear ('she was around then').

Evaluating the work in terms of the key elements for KS1. Both Nicola and Emma's work includes four out of the five key elements:

1 **Chronology:** use of words and phrases relating to the passing of time
   –Nicola, 'my shop wasn't there 50 years ago'.
   –Emma, 'after the war a lot of the shops got built again'.
2 **Historical knowledge and understanding:**
   a. knowledge of aspects of the past
   –Nicola and Emma both show understanding about bombing, the wearing of gas masks, etc.
   b. why people did things/things happened, and the result
   –Nicola, 'they had to take a gas mask nearly all the time in case a bomb could drop and spread poisonous gas'.
   –Emma, 'in the war everyone had to take a gas mask round with them. In case a bomb fell which had poisonous gas in.'
4 **Historical enquiry:**
   a. find out about the past from a range of sources of information
   –Both children found out from oral evidence, artefacts, books, documents, observation of buildings.
   b. ask and answer questions about the past

–Both children questioned Mrs Dolbear and their class teacher to find out about aspects of the war. Nicola answered her own question about her shop's fate in the war.

5   **Organization and communication:**
    –Both Nicola and Emma have communicated what they have learnt through written accounts. The accounts are clear and coherent, despite both being at an age when writing is still a very new skill.

4 Improving Your Own Teaching

Janet, a KS1 teacher, had been on our four day in-service course in January. Now, five months later in June, she was the first to present her fifteen minute report on what she had done since, to other teachers attending the county's Primary History Day. How had she managed to adapt the January ideas in her own teaching? Janet told us that she had been teaching a mixed class of Year 1 and reception children. The topic for the term was boxes. How could she fit history into this? The Trojan Horse, of course!

The Trojan horse

Story The focus she took from January was storytelling. She had a diagram of how the story fitted into the topic. Janet told the children the story of the Trojan Horse using ideas picked up from John Fines' story telling session at the January course. The story was the children's favourite bit of the topic.

Pictures The children drew pictures telling the story in sequence. They were given the beginning and the end of the story, and had to put in the middle section. They took notes in words or drew pictures after she told the story. Each child had a piece of paper folded so that there were six spaces in which to draw their pictures. On display was one child's drawing of the story told in pictures.

Art work The story linked into art work. She had a template of the art work, a Greek pot, with an outline of the horse on it, so that the pupils could design their own pot using Greek motifs. She could have done papier mâché models but that would have been too messy, as experience had taught her. The pupils could copy a Greek design or make one of their own. They researched ideas, using books and other resources. The youngest children were given a blank paper plate to design their own motifs, with the horse already printed on it.

Music She also broke down Greek names into clapping rhythms, long and short. Much to her surprise the children had no problems with pronunciation.

Archaeology – children as detectives She asked the children how we would know what designs to put on the plates. After considerable effort to squeeze out an answer, the bright spark in the class said, 'because we find bits in the dirt'. This led on to talking about the work of an archaeologist.

Artefacts The class then split up into four groups. She had produced pictures of pots and plates that she cut up into jigsaws. The bits of the jigsaw were hidden around the classroom, and the children had to find them. To help the children these were colour coded, for example, a yellow rim to a plate.

Transferring skills

As each of the succeeding teachers presented equally innovative ideas it occurred to us that something dramatic had happened as a result of the Nuffield Primary History Project's five day in-service in January. Each teacher unfolded a different range of strategies for bringing the past to life that they had tried out with their children. The teachers' approaches were based on those that we had explored in January, all of which are included in this book. It seemed that both the underlying principles and practices of Nuffield Primary History had been grafted on to the teaching experience that the teachers had brought with them to the January session. For the first time we felt that we were getting tangible evidence of a general 'transfer', the application in different contexts of teaching approaches that we had introduced. How had we bridged the performance gap between accepting a set of ideas and actual classroom practice?

The only new element in our approach from other courses was the conscious adoption of **Action Research**, a method specifically designed to ensure the transfer of teaching skills, processes and knowledge.

Action Research – What is it?

Action Research provides a systematic, planned approach to bringing about improvement of your teaching. Although teetering on the brink of educational gobbledygook as a term, Action Research means what it says, you act upon research that you carry out. You, the teacher, do the research in question yourself upon any aspect of your own teaching that you feel needs attention – ranging from its planning, resourcing and teaching to assessment and reporting.

Critical reflection Change then can take place through you thinking critically, reflectively and constructively about your practice. The only change, but a major one, from normal practice, is that you consciously review the evidence you have gathered in a constructive, critical way. Did it work? In what ways can I make it better? Okay, it was a bit of a disaster, but what good bits can I save and adapt?

The action plan You should draw up an action plan, outlining in detail what changes you intend to make. When the action plan is implemented, you can review if you have achieved the goals it set.

Action Research provides a specific focus for the improvement of practice. It requires reflective thinking in both detail and depth. As such, it can lead perhaps to more significant changes in attitude, approach and teaching styles and strategies than might have happened before. It forces you to change your mind. Such thinking depends upon having information in a form that helps bring about change. Action Research is how the Nuffield Primary History Project developed its teaching ideas and approaches. Everything that we recommend has been tried out and amended in the light of experience, all of it salutary, some of it disastrous.

How do you do Action Research?

Creating an archive We treat carrying out Action Research as being the same as undertaking a small-scale historical investigation. Here you study books and articles and work upon original sources, usually stored as archives in record offices, extracting from them the information that you feel is relevant. The difference with Action Research is that instead of consulting an existing archive you create your own, your record of your teaching. Once you have the Action Research archive you treat it in exactly the same way as you would one consulted in your historical researches.

Below in the left column are the steps we take in doing our own Action Research. We have highlighted the key elements. In the right column is an example of our planning and teaching of a lesson with a Year 3/4 class on Victorian Britain.

1	What is the **curriculum context**?	We are teaching the Victorian Britain HSU.
2	What is the **problem**? and/or What do you want to **improve**?	How can we introduce the children to the HSU topics and then move on to a study in detail? This meets both the statutory requirement and provides the pupils with some kind of context they can build on

3	What are the **context** and **constraint**s?	The lesson will last for one and a half hours
4	What **solutions** can you dream up?	We decided to take the concept web idea, with the pupils creating their own webs to see the links between topics.
5	What is the **best approach**?	We would build the lesson around the pupils researching topics that interested them.
6	**Planning the teaching.** Turn the dreams into reality on paper!	The class teacher and I discussed the teaching ideas. He had a large collection of topic books, resource and picture cards.
7	**Resource** the plan	Created the post box cards, using the Victorian Britain HSU topics.
8	**Implement** the plan	We taught the lesson and survived.
9	**Record** what happened, that is build up your archive.	In the lesson I feverishly jotted down notes as things happened.
10	Make sure the **records are in a usable** form so you can understand what went on, and hopefully why.	Wrote up the lesson notes as a reflective diary.
11	**Evaluate** what happened, how well it worked.	Discussed the teaching with the teacher and what we had learned from it.
12	**Action** : use what you have learned to inform what you do next.Draw up an **Action Plan**	Revised the actual lesson plan for when we next teach the subject next year. More importantly, reflect on our performance to see how it can help us with the next part of the teaching programme.
13	Repeat the process – starting with step 1	

Each step can be seen as being part of an ongoing, continuous cycle of planning, research, reflection and professional improvement.

Reflection Action Research and your teaching
- If you have not been trained in or engaged upon Action Research, how different is this approach from how you have previously improved your practice?
- How might Action Research help you improve your

How do you do it ?
Action Research
Methods

Because Action Research is usually done by you 'on the job' there are a number of approaches you can adopt. Here is a list you might like to draw upon.

Action Research – Some ways of researching your teaching

1. Tape recording of the lesson
2. Video recording of the teaching
3. Detailed, reflective diary, written up using lesson notes
4. Pupil diary – personal, or in the form of a dialogue with you, the teacher
5. Pupil commentary or review
6. Lesson notes – jotting down things as they happen
7. Colleague taking notes on all or parts of the lesson, using a detailed plan to help.
8. Pupil response
   –assessment task
   –work you asked them to do as a result of the teaching
9. Interviewing, either you or a colleague.
   –structured, with a list of questions you stick to
   –semi-structured : key questions, but with scope for the discussion to be free ranging
   –unstructured : free ranging, open ended discussion
10. Photography : polaroid camera

It is impossible to adopt more than one or two approaches at a time. Our favourite method in the NPHP is to tape record the lesson or jot down notes and produce a detailed, reflective diary.

How often do you do it ? Action Research Constraints

We accept that most teachers are on the brink of exhaustion. Clearly, you can only be very selective in the amount of time you spend doing Action Research, at the maximum two or three lessons a month.

Part of a lesson You have to decide on the when and the what. Thus you might decide to use action research to 'blitz' a particular problem, working intensively upon it employing several of the methods listed above. This might last for only a part of a lesson. We suggest that a blitz approach is okay for one or two lessons at the most, no more. For a longer period it produces a mountain of information that can take days to sort out. It is far too easy to get snowed under.

Long term Action Research You can use one approach, like a reflective diary, to continuously review a programme. Here Action Research can be a continuous, cumulative process.

Conclusion Action Research is an exciting step forward in professional development. It turns the rhetoric of reflective practice into an every day reality. It has definitely worked for us and teachers on our courses. Hopefully it will also bring joy and happiness into your classrooms.

Reflection **Planning your Action Research**
- Take the next history topic you are going to teach, and decide upon the teaching approach.
- Read the relevant chapter in this book about it.
- Draw up a plan to use Action Research to help improve your teaching of the topic.

---

5 Questions and Questioning

The History National Curriculum recognizes the importance of questions and questioning at KS1 and KS2. Key Element 4 of the KS1 National Curriculum History programme is about historical enquiry. It states:

'Pupils should be taught

    (a)   how to find out about aspects of the past from a range of sources of information, including artefacts, pictures and photographs, adults talking about their own past, written sources and building and sites;

    (b)   to ask and answer questions about the past'.

Key Element 5 of the KS2 programme states that pupils should be educated to 'ask and answer questions, and to select and record information relevant to a topic.' Questions are central to historical learning. Questions empower us to select what we find significant and organize it into a coherent explanation. Without questions there is no history, only the past's mountain of amorphous unrelated information. Questioning gives shape and purpose to both children's and our own study of the past. Pupil development of questioning skills enables them to push forward their enquiries. In our own teaching it drives the learning on.

The NPHP view of questioning is based on academic historians' views of the part questioning plays in 'doing history'. An expert on Roman Britain, R.G. Collingwood, places great emphasis on questioning as the key factor driving on an historical enquiry:

> Every step in the argument depends on asking a question. The question is the charge of gas, exploded in the cylinder-head, which is the motive force of every piston-stroke. But the metaphor is not adequate, because each new piston-stroke is produced not by exploding another charge of the same old mixture but by exploding a charge of a new kind.
> (*Collingwood*, 1949, p.273)

A new question can give a focus to an enquiry, no matter how stale the subject matter or how well chewed the evidence. For example, another historian, Professor E. Ives, can get us to look afresh at Henry VIII through the medium of a well directed question :

> Henry the Great ?
> What entitles a ruler to be called 'the Great'? Alexander, Charles, Peter, Frederick, Catherine, and from this side of the Channel, Alfred. And there are popes too: Leo I, Gregory I. For some years after the death of Henry VIII there was a possibility that he also would receive the accolade. He had ruled for only a few years less than Charlemagne and nearly a decade more than Alfred … He was powerful at home and notable – perhaps notorious – throughout Europe. Even today his name is the one which foreigners recognize in lists of English kings. Yet 'Henry the Great' did not stick. Why? (*Ives*, 1994)

By asking the question, 'Henry the Great?' Ives not only asks us to consider Henry and his activities; he also asks us subconsciously to decide which criteria we attach to the title. These kinds of terms – 'Great', 'Bold', 'Weak', 'Lionheart' and so on – when attached to kings, or anybody else for that matter, well repay examining in detail. With children we have found it a source of fascinating enquiry. What makes Manchester United a great football team? Are Arsenal boring? These are questions that generate interest in even the most apathetic pupils.

Such questions project our opinions, based upon interpretations that arise from our initial questions and the answers that we have teased out of the sources. Asking and answering questions is seminal to both teachers and pupils creating their own histories. Not all questions are of equal weight. What makes a significant history question, such as the one Professor Ives asked? At its simplest a good question should help us develop our understanding of the past, giving us a starting point. It hooks us into the topic.

Questions and teaching history

Theory is fine, seeing good and great historians practise the idea is illuminating, but how in reality do we get our children to engage in answering and asking questions?

Relating to this, the exercise below asks you to work out the questions that a project team member might have asked when teaching a class of Year 5 and 6 pupils using maps to learn about Life in Tudor Times.

Question exercise   In the left-hand column, list the questions that might have been asked during the teaching.

Possible questions	Account of the teaching
	• We discussed the purpose of maps today by looking carefully at an up to date Bartholomew's road map which showed tourist information. The children used the copies of the map and a key in pairs and brainstormed their ideas. They decided that we needed maps today to find our way, to learn where parts of the world are, for walkers to use, for transport routes, for planning, delivering, for learning and for estimating distance.
	• When the map was distributed the pupils discussed and made notes about what types of information it gave us.
	• They drew up fourteen differences which included many interesting points such as less houses, more fields, different names for places, no airports, less leisure buildings and places as people would have had less leisure time. It would not be printed but drawn.
	• They were then given copies of John Norden's map of 1595. After a time for observation and discussion they were asked to draw up a list of questions about the map that they would like answered.

Types of questions   Study Illustration 6. Draw up a list of questions you would ask KS1 pupils when teaching about this picture. Put your questions into the order you would ask them. Discuss the categories into which your questions fall.

Illustration 6   *A section of the Bayeux Tapestry*

Illustration 7   *Richard the III*

The driving force of questions

Study Illustration 7. It is a portrait of Richard III, king of England from 1483-1485. Richard seized power in 1483. He sent the two young sons of the previous king to live in the Tower of London, a royal palace. The oldest would be king when he grew up. The two boys, the so-called Princes in the Tower, were never seen again. Many people believe that Richard had them killed. In 1485 Richard's enemy, Henry Tudor, invaded England. Henry defeated and killed Richard III at the Battle of Bosworth and was crowned king as Henry VII. Henry's family, the Tudors, ruled England from 1485–1603. Using this information draw up a list of the different questions you would ask a class of Year 1 and Year 2 children about the picture and the order in which you would ask them. Now read Questions in the history classroom, below. Compare the kinds of questions that you listed about Richard III's portrait with those in this section. How do they differ? Compare your questions with those below. If they are better than yours, why is this so?

Questions in the history classroom: an example

Richard III's portrait Let us start with questions that will help pupils begin to explore historical sources. Here we are, confronted by the famous portrait of Richard III. We want to learn from it, but it won't speak to us directly, only responding to the right enquiries. So we might begin by saying 'Is there anything in this picture of a king that surprises you – what is unexpected?' Now the children have a way of looking at the portrait that makes the job conceivable – we don't have to look at everything, just the surprising bits. Okay, why no crown? The children have now raised a question of their own. Let us concentrate on that – write down at least three reasons why a king should have his picture painted not wearing a crown. We get a list – the list raises its own questions – which of these reasons is most likely and what does that tell us about our subject?

Already, by focusing the questioning down to one area we are in the middle of a rich vein of speculation where the children are using their minds and working hard. Here we don't need closed questions to check up on them – their answers to open questions will tell you straight away where they are, what they understand and where they can go next.

We can begin to broaden the enquiry. The children may be making observations on the meaning of the picture already and saying ' He looks nervous, ill, worried.' Now we can begin to control our speculation a little by looking at the distinction between information and interpretation. Thus we can say 'his forehead is wrinkled' and all agree that this is a piece of information. But when we say 'his forehead is all scrunched up because he is thinking hard' or 'because he is worried' or 'because he is ill' then we are in the domain of interpretation. We have a theory about what we see, and now we must ask questions to support or test the theory. Is there any other evidence to suggest that he was ill?

As the research goes on we need to put questions that will make us understand the subject in context. Thus we are seeing Richard with 20th century eyes; how might they have seen the picture in their days? Here the teacher might use role cards to help children look. If you were Richard's son, how might you have seen your dad in this picture? If his wife, if his doctor, if his tailor, jeweller etc.? So we get to know a set of different readings of the source which again take us back to the deepest question – where is the real Richard?

Thinking about questions

We start off with a stock of experience of human nature and activity, some skills of interpreting evidence, and some knowledge about the past as our base (the second record). Out of this we might generate a question about the past – most often a very general question, such as 'Why have people so readily had to recourse to war?' We might, on the other hand, formulate questions from our reading of historical accounts and historians' treatments of the past (as evidence about the past, they are part of

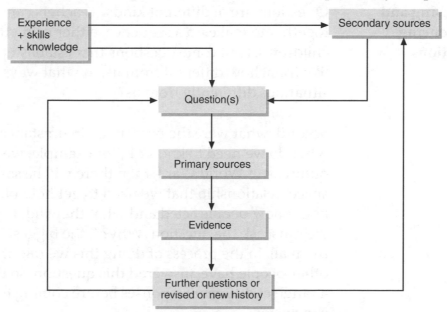

Illustration 8

the first record). Our reading might generate all sorts of questions, but mostly more specific ones, such as 'Is this account of Alexander the Great fair?' Or 'Why did he burn Persepolis?'

Having established a question or many questions we go back to the primary, or first-hand sources, that is the information which comes to us untreated from the period about which we are asking (the first record). From the sources we will select those pieces of information (that is, evidence) that will help us to answer our question, and we must try to understand the evidence, weigh it, and see how far it can take us towards an answer. Usually what happens is that this process only raises new questions, but occasionally it helps us to revise our view of history.

The point in this model where the experience, skills and knowledge are most required is at the stage of processing the evidence (see Illustration 8). To do this effectively with, for example, a document, we need to know who wrote it, in what circumstances, with what intentions and for whom. We also need to know the context of the document in order to make meaning – we must be able to recognize the names he mentions and know who the people were. We need experience and skill in order to help our intuitive reading of the document to try to read between the lines to ascertain the deeper meaning (the second record).

Choosing and sequencing questions

Questions are of different kinds. Teachers can thread questions together to make up a sequence, either using their own or the children's. First come questions that establish period – what was it like then, how different from us, in what ways did they respond to situations differently from us?

Second, what were the particular circumstances we are looking at – what do we need to know? If, for example, we are looking at the outbreak of World War I, then there will be some details of time, space, relationship that we need to get hold of. Third, we need to know how people acted and what they did, in some detail. Finally we must ask the question 'Why? ', the biggest history question of them all. In the process of doing this we might also look at how other people have answered this question, so that we can consider a range of different responses before coming to our own conclusion.

When working with children to try to get them to understand this process of questioning the steps laid out can be in this way:

1 What is it we are looking at?
2 Where and when did it all happen?
3 How did it come about?
4 Why?

A whole class approach to key questions

The role of a set of carefully structured questions is shown in the example below, an account of an introductory lesson on Roman England to a Year 5 class. The teaching strategy has six linked stages:

1 Whole class introduction to the key question.
2 Group work in relation to the key question with children working on the same set of sources.
3 In turn each pupil in the group gives an answer to the rest of the group who have to answer a list of subsidiary questions aimed at judging how well the pupil has answered the key question.
4 The teacher copies each child's answers for the rest of the group. They then produce a collective answer to the key question.
5 The group answers in turn are copied and each group gets a copy of each of the other groups' answers.
6 The whole class discusses the answers in relation to a second list of questions.

The strategy in action

We started with the key question, 'What was Roman England like?' The children worked in groups on a set of contrasting visual images of Roman England. The pictures showed scenes with some aspects that were familiar to the pupils, such as cooking.

The role of subsidiary questioning in pushing on with answering the key question was crucial. In their groups each pupil in turn picked up one picture and told the others what she/he thought was happening in the picture. The other pupils then had to answer these questions:

- Do you agree with the description she/he has given?
- If you disagree, say why.
- Is there anything you want to add to the description?
- What do the pictures tell you about Roman England?
- Would you have liked to live in England at that time?
- If so, why?

The group members then worked together to answer the original key question, each person producing an answer. The teacher copied the individual group members' answers, used these as the basis for group discussion, and the production of a collective group answer.

Next the pupils wrote their individual answers to the key question. In turn these answers were copied and given to other groups. The whole class then discussed the separate group reports through the medium of a series of questions, beginning:

- Do you think this is true?
- Where did this person get this information?
- Do you agree with the description she/he has given?
- If you disagree, say why.
- Is there anything you want to add to the description?
- What do the pictures tell you about Roman England?
- Would you have liked to live in England at that time?
- Why or why not?

Reflection Questioning and planning the teaching of a **History Study Unit.**
Review how you planned and taught a HSU in terms of questions and questioning.

- How did you select the area for the children to study ?

- What part did the framing of questions play in focusing in on the specific elements ?

- Did the pupils have a role in framing questions ? If so, what kinds of questions did they ask ?

- How might questioning play a part in your initial planning ?

Children asking questions

Key Element 4 of the History National Curriculum states that children should ask questions. Children's questions can provide them with the impetus to push on with an historical enquiry, and serve as the basis for their learning. The pupils' asking of questions at the start of a history-led project can serve many useful functions. It provides the children with a personal view and a constant point to which later study can be referred. It provides the teacher with a wealth of material if, as is the intention, the questions are used as the basis for the project content. Quite simply, the children ask the questions and together teacher and pupils begin to answer them.

A simple strategy is to ask pupils to write down at least three questions that they would like to ask about a topic. They can work in pairs or threes, and draw up a list as long as they like. These we then pool on the board, discuss, categorize and select. Typically the children come up with over 100 questions. Their questions can form the basis for subsequent investigation. Children soon become well versed in framing questions. Learning to frame questions should be central to pupils' historical training. How have we consciously tried to build children's questioning into our teaching and learning?

Introducing a History Study Unit We began our work on Saxon England through getting the children to prepare a holiday guide to the country. In pairs they drew up their own questions. Taking one question from each pair, we pooled their questions on the board as a concept web.

Using topic books the pupils researched the questions, coming up with answers based upon what they had discovered. This material served as the basis for creating their travel guide to Saxon England.

Pupil questioning and topics Pupil questioning can be used for any history-led topic. Most teachers plan quite carefully and might be worried by the idea of waiting until after the first lesson to produce their detailed plan. However, this is not the problem it might seem to be. The teacher should have a broad idea of the way in which the project is to develop. The questions on the Saxons fell into distinct bands – daily life, technology, political and social history. Teachers can work out in advance the types of questions which will be asked and plan accordingly.

The final point is one raised by a sceptical teacher who asked what to do if a child asked a question which could not be answered. This will, of course, happen. It is one of the enduring frustrations and delights of this subject that we will never know all the answers. It is therefore important that children realize this too. A simple 'I'm sorry, we just do not know, but we could try to find out', is usually sufficient.

The message is clear enough. Allow the natural curiosity of the child to contribute to the perceived planning and you unite teacher and child in a common purpose. Succeed in this and you open the door to a learning process of supremely high quality and depth. We can use children's questions at all parts of the learning process. The examples below illustrate the process at work in both KS1 and KS2.

Children asking questions at KS1: an example	Here is an example of historical enquiry on the topic of Columbus done by a class of Year 2 pupils over a period of four weeks. Most of the teaching was done by the class teacher, Lynn Cowell. I observed parts of the teaching, taking part as an 'in role' sailor of Columbus. At the end of the topic Lynn lent me her teaching notes and examples of the children's work. I was particularly interested to see how young children coped with using various sources of information in relation to asking and answering questions.
Planning	Lynn decided to focus on the question, 'How can we find out about a person who lived a very long time ago?' She then listed a number of sources of information for the children to use: pictures, story, maps, 'in role' work by a visiting teacher, ship artefacts and models and reference books on explorers and ships
A whole class brainstorm	What does an explorer do? The topic began with a brainstorming on the children's ideas of explorers – what is an explorer? What does an explorer do? The pupils' preliminary ideas were listed on the blackboard and categorized under headings suggested by them. Lynn told the class that they were going to test their ideas by listening to a story about a real explorer of long ago – Christopher Columbus – and proceeded to tell the story of Columbus using five or six pictures to illustrate some of the episodes. She focused attention on a large poster-size picture of Columbus asking the children what they observed about his dress, appearance and what the picture told them about the past. From their responses she built up on the blackboard a table showing ways in which the past differed from the present.
Group work on pictures	In the next phase of the topic pupils, working in groups, were given sets of identical pictures and asked to select eight which showed what they considered to be important parts of the Columbus story. They then sequenced the pictures chosen and prepared a caption for each picture. Both pictures and captions were mounted on a card and made into a ziz-zag book. Each group showed its book to the rest of the class, telling their version of the story whilst Lynn drew out the differences between each group's account. At the end she asked the class why each version was somewhat different. Some of the pupils began to recognize that different people remember things differently and that the choice of pictures would influence the ways things were told, certain events becoming the main focus of the story depending upon which pictures were selected and how they were interpreted. This was an important step in the children's awareness of historical

interpretation and their recognition that there are many versions of the Columbus story.

How are famous people remembered?

For the next phase, Lynn began by asking the children how famous people are remembered. Lots of ideas were mentioned including that of commemorative shields or coats of arms. This idea was taken up by the children, designs for a shield were prepared and finally the idea of a quartered shield emerged and in groups they designed four pictures which they considered were illustrated episodes from Columbus' life. Each group was asked to justify their choice of pictures to the whole class before being shown the actual coat of arms given to Columbus by Queen Isabella.

The children's questions

By this point in the topic the children were starting to build up their own mental images of Columbus and Lynn felt they were now ready to begin to raise their own questions about the explorer. She explained that I would be visiting the school in the role of a sailor who had sailed with Columbus. What sort of questions would they like to ask him? Some time was given to devising questions by going over the previous work. Working individually and in groups the children came up with a range and depth of questions that I found impressive. We did an analysis which revealed that the questions fell into the following groups:

Personal beliefs, motivation and feelings
Why did you leave your family to sail with Columbus?
Were you a prisoner or a sailor?
Why did you go on the voyage?
How was your family (when you got back home)?
What was your mum and dad's names?
Did you like sailing with Columbus?
Why did you think the world was flat?
Was it scary when you saw the sea monsters?
Were you sad to leave your family?
What was it like when you sailed off?
Did you fall off the edge of the world?

Time questions
How old was Columbus?
What was the day he set sail?
What time did you go?
What was the day of the week you landed?
Is Columbus dead now?
How did Columbus stay alive all that time?

Living conditions on board the ship

Where did you sleep?

How did you get the food?

Was it cold?

Were there any fires? (accidentally started)

What was the boat like?

Where did you go to the toilet?

What did you have to drink?

Did you have chairs on the ship?

What sort of clothes did the sailors and Columbus wear?

Where did they keep the rowing boats?

Did the food go mildew?

Did Columbus have blankets on his bed?

Did you have turns to watch in the crow's nest?

What weather did you have?

What did the crow's nest look like?

Evidence for the sailor's story

How do you know the answers to these questions?

The Indians

Were they nice?

What did they look like?

What were their names?

What did you think when you saw pipes in their mouths?

Did you see Indians when you were sailing along?

What sort of present did they give you?

Columbus

Did they have any books about Columbus?

Is he dead now?

How did he stay alive all that time?

Did he have blankets on his bed?

How old was Columbus?

Did you like sailing with Columbus?

The Crew

Were there any girls on the ship?

Can you remember the sailors' names?

How many boys were on the ship?

What was the cabin boy's name?

Lynn added the following questions: Was Columbus a kind man or grumpy? Would you have liked to stay on the island? Do you think it was a good thing that Columbus made his voyage? Did you ever meet the king and queen of Spain? Would you go again if you had a chance?

Questioning can also be used in assessing pupils, as the following KS2 example shows.

Children asking questions at KS2

The children were all in Year 4. They had covered several aspects of National Curriculum History and had a wide range of historical experience. The school owns a large number of replica artefacts which the children have used on several occasions. In addition, the children have become well used to posing their own historical questions and therefore this type of assessment procedure fits in quite naturally with their own working practices.

It was decided not to make the assessment relate specifically to any of the study units which the children had worked on. Over the past year the children had studied food and farming, the Egyptians, the local environment, including an element of local history. The children were fairly confident in using different sources of historical information.

The assessment

The various tasks set out below were given to the children as a set of written instructions. Six facsimile pots were placed on different tables. These ranged from a Saxon burial pot to a Stuart three-handled jug. The children had not worked with these pots before. As can be seen from the instructions, the children were specifically told to work on their own rather than in small groups. Besides the rather obvious statement that we wished to assess the ability of each individual child, it was also considered important that the children be allowed to show what they could do without having to endure endless interruptions from their fellow pupils.

The assessment activity instructions

1 Go to the table with the pot you wish to work on. Remember, you are working on your own so it should not matter where your friend is going.
2 You have plenty of paper. Two pieces are for the final answers but the rest is for drafting; do try to use them.
3 **Task 1** Write at least 10 questions about the pot. These can be anything you want but the more unusual ones are often better. Draft these and when you are ready copy them out in best. You may use borders.
4 **Task 2** Draw the pot underneath the questions or on a different piece of paper if necessary.

Illustration 9 *Children working with the pots*

5 **Task 3** Take three (or more) of your questions and answer them as well as you can. Write as much as you can for each answer. You may draft first and then copy your answers out. Is there more than one possible answer? If so, which is the best ?

5 **Task 4** Finally, you have been asked by the museum curator to write the label for this pot. It must be no more than four sentences. What will you write?

The assessment explained

Task 1 requires the children simply to examine the artefacts and to pose questions. At this stage there is no need for the children even to consider how to answer them.

Task 2 was not assessed.

Task 3 begins the search for more advanced skills. Here the children are expected to select at least three of their questions. This selection process itself contributes towards the assessment, for the more able child will choose questions which are open-ended rather than the simplistic 'What was the pot used for?' type of question. The child who successfully selected three questions had then to research possible answers. For this purpose there was a range of books available within the classroom. As the pots were from different times these books covered a wide historical timescale.

Task 4 From the information the children had discovered they had to select the four most important elements. As an extension of this exercise they then had to justify the inclusion of the information of their choice, as opposed to the rejection of other material. This was done verbally to the whole group at the end of the session.

The children's responses

Below are the responses of two contrasting children to illuminate the extent and nature of children's questioning.

Example 1: Kim

Kim is a child with major learning difficulties. He is not statemented but is approximately two years behind his peers. Kim receives additional support both in whole class and in small group work. He has a poor concentration span and needs substantial assistance with written tasks. For the purposes of the assessment activity he told me what questions he wanted to ask and I wrote them down for him. He then copied his questions onto paper. These were his questions: Who made it? Where was it made? When was it found? How was it made? What was it for? Who was it made for?

Despite his inability to write, what is interesting here is the kind of questions he asks. He has clearly concentrated upon the physical presence of the object and has no real understanding of context, although he does discuss its use and role. Given the time available he did not get to begin to answer any of the questions but because of his difficulties he would probably have experienced great problems with this.

Example 2: Lauren

For the second example we have chosen Lauren, probably the brightest child in the group. She is very able but often does not produce the work of which she is capable. In this instance, however, she was interested and motivated and did well. She wrote more than 20 different questions of which these are a random sample: How old is it? Why is it this shape? What sort of food was cooked in it? Who was first to use it? Why has it got a pattern on it? Why is it all black? Why is it thinner at the top and the bottom? What did the food taste like when it was cooked in there?

With her question about the thickness of the pot she is considering reasons for why it looks like it does. For her selection of questions to answer she chose the following:
Why is the pot black? The pot is black because the Vikings did most of their cooking over open fires. If you put something into fire it goes black!

What sort of food was cooked in it? Herbs, porridge and a meat stew were the kinds of food cooked in this pot.

Why is it this shape? It is this shape so the heat can spread evenly and so you can get lots of food inside.

Lauren then drew pictures to show her answers in pictorial form. These were accurate and informative with correct labels. Finally she came to writing the label for the museum. This is what she wrote: 'This is a cooking pot that the Vikings used. It was used on an open fire. Things like herbs, porridge and meat stews were cooked on it. It was probably made on a wheel.' Lauren did a certain amount of research for her answers to her questions. She has been able to communicate her findings in a variety of forms and her conclusions are reasonable given the information she has discovered.

Reflection Questioning and the teaching of a History Study Unit

- As you read the account, jot down how questioning shapes the pupils' historical learning.
- Consider how this approach might influence your future teaching of history.

6 Speaking, Listening, Discussion and Debate

One of the tangible benefits brought by the National Curriculum was the clear statement that we need to teach our children to talk and listen. The ability to talk – to discuss, argue, debate, describe and express ideas, thoughts and feelings orally – is indeed one of the most important skills anyone can have. I recall some years ago a series of programmes on adult illiteracy and although they showed well the problems these people faced, they also showed how well they got round them by talk. A lorry-driver 'just asked', others got into conversation and learned by the incidentals of the debate, others just listened with skill and got by.

It is not to denounce the skills of literacy that we in the NPHP have set such a high price on talking and listening. Of course we must struggle as hard as we can to get children to read and write all the time, never giving up, but when we see daily how hard, how unachievable the goals seem for so many children, then we must also value the skills they can learn.

Listening

The skill of listening is perhaps one of the most important we can encourage. To listen requires a certain discipline, a self control that children mostly do not have naturally, and they must learn it. As they realize that waiting gives them a chance to learn from what other people are saying and a chance to put together a more coherent contribution next time they intervene, they learn skills of co-operation that are vital in the world at large. Above all they begin to see in practice, in a way that all can understand, how to chain an argument, how to present a case, how to be convincing. What better skill could we offer children going out to find a place for themselves in a hard market?

Many children find reading and writing so difficult that they have learned during their years of schooling to put up insuperable barriers. Imagine (and of course the fact that you can read and write makes this act of imagination much more difficult) if you had spent, say, four or five years training to become a skilled poker player, or a high wire artist, or a juggler, and you had failed all the way through, what would your reaction be when asked to join a game, put your foot out or take the clubs into your hands!

Debate

We have offered such children the chance first to try the domain of talking, and it is interesting that in debate it is often those children of least literary ability who come to the fore. I recall one such child who would beg every lesson 'When are we going to have a debate?' because he knew he would shine there, and when we did he would go out of the room punching the air and saying (very loudly) 'Best lesson ever'. He loved it because he was a success and I loved it because I could begin to break through his resistance to learning and actually teach him something.

Orderly thinking

One of the main elements of teaching and learning is the discipline of orderly thinking. At first children see debate as a battle – shouting opposition at one another. This is fun, but they must begin to learn to listen to their opponents, if at first only to make a case against them. 'You say the Emperor had to keep control and so he was right to be hard, I say the harder he was the harder he got'.

The workhouse debate

Let us now to look at one example of debate and discussion in action. As with much of our work, role play is frequently employed to help the children examine an historical situation from 'inside' rather than 'outside'. In this example the class (30 ten year olds) was doing a local study and had focused on a building that was the local union workhouse. In the first phase of this part of the topic, they were thinking about the character of the beadle. Sue Edwards, the class teacher, was working with me.

In the third lesson we discussed workhouses further and several children who had seen 'Oliver' gave us their memories. We looked at the figure of the beadle (and after some confusion with Jeremy Beadle) found a character to play with. At their direction, I became a rather horrible beadle, greasy to the visitors, grasping with the residents. The children enjoyed the role play vastly and would gladly have gone on.

In the fourth lesson we explored how this situation could have come about. We looked at the payment of a parish rate to support the poor and the children (again in role plays) quickly established the point that people wouldn't have been eager to pay a high rate. Perhaps this was the root of the problem?

But they still wanted to hammer the beadle and in the fifth lesson we gave them their way. I played the beadle, Sue, the judge and we had lawyers, witnesses (with carefully made up 'wounds') and set the scene in a cleared classroom. The beadle was sent to serve a long term in gaol to the great satisfaction of the children.

At the beginning of sixth lesson I told the children that the beadle was having a hard time in gaol and they all said 'good'. But the story was by no means over – there were still paupers in Midhurst, people were still not anxious to pay the rate, and something must be done. For a while they struggled hard to think of ways of making money, and again we tried these out in role, but alas they didn't seem to work. At the end of the lesson I took on a new role. I was from the Petworth Emigration Committee and I would 'buy' as many paupers as would go to help populate Canada. Some children breathed a sigh of relief, but others smelled a rat.

In the seventh lesson I introduced the children to the scheme, using photocopies of the original documents. They were fascinated and much appreciated that this was still 'real', not invention. The document was hard to read but the children took great care and held fervid discussions, saying those who didn't want to go must stay and be supported in the workhouse. The volunteers were kitted out as best we could afford – there was considerable argument as to whether they all needed bibles and changes of clothes, but finally, off our twelve emigrants went. I left the children to write letters from Midhurst to Canada and from Canada to Midhurst.

We then spent a long time reading the childrens' letters and comparing them with some originals from 1832. The children were quite moved and declared that emigration wasn't the whole answer; we had to care for our own poor. It was a good moment to stop, and yet we went on.

A contemporary comparison

After all the children now knew a lot about the problems of poverty in the past and it seemed a shame just to leave it there, so I asked them in the next lesson whether they could think with me about today. They eagerly accepted the challenge, so on the spot I magicked them into being DSS officers, and introduced them to four sad cases, which I role played, lightly but clearly.

The first character had been a highly successful car salesman who had spent freely and when he was suddenly made redundant had considerable debts and a big mortgage. The second was a cleaner who possessed very little, whose low salary had been cut in half by the firm that employed him. The third was a deputy bank manager who had come to the end of his six months sick pay but was not yet well enough for work. The last was an illegal immigrant from Bosnia, a lady with little understanding of the English language or customs, who lived in a hostel and believed she needed to have money to pay the police not to deport her.

The children interrogated each character with a great deal of care. They dismissed the first as worthless, because he had wasted his money and confessed to having been a bit of a gambler. The children had ideas on how he might cope, but were determined not to throw good money after bad. The cleaner was given money without question. The sick man they felt needed support, and they gave it, not enquiring too deeply (because they never asked, they did not know that his illness was alcohol-related). The Bosnian lady was told she was breaking the law and must go home. No one questioned her idea that the police needed bribing. Several children had good ideas on how to help her, and some protested vigorously at her deportation.

In between this and the tenth lesson I consulted the DSS by telephone and got advice on each of the cases. I was told that the first man would be quite favourably treated, the second given no support, the third would have to have a lot of tests, and in the case of the Bosnian lady, they quite agreed with the children.

The children listened to my report back pop-eyed. *Surely* I had got it wrong, this *can't* be right. So they wrote to the DSS, and got a reply.

Debating and power

We have used a great range of debating topics within the NPHP, and interestingly, many of them have, like the above example, been about power. We find it useful to base the discussion, within a role play context, around a key question. In the example above the key questions were:

If the committee wouldn't give the beadle enough money to treat the inmates well, was he justified in treating them badly?

followed by

How should modern DSS officers decide upon the claims of four applicants?

In order to add a sense of reality to the debate we took the trouble to consult the DSS by phone and got advice on each case. In another example when we were considering the role of the beadle in the workhouse, we spent a long time balancing the power of the committee (who controlled him) and the power he had over the inmates. Thus the children had to consider the complex question, 'If the committee wouldn't give him enough money to treat the inmates well, was he just in treating them badly?'

Arguing with the teacher

Another glorious feature of this work for me was to see children discovering that you could disagree (not least with the teacher) without fighting and that debate can be immensely invigorating. This is the beginning of political education, the foundation stone of democracy, and as a society we are lost without it. I think of one small boy who was for me a bit of a touchstone in this class. If I could stir him then I could guess that the rest would be all right. He had a difficult background in education, had been seriously let down far too many times in such a young life, and had decided that he would, in future, slide out and under. He wasn't going to be caught again, no fear, and was fast becoming that most difficult of problems, a sly boy. As we worked along he kept, against his principles, getting slightly interested and half raising his hand. On every occasion I pounced and jollied up what he had to say to a pitch of cleverness where he scarcely recognized himself. The class teacher caught him fully, about half way through the project, when he volunteered a plan to save the workhouse. She immediately took on the role of a hostile beadle and fought him vigorously. Although he was shaking his head by the end of the process, he knew he had enjoyed it, and was soon to be seen raising a proud hand to say 'I disagree'.

Likewise, when we were considering the impact of the National Health Service on hospitals, we had children who knew that fruit juices were important for tonsilitis patients debating the expenditure with politicans who knew they must somehow cut their costs. When children, who had pleaded for a diptheria poster campaign to warn parents of the disease's first symptoms, met a policitian who said, 'Why is this child dying?' then the debate was clear and open, and hot as it could be.

Debating and evidence

Part of the business of debate is getting your authorities right. Children quickly learn that it is no good simply asserting something because the opponents will equally simply reply 'prove it'. As we run up to a debate it is important to get the children to value the role of research and to prepare evidences so that they will be available in the right format when they need them. Debaters need notes – not notes of what to say, but notes of evidences to support what they say.This is not to deny the fact that discussion and debate often lead to the need to find out more evidence or to check back on evidence. Thus researching evidence will certainly be a preliminary activity to discussion, as well as something to return to afterwards.

Setting the debating scene

Yet of course what you say is of the essence and this is one of the ways in which children learn most effectively from discussion. It is important to know what you want to say and to have the vocabulary with which to say it most effectively. It is useful before any discussion to spend some time round the board thinking about the words we might use and categorizing the range of ideas that might fruitfully come under the question we are debating.

As children see that careful preparation will give them the language they will need in the debate, so they will be the more willing to spend time on it, and as a by-product they will write a great deal without grumbling about what they are doing. However it is always important to make clear to them that they will not win by reading things out, although initially it must be admitted that some children need the support of a piece of paper in front of them. The aim will be to reach the conviction and clarity of extemporaneous discourse that will eventually get them the rewards they so strongly need from lively discussion and debate.

Testing ideas

Within the process of discussion and debate children will discover the facility of testing their ideas, seeing how they work and considering how they might reformulate them in written discourse. For above all things discussion and debate are best used as preliminaries to writing.

The teacher's role

Children approach a debate with their usual happy confusion about what they are supposed to do. They have some ideas, some convictions and they are ready to do battle for these. Yet as the debate goes on, and as the teacher guides what is being said by reminding the children what the question at issue is really about, so the children begin to understand that some of their contributions are irrelevant, some of them focused, some of them convicing, some of them not so. Here we have the ideal preparation for writing, and nothing could be better.

Yet the children need to know what is happening, that this is not just a gladiatorial combat but really a testing ground for their own thinking. They should observe when the teacher is saying – 'Yes, that seems to me to be a strong argument' and when the teacher is saying 'Tell us more about your idea. I don't know yet what it has to do with the question we are debating.'

Guidance

The teacher's role in discussion and debate is as ever most important. Above all the teacher must guide the discussion along the lines of the question stated, but must be prepared to open out novel lines from pupils where they seem productive. Thus in a debate on Ancient Greek democracy it is easy to get stuck on 'Why are women allowed no place here?' but to be able to strike out on 'What issues in Ancient Greece might women have been able to contribute to?' The teacher must listen hard for the child who can lead the debate on to higher grounds – it is no good trying to introduce the issue oneself. The one person children find it very hard to listen to is their teacher!

The teacher as controller

Yet the teacher's role in control remains absolute. Children are not born listeners and do not give way easily. It is useful to have some symbol of the power before being allowed to speak – a hat (as in the House of Commons) or a ring (more powerful as a symbol) or a stone or any other object that may be held as 'the right to speak'. The symbolic object must be given by and handed back to the teacher on every occasion, marking a useful pause for calming down and thinking out the next step.

History and debate

All of history is a debate, and if children are to see history fairly and truly, they must engage in that debate. The past is not what we see, but how we see it, and our skill as historians lies in our ability to convey our vision to others. Part of the joy of all this is in the conflict it involves. There is no doubt that historians (adult, professional historians that is) love to contest each other's vision of the past. Their debate is often hot and hard, so when you are feeling that things may well have gone a shade too far, think again that this might be another example of children doing history.

Discussion and debate at KS1

As a contrast let us look at an example of discussion and debate with a Year 2 class. The children and their teacher, Lynn Cowell, had been doing a topic on Columbus which has started with a story and picture sequencing followed by some research into the life of Columbus (see pages 58–61). For the second year running, I was invited to take the role of a sailor who had sailed with

71

Columbus and answer the children's prepared questions on the journey. After discussion with Lynn I decided this time to take the role of a sailor who was very critical of Columbus and whose answers to the children's questions would challenge their, heroic views of the explorer. I took the role of Francisco Pinzon, the brother of Martin Pinzon who had captained the *Pinta*, which sailed alongside the *Santa Maria*. In answering the children's questions in role as Francisco I cast doubt on whether Columbus was such an heroic figure.

Following the interview, Lynn discussed with the class Francisco's opinion of Columbus. First, did they believe his account? Initially all the class accepted absolutely all Francisco had said about Columbus. Then Lynn gently suggested that maybe Francisco had been jealous of Columbus' success and great welcome back to Spain by the King and Queen. Gradually the children began to modify their initial views of Francisco's opinions of Columbus until eventually about ten children expressed doubt about Francisco's views whilst others strongly held to their original opinions. With children of this age the discussion needed careful guidance by the teacher – careful, but also sensitive in holding in balance the heroic view alongside the critical.

For these children, this was probably the first time they had been asked to reconcile two opposing points of view on an historical figure. Lynn tape-recorded her discussion with the class to provide evidence of young children's ability to discuss evidence of a conflicting nature, as well as evidence about her handling of a tricky piece of teaching.

Leading the discussion

Initially, the discussion had begun by Lynn getting the class to recap points about the interview with Francisco. This was simply recall of the interview which most the children did accurately. She next moved on to Francisco's opinions of Columbus as a leader and again the children recalled accurately. Then came the key question 'Do you believe what he said about Columbus?' Response from everyone was 'Yes'. At this point Lynn could have simply closed down the conversation. Rather than taking that course of action, Lynn gently suggested that maybe Francisco was jealous of Columbus and let this idea simmer for a while. Patience and pace are both important at this stage of such a discussion, as well as listening carefully to the class. One boy tentatively suggested that without Columbus there would not have been a voyage of discovery at all. Lynn mused with the class on this idea. Other ideas slowly emerged – if Columbus had acted like Martin Pinzon, Francisco's brother, then he would have been a really great man. Again Lynn mused with the class on this idea. At this crucial stage of the discussion far deeper ideas were beginning to emerge – not necessarily in favour of Columbus, but going back over some of Francisco's critical comments. Was Columbus really the gold-greedy man portrayed? Did he treat the natives badly? Did he cheat the sailor who first spotted land unfairly in claiming the reward of money from the King for himself?

Finally, Lynn told the children that they would be writing a report on the Columbus voyage for the newspaper. As reporters what would they write? Each pupil in turn was asked this question. This is a good way of getting young children to sum up their views. Some children stuck firmly to Francisco's evaluation, while others had modified their initial views expressed early on in the discussion. A few still held to an heroic view of Columbus.

Undoubtedly, the structuring of this exercise was important in the setting up of the interview, using the children's own questions with a critical interviewer of Columbus, the careful and sensitive discussion after the interview with the class teacher, the timing and pace of the discussion, and the drawing together of ideas through the medium of a newspaper report (not historically accurate, but a recording idea young children living today can understand).

| **Developing pupil talk** | Pupil talk clearly goes through a series of stages, from the initial encounter with the task and resources through to the resolution and presentation. Starting talk is exploratory: uncertain, stumbling, inchoate, discursive, confused, ignorant. Steadily as confidence and understanding develops it become fuller, more rounded and directed with focus. Within this context of developing understanding there has to be full rein given to the pupils to run along apparently unfruitful lines, to toss ideas around, to argue to apparently little purpose, so long as all are related to the task in hand. |

Such talk needs careful development, with the teacher playing the key role in regulating, controlling, directing and enriching. It should occur in a structured situation. It should have a clear set of goals, a deliberate function. It can be regulated to occur within a prescribed period of time, 'you have x minutes to discuss this', then you have to report back. Within the context of discussion we need a set of guidelines, rules, to help promote learning. You can get the class to draw up the rules, or give them a sheet based on the points below.

Guidelines for discussion

1 Our only rule is that when another person is speaking, you listen. This relates to working as a whole class, or in groups or pairs. Good manners are essential. Respect the other person.
2 Remember you are taking part in a discussion:
   a to learn
   b to help other people learn
3 Ask for anything you do not understand to be explained.
4 Do not be afraid to ask even if you think you might appear to be stupid. It is the job of the speaker to make sure that everyone understands what is being said.
5 Stress points that you think are important.
6 In a group try and sort out misunderstandings.
7 Make sure that all members of a group have a turn to say what they think.
8 Always be ready to change your mind.
9 Don't shout people down.
10 Always make sure that you take part in a discussion even if you are shy.
11 Listen carefully to what everyone has to say.
12 Have a pencil and paper to make notes as you go along.
13 Make sure that one person in the group has the job of summarizing ideas and presenting them to the rest of the class.
14 Take turns to do this job.

Reflection Debating with Children

- Consider when you might hold a class discussion and debate with your children
- How would you go about it?
- Consider the following points about discussion and debate in the classroom:
  The key question
  Researching the evidence
  Setting the scene : pooling ideas
  Controlling the debate – teacher as chairperson
  Orderly thinking
  Writing and resolution

Pair and small group talk

In 'doing history' talking in pairs and small groups plays a major part. What is needed for successful pair and group talk?

- Being sufficiently interested in others to ask them questions, and listen to their answers.
- Being prepared to let someone have his/her head, allowing him/her time and space to formulate and re-formulate an idea without interrupting him/her and to support him/her with little encouraging noises.
- Being prepared to hold one's own point, or interest, temporarily in abeyance so that one can help others in their formulations, so that the main thread of the discourse is not lost.
- Being prepared even to lose the chance of voicing an idea because the other person or the mainstream of the argument is more important.
- Being able to participate in the formulation of a group construct to which all have contributed and now subscribe.

This means that the pupil has to have the self confidence to shut up, listen and cooperate.

Reflection **Pair and small group talk**
Review your next piece of history teaching, and consider when and how you might introduce pair and small group work along the lines suggested.

---

7 Reading Books

Without reading and writing there can be no history. Children often find reading and writing difficult, and because of this they are prone to say that history is hard, sometimes it is too hard. Some 15-20% of our Year 3/4 pupils read and write fluently. By Year 6 the figures will have dramatically improved, but there will still be a large number who struggle with reading.

Yet children must read texts, look up information, make notes and in the end communicate findings. Later we address the issue of children reading documents; here we examine the use of books.

Books are often very much more difficult than they look. Publishers are skilled at making books look good and we often buy by the look of the thing. But we should notice how very rare a good information book is. Most history books are still written as sequential readers, even though nobody wants sequential history readers any more. Thus a child trying to find information is blocked by entering a story at a particular point.

Equally books that are designed to give information either overcrowd the page or give such trivial information that they are no use and simply annoy the child hunting for the particular.

For example, one very angry small boy reported, 'I have hunted and hunted through all the books in the library and I cannot find a word about Alcibiades'. Of course the immediate answer is 'Look in the index, dear,' but we should pause and examine the quality of indexes to children's books before using this nostrum. Often pre-tagging books with sticky labels ensures that children get to the right spots. It may be a bit primitive to say 'Orange labels for games, blue for villas' but it does actually get children started on reference work.

Reading for information

History has the advantage of seeing reading in many different contexts, not just as reading text. Pupils need to read pictures, maps, sites, every kind of source we use. Children should practise reading skills in these areas which they might think are 'easier' than text. We must formulate questions, we must learn to scan surfaces, we must ask ourselves what the evidence we are discovering means. As we sit examining a picture, we are practising reading skills because our kind of reading, reading for history, has universal applications. We must learn to stop, to enquire, to extract, to organize information into a meaningful pattern and sequence. And this requires time and patience.

Reading books

We need to spend time training children to use books. For example, most children regard illustrations as merely decoration, and do not think of them as sources of information. There are some bad illustrations, but these days in many books the illustrator has done more research and taken more trouble than the writer, so this is worth pointing out.

Questioning

Another bit of training we need to do is to get children to question books, not just in terms of finding out answers, but critically, 'What is this version saying, as against that?' Looking at a number of books on the same subject area does help us see that an author has a particular vision, and indeed has heard particular stories. We need to question what this has to say to us, the searchers.

Reading and the story of Theseus

Below is an example of work undertaken with a mixed age class of Years 4, 5 and 6 using reference books to find out about aspects of life in Ancient Greece.

Session 1 I told the children the story of Theseus and the Minotaur and followed up with a discussion on the sort of people who might have created such a story. The class then began to research this question in groups using reference books. Finally I made a blackboard summary of the pupils' findings.

Session 2 The class was divided into three groups with each taking responsibility for an area of research.

    Group 1:   Temples, Religion
    Group 2:   Soldiers, Sailors
    Group 3:   Drama, Theatre and Masks

We selected these topics from the blackboard list of items the children had reported on at the end of the first session. The children were asked to record their findings under three headings: Title of book, page number, evidence.

Although each group tended to interpret the task differently – one recording the information in full as they discovered it, another making notes for future reference and the other fully discussing its findings – the children responded extremely well to this challenge and successfully identified appropriate items of information.

Session 3 Groups were increased to four and the research topics were modified to allow the children experience of researching four new areas of information: Gods and Goddesses, Weapons and Armour, Food and Drink, Ships and Sailors.

Each child was challenged to record five pieces of information on a prepared form and to select the piece of information they considered most important.

The children tended to look for their information under chapter headings which were often of little help. When they found references they found it extremely difficult to identify five pieces of information from the material in the books. Few were able to respond with any conviction to the last task. 'I just put any old thing' – Alison.

Analysis of the work done by the pupils in Session 3

Of the eight Year 4 children, seven made careful reference to their source, the only one failing to do this having been away at the start of the exercise, therefore not fully understanding the instructions. Three of them found two pieces of information, one found three, one found four, and three found the full five pieces. The three who found the five pieces of information also made a choice and gave an explanation. Their choices seemed fairly random but the explanations made sense of what they chose – thus Cal chose an item about breakfast and explained that you need a good breakfast to keep you going through the day. Kyle chose the word 'hoplites' as his most important piece of information on the grounds that it was about the soldiers themselves and not just about their equipment.

Of the three Year 5 children, all gave five pieces of information and all gave sources. Two gave choices and substantiated them, with perhaps slightly less reasoning that the Year 4 children.

Of the six Year 6 children, all gave five items of information and their sources. The only one who didn't make a choice was Gracara, which is strange, because her listings were some of the most careful and sensible. Again the choices seemed random and the

Name:

Topic you have been researching:

The five pieces of information I have discovered are:

Title of book and page

1.

2.

3.

4.

5.

The most important piece of imformation from the five is:

The reason I think this is because:

Illustration 10 Book research form

explanations merely extensions of the statements except in two cases. Karis chose a list of gods and goddesses and their symbols clearly because it was useful. Jemma firmly declared that all of her pieces of information were equally important.

Reflection
- Review how you use books in your teaching of history.
- What changes to your practice will you introduce in the light of the above?

8 Reading Documents

We define a document as a written or printed piece of raw source material that we use to write history. Documents that we have used to teach KS1 and KS2 children range from Dark Age charters and land grants to modern autobiographies, trade directories, census entries, diaries, newspapers and computer printouts. Through reading documents and working upon them, children come face to face with people from the past in their own words. A document forces the pupil to participate at first-hand in a dialogue with the past. But, how often do you sit down with your children to read carefully through a document and then squeeze it dry of what it can tell us?

Reflection Review your use of documents by answering these questions
- In which ways did you use documents in the teaching of your current or last HSU?
- How might you use documents in your current HSU or the next one?
- What problems might Specific Learning Difficulty pupils have in using documents? What steps would you take to overcome their difficulties?
- What problems might the exceptionally able, fluent readers experience? What steps would you take to help them?
- What other difficulties might present themselves when using documents with your class? How could these be overcome?

Reading documents with children

Many teachers, when they realize how deep the literary requirements are which history makes on the young learner, will hastily declare that their own class is either too young or too poorly skilled in reading techniques to cope with the proper study of history. Instead of seeing history as a useful area of practice, in which pupils may improve their literary skills, they simply declare that the hurdles are too high, and attempt to retreat from the race. While we would all agree that there is room for improvement in the teaching of reading to KS1 and KS2 children, the true problem lies elsewhere: teachers do not realize that they have given the children the tools to read even the hardest document.

Accessibility

There are many ways of making documents accessible to children. We have done a considerable amount of work using documents on audio tape with pupils, so that after going through the text with the whole group we can set everyone to work on further study, but with some pupils using the tape as a support to their reading. It is a good way of slowing the process down to the reading ability of the pupil – if you read at the pace of a voiced rendition of the text, then it does become an easier task. Amazingly, young children will often find reading texts in the original handwriting much easier than one might expect, because we recognize that this will be a slow process of decipherment where we are not expected to dash through with immediate understanding of everything. Even the hardest of texts can be used if if the teacher prepares properly. This means being very clear about the learning objectives and breaking the learning process down into bite-sized pieces, with teacher support at every point.

We must, as teachers of reading (and we are all that), learn to stress the positive, and not to underline the mistakes children make. I remember to this day with the deepest distaste a teacher who started a dictation by giving pupils twenty marks each (seems nice) but took a mark off for every mistake, thus ensuring that careless little me ended usually with minus 20 as my reward. My French remains inaccurate to this day as a result. We must work with children on the words and phrases they can understand, not on those that give them pause. The very worst way to attempt any text is a word by word, line by line reading, attempting full comprehension at every stage.

A subsidiary cause of a failure of confidence in the pupil is that reading is often an isolated, almost competitive activity. Children are often left to read alone, without any clues as to how to do it or what it might be for, and they are often forced to take part in the disastrous activity of 'reading round the class' in which they are shown up as poor readers to the impatience of all concerned. If a teacher wants everyone to share a text at the same time there is only one way to do it – the teacher must read him or herself, or must prepare a taped version that all can listen to – and even if it is your own voice on the machine, there is a magic quality in all listening together to one reading.

We expect you are saying, 'It's easy to criticize, but if we are not to read serially, not to read in silence, not to read round the class, what the devil are we to do?' Fair question, and the answer lies entirely in the goal of confidence-building, making pupils believe they can read, that the task is possible, and that they will be able to do it themselves. To achieve that we need to have five activities in our classrooms:

a) **whole class teaching**
b) **constant rewards for success**
c) **rapid scanning of the text**
d) **repeated scanning of the text**
e) **tasks of carefully graded difficulty.**

Let us consider these points in order: first, you need to work with a whole class on a given document reading exercise so that you can know what is happening in every part of the class. We bring the whole class to the front, close enough for real eye to eye contact. When you are working with the whole class you must of course abolish that stupid notion of 'hands up'. This is a supposed contract of fairness whereby you the teacher promise to listen to the first person with their hand up, while the class promises to maintain good order by not calling out. In truth, however, this bargain may not be kept, and teachers keep the bright pupils who always answer first with their arms aching in the air whilst they appeal for answers from other children.

It is nothing but a farce, and in its place the teacher should put the simple technique of posing questions to named individuals, and being prepared to take a number of answers when the question is open (as most good teaching questions are). As the teacher spins the questions round the whole room, so he or she takes the learning temperature of the class and may slow down or speed up without doing all the work themselves and leaving the least able resting quietly in the conviction that clever Sarah will do it all.

Praise and reward   Secondly, at each stage every pupil, whatever their ability, will need the reward of praise. In so many classes, we see teachers who reprove and never praise, and their children will never have the self esteem required for proper learning. On the other hand, teachers watching me in action often query the amount of praise I use, feeling quite sickened by the atmosphere of mutual congratulation, and they ask whether it is sincere, whether or not I am being hypocritical in saying 'Well done, you clever, clever girl,' when indeed only a moderate response has been given. Maybe sincerity is not what we want most, for in my classrooms children do flower under my praise, and want to move on to gain more. Thus recently when we were using The Battle of Maldon with some average to poor reading eleven year olds we said good words about their reading of the translated text, and soon they were happily struggling with the Anglo-Saxon version. It is the 'happily', we want to emphasize here – if children work willingly and confidently they will work well, whatever their ability.

Gradual immersion in a document

So the **first stage is to rush them through the whole of a document** so that the pupils can feel they have at least galloped over its surface. So we may say 'Just glance through it for me, don't read it yet, just flicker through it and sort out the people involved – they will have capital letters for their names, so they should be easy to spot – just do that for me in two minutes, please.' The 'please' is quite important, as is the time – to give them a short period of time is a gamesome way of getting them to work with a will from the start, and it boosts them into activity with added motivation.

We then need to take **many more quick swathes through the whole text** – look for places for me, look for dates – whatever you can find to ask the children to look for that will take them at speed through the text. Each time they go through it, of course they pick up more and more of its meaning, and more and more confidence in their power to understand. One special way to reward the children's findings is to use the blackboard to record them, either writing them yourself or giving the children who have found something the chance to write it up themselves.

Next we **need to ask increasingly complex and demanding questions** that require a critical capacity, an individual reading, real thinking. But we must not get too excited and ask too difficult a question at the start – something broad and general, something everyone can answer will suffice. So we say 'Now, I want everyone to think very hard,' (signal that a question is coming up) 'about the way the writer of the poem thought about soldiers. About what qualities they needed – the things that made them good, really good soldiers. Look at the text again, and then discuss with your neighbour whether you can come up with one word to add to the end of this sentence. 'In the Battle of Maldon the poet thought soldiers should be _____.' Note how the question contains many repetitions, many restatements, all designed to make it very clear to every child what they have to do. It is important to receive all the answers, however trite, to reward them and to record them. It will require patience from you, and patience from the class, but listening to everybody is part of building belief that everybody is important, and everybody can do it.

The big question

There may be several steps in this sequence of questions of a rising order of difficulty. But we must ask the big question eventually and see what we get in reply: 'Can you see any difference between what the Anglo-Saxon poet saw as good qualities in soldiers, and what the Viking poet saw in the poem we studied before, and what is the difference between both of their views and what we see now as the best qualities of the soldier today?'

Once one has asked the big question, it is important to allow plenty of time for talk between pupils trying to bring their own ideas to the surface, and talk between them and you trying to express what they want to say. Often children sound very naive at first when they are trying to say something profound, and it is important to wait, to listen carefully and sympathetically, and to probe for what lies behind the surface of what is being said. And then we must use what we have found from our reading – first to learn new things, looking up all those bits and pieces we didn't understand, and which might help us review the meaning we have made of our reading once we know it all. And of course we must communicate what we have found – we must tell in some way, writing, speaking, painting, acting – any one of a hundred ways of expressing the statement 'Look what I have found out by my own effort.' With a little bit of help from the teacher, of course.

Reflection Working out a pattern for teaching with documents

Consider the main points above about how to teach children to read documents:

> the big question
> whole class teaching
> constant rewards for success
> rapid scanning of the text
> repeated scanning of the text
> tasks of carefully graded difficulty.

How does this contrast with your current practice?

Teaching with documents	The key to involving children with documents is to present the document in a form that they can work upon enthusiastically. You can draw upon a number of strategies to make the most intractable source accessible to children. One approach is to read the document out, or having taped it, to play it to the form while they follow the original. For example, in our work on children during the Second World War we deliberately taped a Japanese girl's account of life at the end of the war, and played it back to the class, stopping it frequently to tease out the meaning of the passages. The tape took us all back in time, we were all quaking from fear during the bombing raids, drinking polluted water, living off handfuls of mouldy rice.
Teaching the Victorian school	This is an example of using our repertoire of approaches for teaching with documents. The clear topic was Victorian schools. The class teacher and I were teaching a mixed class of thirty-one Year 4/5 pupils. Central to our teaching strategies is to move from what children know, understand and can do to an unknown and unfamiliar area that relates closely to the known. Thus to introduce the idea of creating history from sources, we had just investigated a bag containing evidence about a boy, Tom. The pupils became heavily involved in the investigation and excited by it. We then moved on to finding out about Victorian children using documents, the investigating documents being analogous to examining the contents of the bag. The class had never done any document work. I explained that next they were going to look at some far more difficult clues than those in the bag, primarily because these clues came from 1839 ('Almost a hundred and sixty years ago,' said Adam) and things were different then from now. We discussed the central point – that we had recognized and understood the clues about Tom because they were from today. We were going to try to read something which was written over 150 years ago; people didn't speak quite the same then as they do now and the world they lived in was different.
The Document : Eastbrook School for Infants	Copies of the Eastbrook School for Infants document were handed out. I read it aloud, to ease the pain of the children's first encounter with a page of turgid Victorian prose, while they followed the text. 'What's this all about? What is it?' I asked. John put up his hand. 'A very hard piece of writing, Miss.' The next volunteer, Sarah, pronounced: 'It's an advertisement.'

Illustration 11   *Pupils using Easterbrook School document*

Teasing out the meaning – questions and discussion

The next twenty minutes were spent teasing out the meaning of the document. The only two words the children needed explaining to them were 'benefactor' and 'morals'. The first specific question about the document was: 'What ages were the children in this school?' We chose this deliberately as the starter question, as the children were obviously intimidated by the text. I knew that they would succeed in reading the children's ages and therefore gain confidence. The pattern of questions which enabled the children to understand the document's meaning, purpose and context was as follows:

What ages were the children?	Easy initial textual question to allow the class to broach the document successfully.
So, what kind of school was it? Was it like ours?	To establish a mental picture of the school in the children's minds, through stimulating them to search the document for clues.

What did the school say it was going to teach the children? Why, do you think, it taught these topics?	Open questions to encourage speculation.
What kind of people is this 'labouring advertisement for?	Extrapolating – not only classes', but people at work all day.
	(We held a quick poll to see how many of them had both parents working. Most did. Who looked after their pre-school brothers an sisters?)
Sarah spotted that this was an advertisement, and adverts try to sell us things. Is this advert doing this? How?	Analysis question. (The children picked up the promise to teach religion and obedience, and also the 'keep them off the unsafe streets' argument.)
Why should running about the streets endager the children's health?	Again, a question to encourage hypothesizing, extrapolation and comparison with the situation today.

A long discussion about early Victorian town streets, labourers' homes, and communal loos ensued. Several children remembered outside loos at the homes of older family members. At the end of this section, I praised the class fulsomely about how clever they had been to understand such hard Victorian writing. In the next lesson we worked on a copy of the Eastbrook School Rules. The children were now so confident that they declared they could work on them alone.

Hopefully this example has helped you grasp the central ideas of breaking the reading task down into easy steps that children can master, and of using questions at each stage to drive the enquiry on.

> **Reflection** Reading documents in the classroom
> - Read Teaching the Victorian School
> - Work out how the teacher made the documents accessible to the children and built upon this to deepen their understanding of the topic. In particular, how did she make sure every child from the start could read something in the document?

Documents come in many shapes and sizes; prose, poetry and lists are among the most common. Use of *The Diary of Anne Frank* illustrates our strategy for handling documents.

The diary of Anne Frank

Year 5/6 pupils had been working on people's experiences during the Second World War, and knew that they were looking at the war through the eyes of a child, in this case Anne Frank. They had done some background work on the Frank family, and knew about them going into hiding when the Germans took over in the Netherlands.

Our resources were:

- a copy of the letter – in Dutch, original

Anne Frank, Het Achterhuis, Dagboekbrieven

Dinsdag, 6 Juni 1944

Liefste Kitty,

'This is D-day' zei om 12 uur de Engelse radio en terecht, 'this is the day, de invasie is begonnen!'(1) Vanochtend om acht uur berichtten de Engelsen: zwaar bombardement van Calais, Boulogne, Le Havre en Cherbourg, alsmede Pas de Calais (zoals gewoonlijk).(2) Verder een veiligheidsmaatregel voor de bezette gebieden, alle mensen die in de zone van 35 km van de kust wonen, moeten zich op bombardementen voorbereiden.(3) Zo mogelijk zullen de Engelsen een uur van tevoren pamfletten uitwerpen.(4)

Volgens Duitse berichten zijn er Engelse parachutetroepen aan de Franse kust geland.(5) Engelse landingsboten in gevecht met Duitse mariniers, aldus de B.B.C.(6)

Discussie in het Achterhuis om negen uur aan het ontbijt: Is dit een proeflanding net als twee jaar geleden bij Dieppe ?(7) Engelse uitzending in het Duits, Nederlands, Frans en andere talen om 10 uur.(8) 'The invasion has begun!' Dus: de 'echte invasie. Engelse uitzending in het Duits 11 uur: speech van de opperbevelhebber generaal Dwight Eisenhower. (9)

Engelse uitzending in het Engels 12 uur.(10) 'This is D-Day'. Generaal Eisenhower zei tegen het Franse volk : 'Stiff fighting will come now, but …(11)

- a translation of the letter from *The Diary of Anne Frank*, (Pan Books, 1954, p. 203)
- an extract from a textbook, *The 20th Century*, M. Duffy, (Basil Blackwell, 1974, p. 151)
- a dictionary of Dutch words and their English translation.

The learning objectives were to develop skills in handling an original document and to get pupils to develop an idea of what was going on in the mind of Anne Frank.

The teaching

This seemed a really crazy idea, getting the kids to work off the original Dutch. So, we came in and gave out the letter face down. First we sketched in the background to D-Day, the pupils already having done some work on the German occupation of the Netherlands.

Now we turned to the reading of the diary. We asked the class, 'Can you read Anne Frank's diary ?' A chorus of 'Yes, of course', with the occasional well curled sneering lip of condescension or worse. Repeated the question, 'Are you sure?' 'Yes, no problem', with them bordering on contempt in their reaction.

Quick, skim read 'Turn over !' And there it was in Dutch!!! We asked the children to scan the piece quickly, and then asked them what impression it gave, what it was about, what ideas did they have. Here the shape of the document was useful, we asked what kind of document it was. Working out that it was a diary entry and a letter helped with words like *Liefste Kitty*.

Slow read They then read it through the second time carefully, underlining all the words and phrases which they thought they could understand. They wrote in any words they could translate.

Class work We went round the class, collecting ideas and putting them on the blackboard. The rapid pooling of knowledge, with them moving from despair to slow grasping at meanings, went well.

Individual/pair work. The next step was to hand out separate sentences of the document, with each pair or group of three working on a sentence. When they had agreed on a word or phrase's meaning with their group, they wrote them in on the space underneath the text.

Research Then we asked where they could find out more about the diary entry – and got the reply of books and textbooks. So we gave out the Duffy extract, and had the pupils reading around the class, two or three sentences at a time. We gave out the dictionary words, and the class used them to translate their sentences.

Resolution We went around the class, starting with sentence one, chalking up a translation on the board. The whole class joined in. Slowly the meaning of the document emerged. We then moved on to building up a picture of what life was like in the attic. This served as the focal point for this topic, using expressive movement to tell the story of Anne's life from the family going into the attic until the German soldiers broke in, arrested them and sent them to the concentration camps (see Chapter 15).

Poetry

Poems are a vivid way of seeing into the past. The account below shows how the ideas in this chapter can be applied to a poem. I stumbled across this poem reading an unpublished history of Crediton in the local reference library when preparing to teach the Local History SU. The poem tells us what a farmer felt about both the Roundheads and Cavaliers.

THE DEVONSHIRE DITTY

Ich had six oxen t'other day
And them the Roundheads took away
A mischief to their speed.
Ich had six horses in a hole
And them the Cavaliers stole,
I'se think they be agreed.

They cut my corn, my beans, my pease
I'se dare no man to displease,
They so swear and vapour.

How did we read this with our class of thirty Year 3/4 pupils? Our teaching diary follows:

The teaching diary

We asked whether there are any fights or quarrels in the playground, and what they are about. With the idea of conflict in their minds, we asked if they had seen any fighting on television lately? We pooled responses, and Tom came up with the idea of civil war.

The pupils were asked to shut their eyes and pretend they were going back a long time, four hundred years. When they opened them they were in Crediton, with an army marching down the road outside the school, for we are in the middle of a Civil War! We told them there was a Civil War in England, and we marked it on our timeline.

We got the smallest pupil in the class to come out, and said that he was the king, Charles I. Did anyone know who fought for the king in the war? The word cavaliers came out. Now we asked for the tallest child to come to the front, and he was Cromwell. Any ideas about who fought on his side? Out tumbled Roundheads and Cavaliers. On the board we put up Roundheads and Cavaliers under their leaders Cromwell and Charles. We told the children that both armies came to Crediton, and that Cromwell gave his name to Cromwell's Hollow just over the hill (Two years later Tom brought into school a horseman's spur from the Civil War period. He had found in a local field and taken it to the museum to find out when it was from. He talked to me about the spur in relation to this lesson two years earlier!).

We gave copies of the peom out. The children read it through quickly, and were asked to say one thing that they thought it was about. These ideas were jotted on the board. The pupils then underlined any words they recognized. We cut the poem up into sentences, with pairs or threes working on the meaning of each sentence. The pupils talked about their sentences, looking for meanings in them.

Pooling ideas

Buzz words We went round the class to get their ideas about what thoughts and feelings the poet had. We put up the words on the blackboard, with the pupils sitting around the blackboard at the front. The list ran:

frightened	complaining	strange	mischievous
bloody	upset	farmer	ran away
took horses	sad	food	stealing.

Now we worked slowly through the poem, sentence by sentence, putting up the meaning we worked out on the board. We translated the poem into modern English.

We extended the idea into the next lesson, using drama to organize an attack on a local farmhouse. In this we wove the words and

Census Entry

Address	Name	Son or daughter	Age	Job	Where born

Census Entry

Address	Name	Son or daughter	Age	Job	Where born

Census Entry

Address	Name	Son or daughter	Age	Job	Where born

Census Entry

Address	Name	Son or daughter	Age	Job	Where born

Census Entry

Address	Name	Son or daughter	Age	Job	Where born

Census Entry

Address	Name	Son or daughter	Age	Job	Where born

Census Entry

Address	Name	Son or daughter	Age	Job	Where born

Census Entry

Address	Name	Son or daughter	Age	Job	Where born

Illustration 12   Census form

93

ideas of the poem into what might have happened, from the troops waking up in the morning, to storming the farmhouse, looting and burning (see page 20 for an example of a pupil's writing about the incident).

Working on tables of information
Censuses, trade directories and inventories are three very common documentary sources. They are packed with information and ideas about societies in the past.

Working on a census
The census is a marvellous sources for bringing your local Victorian community to life. When using the census with Year 3/4 pupils our teaching objectives were:

- To build up an idea of what life was like in Crediton in the 1850s
- To develop the skills of working on a source like a census.
- To give the pupils roles for them to participate in an historical drama.

In our teaching we move from the familiar to an unknown source that is similar. So, we started with the class doing a census of itself, using a blank census form.

The lesson plan

1 **Introduction – class census**
- Ask the class how the government knows where people live, how old they are, what jobs they do. Lead on to the census.
- Say we are going to do a census of form members – hand out the census slips for them to fill in. Tell them to put in jobs they would like to do.
- Pool and work on the data to produce a map of where pupils live, the places they were born, average age and so on.
- Tell them they have created their own census.
- Tell the class that we have had censuses for around 200 years.

2 **Studying the census**
- Handout the Census Sheet for 1851, one sheet each pupil.
- Quick scan. Give the pupils two minutes to scan the document. Ask them to say what they think the document shows.
- Discuss ideas, put them on the board.
- Slow read. Ask pupils to underline any words, names and numbers that they recognize, or, if they are good readers, words they do not know or understand. There was great

Name of street, name or no. no. of house on night of 30 Mar 1851	Name and surname of each person who abode in the house	Relation to head of family	Condition	Age M	Age F	Rank profession or occupation	Place or road where born
2 High Street	William Smale	Head	Mar	39		Butcher	Sandford
	Mary Smale	Wife	Mar		39	Assistant	Sandford
	Ellen Do	Dau			9	Scholar	
3 High Street	William Bishop	Head	Mar	57		Baker	Zeal Monacho
	Julia Do	Wife	Mar		57	Do wife	Wemburthy
	Geo Do	Son	U	17		Tailor Ap	Crediton
	Fanny Do	Dau			12	Scholar	Crediton
4 High Street	Susannah Mansfield	Head	Mar		32	Housekeeper	Crediton
	Jas Do	Son	U	24		Carrier Ap	Do
	Sabina Do	Dau	U		16	Shoe binder	Do
5 High Street	John Madze	Head	Mar	41		Ag Lab	Do
	Grace Do	Wife	Mar		43		Do
	William Do	Son		9		Scholar	Do
	Ann Do	Dau				Scholar	Do
	Eliz Do	Dau			3		Do
	George Holgrove	Lodger	Widr	75		Chelsea Pensioner	
16 High Street	William Stone	Head	Mar	46		Cordwainer	Colebrooke
	Ann Do	Wife	Ar		4319	Weaver	Crediton
	Jn Do	Son	U	17		Cordwainer	Do
	Anne	Dau	U			Shoe binder	Do
	Will	Son		14		Cordwainer	Do
	Edwd	Son		12		Do	Do
	Geo	Son		9		Scholar	Do
	John	Son		6		Do	Do
	Sam	Son		3	Do	Do	Do
17 High Street	Mary Stone	Head		37		Dressmaker	St Thomas Exeter
	Sarah Seldon	Lodger	U		60	Retired	Crediton
19 High Street	Robert Stone	Head	Mar	44		Grocer	Do
	Ann Do	Wife	Mar		40	Assistant in shop	Do
	Ema	Dau	U		16	Do	Do
	Edwd	Son		9		Scholar	Do
	Will	Son		5		Scholar	Do
	Louise	Dau			1		Do
	John Cornish	Visitor	Mar	40		Butcher	Do
	Ann Stone	Niece	U		16	Dressmaker	Colebrooke
20 High Street	Elizabeth Reed	Head	U		40	Laundress	Kingsbridge
	James Emes	Son in Law	Mar	23		Carpenter	Sandford
	Mary Emes	Dau	Mar		22	Milliner	Crediton
	Eliza Martin	Servt	U			House Servt	Do
24 High Street	Elizabeth Burridge	Head	W		37	Parish relief	Winkleigh

Illustration 13   *1851 Crediton Census list*

excitement here, with pupils recognizing family names and streets where they live. Go through these with the class.

- Get pupils to write out one row of information under headings.

3 **Asking questions**
- Get class to think of questions they would like answered about the people on the list.
- Split up the census into families, and give each pair or small group of pupils one family.
- Say that they will be taking the role of that person, and will be doing the job on the census form.

4 **Day timeline**
- Make out a chart/timeline on a small piece of card of how they would spend a normal working day as that person.
- Research. If possible using books and materials, they could try and find out from them about what their job was like.

5 **Mime**
- When pupils have a clear role identity, they mime it in front of the class, who have to guess what their job is. The whole class should join in trying to work out what the jobs are.

6 **Interview/Hot seat**
- Each family can be interviewed by the form as to their home, work and lives.
- There should be lots of feedback from each family.

The census is an excellent springboard. In another case, I used the 1851 census with some Year 5 children as the starting point for them to create their own Victorian biographies.

The trade directory   In working on a trade directory we took the same approach, breaking into the document and once we had understood it, using the information from it to bring the past to life. The class was going to a local museum which recreates a Victorian parade of shops. We decided to use an 1857 Trade Directory for our town, Crediton, to bring a Victorian shopping street to life before the visit. Having split the document up we brought the street to life by creating its shops.

The pupils designed their shop signs, then we used clothes pegs to hang the pupils' signs on a piece of cord in the order of the street's numbers on our timeline, thus recreating the High Street in the classroom. We taught this lesson to three separate classes, and each ended up with their own Victorian High Street. The list of shops in our first class was typical:

baker	blacksmith	boot and shoe maker
butcher	carpenter	chemist
coal merchant	dress maker	glazier
grocer	hat maker	ironmonger
plumber	sweetshop	toy shop
	wine shop	watchmaker

Then the pupils took part in a Victorian trading game. What a buzz there was when we visited the local museum! There were the things they had been buying and selling in their recreated Crediton High Street!

Inventories/lists of contents of houses and rooms

The same basic strategy is applied to using inventories and other lists. Here we take the contents of the list and get the children to translate the objects into a plan of a room or a building, drawing in the features. They can then arrange for a tour of their building, with them serving as guides, be it for Queen Elizabeth or a Victorian nanny coming to see the nursery.

Reflection Preparing a document for teaching

- Select any document you would like to use in the teaching of your current or next HSU, either a piece of prose, a poem or a list.
- Photocopy the document, cut out the part for the class to study, and then run it off actual size or enlarged.
- For easier access, you can cut the document up into sections or sentences for individuals, pairs or groups of pupils to study.
- Work through the relevant section in this chapter on how to read such documents with children.
- Plan the lesson of how you would use the document with the class.
- Teach the lesson, keep a record of what went on and revise the lesson plan accordingly based on your practical experiences.

---

9 Children Writing

Getting ready

Before actually putting children to paper and pencil, it is useful to spend some time clarifying the issues relating to the written task through other verbal approaches. This clarification will help, above all, the least able pupils. We have found the following activities help children prepare for writing at this stage:

> debate and discussion
> role play
> simulation games
> hunting for suitable vocabulary items

Thus we may ask the children to debate the question 'What shall we do when the King dies?' As they consider this question and struggle to put forward their points of view, and hear others' ideas (for the purpose of mixed ability teaching is that all should profit) they become clearer in their minds about what they want to put on paper. The blackboard is frequently used to record ideas about vocabulary relevant to a given topic. We do this in a whole-class session, often asking children to work in pairs to describe, for example, how different the Ancient Greeks were from ourselves. As the words tumble out and appear on the blackboard the children gain confidence in their power to control language. As a culmination of this activity we ask them to look at the board and choose the five most appropriate words and to justify their choice. This is a harder task, but it helps them concentrate on the linguistic problems ahead.

Setting the task

When setting the task it is important to be clear, to give a concise statement of the title and several models of how it might be attempted, selecting from the ideas below. Children might be given some flexibility in how they respond, but this is subject to negotiation. Do you want an empathy exercise? Is poetry really within the grasp of this child? Would a simple report on a site visit do? Tell them what you want.

| **Concept of audience** | We also consciously use the concept of audience as a way of allowing the children to express themselves as fully as possible. For whom is the child writing? The following ideas influence me all the time in preparing written and spoken tasks. Is the audience: |

1 Child to self
2 Child to trusted adult
3 Child to teacher as partner in dialogue
4 Pupil to teacher as examiner or assessor
5 Child to friend
6 Child to working group
7 Child to whole class
8 Child to wider audience, for example, an old people's home
9 Child to unknown audience?

We are also very keen to allow a full, free expression of views and to encourage children to put ideas on paper during the early, draft stages of writing. This expressive phase is crucial in allowing the full flowering of both imagination and understanding. It can be spontaneous, unstructured, a set of jottings and brainstormed thoughts. But, it is an essential element in the development of written work.

| **Expectations** | Above all it is important whenever children set out to write that you show them you want them to do well, and that you are expecting great things from what they are about to do. |

| **Timing** | But be realistic with the time you are going to allow for a written task. Open-ended schedules invite children to waste time. Far better to specify a time limit – by break time or the end of the morning – then collect it in. Children must know the rules, and when they do they work to them. |

| **Marking** | When you mark try above all to mark the individual child's work. Don't compare the work of different children – comparisons are invidious. Ask yourself, and the child, is this piece of writing better or worse than his or her last piece? In what ways? Why? What goals should we now set for the future? |

You can write these goals down, but nothing replaces telling children. First in public, 'I want to read to you some of the best pieces that were handed in. I shan't say the names, but the authors will know'. This models for the whole group what you consider to be good work. Then, individually, go through the piece carefully with each child, explaining your views in detail to the child. It takes a lot of time, but it is worth every minute, and whilst you are giving individual tutorials the other children can be busy reading some historical fiction, or doing other work.

Achievement

Above all one must recognize achievement. When children write really well one must recognize this publicly. We have set up a 'book of excellence' in which the best work is preserved for pupils to look at and see what they might aim at. Model the best, and the rest will follow, or at least try.

The telephone project as KS1

As an example of children's writing in history we have chosen a project done by a Year 2 class on old and new telephones. The main written activities took place towards the end of the project, but we have described the earlier stages so the readers can put the written work into context.

The telephone project was designed to investigate the use of artefacts. Lynn Cowell, the class teacher, and I began by showing the children four telephones: a candlestick phone, an old bakelite phone, an early plastic phone and a modern phone with the dialling mechanism in the handset. The first activity was a discussion on the differences between them. The children examined each phone and quickly noted differences in shape, weight and colour. We next moved to considering which phone was the oldest, which the most modern and the reasons why the children thought this to be so. Whilst there was agreement on which was the most modern phone, opinions differed about the oldest. We arranged the phones to reflect the pupils' judgements. At the end of the first session the pupils were asked to try to work out how the candlestick phone might have been used to make a call, as they had already discovered that this phone had no means of dialling a number. During the following week the class had time to examine and play with all the phones.

On my next visit the class were asked to explain how the candlestick phone may have been used. A variety of interesting ideas emerged, some of which were quite plausible and others not. Each idea was discussed by the class, after which we moved on to look at some large pictures of old phones. The pupils were asked to try to match up the pictures with the four phones we had in class. Some of the pictures were different from our artefacts and in these cases the children were asked to place the pictures near to the phone which they thought was similar, or if the picture looked entirely different, in a separate pile on its own. This proved to be a useful way of getting the children to look carefully at the artefacts and pictures.

Towards the end of the lesson, I produced a large picture of a 1927 Telephone Exchange. What did the pupils think this picture was about? Was it a picture of something today? Why? This led to a lot of discussion and ideas, which we noted on the blackboard. The children established links with the telephone, but not as yet with the idea of a telephone exchange. During the following week Lynn spent time discussing these ideas with her class and in using role play to help the pupils investigate the work of the switchboard operators.

On my next visit different pupils took it in turns to demonstrate making a call using the candlestick phone. Each demonstration was followed by discussion. What did the other pupils think? What exactly had the demonstrator done to make the call? What did the switchboard ladies do? Gradually we modified and refined our conclusions and compared the method with using a modern phone.

It was at this point in the project that Lynn asked the children if they could write out some instructions on how to use a candlestick telephone. By now the children were confidently and correctly using terms like 'switchboard'. 'ear piece', 'operator', 'headphones', 'receiver', 'transmitter', 'press button' and 'dial', in their oral work. They had also worked out in role play the sequence of operations required for making a phone call with the old telephone. Using the blackboard Lynn had bult up a vocabulary bank. Here are some uncorrected examples of what the children wrote. The detailed attention given by these children to the possible sequences of operations in making a call are the result of the time spent working through the various demonstrations with the class.

Pupils writing about telephones

'To use the candlestick phone you pick up the earpiece and rattle the earpiece holder. By doing this you will get the operator you would say the number you want. The operator would hear your call on a set of head phone's. The operator would get a wire which comes from your home and plug it in to your friend's wire. The people in the picture are wearing skirts and aprons.'

'How the candlestick telephone works. First you pick up the

receiver and you put it to your ear. Then you say the number into the transmitter. My number's 257298. Then the women at the peg board would put you through to the person you wanted. They wore head phones and a transmitter over their mouth. When you said the number your number would light up and she puts a wire into your hole and she puts the other end of the wire into your friends hole.'

'Yesterday Mr Verrier came to school to talk to us about telephones. Mr. Verrier's own phone had a black base and a green phone with push buttons and the inside was black. There was a black telephone and a cream colour. My favourite was the candlestick telephone. It has a round bottom and a thick stick up the middle. The bit you speak through is called the receiver. The receiver is sticking out at one side. The transmitter is also sticking out at the top. This is how I think it works. First of all you take the receiver off its holder. Then press the holder down two or three times. Then you speak to the operator and lets say that your number was 596458 you would say could you please put me through to this number.'

'Mr. Verrier came into class 6 on Tuesday June the 9th to tell us about telephones. He brought in 4 telephones. They were all different. One was modern one was older than the modern one and so on. He told us about the candlestick telephone. The candlestick telephone is taller than the Press Button telephone. The candlestick telephone had got the transmitter stuck on to the telephone. The press Button Telephone had got a black base with a green phone on the base. Now I'll tell you about the dial telephone. He brought in 2 dial telephones one was like my home telephone and one wasn't.'
(*spelling corrected*)

Children writing: structures, scaffolding, writing frames	A new concept in the process of helping pupils start the daunting task of putting things down on a piece of paper is simply to provide a framework for writing, breaking material down into its constituent elements, so children have the scaffolding to express their understanding of a subject.
	The idea of scaffolding and structuring was developed by Exeter Extending Literacy project (EXEL). The section below is drawn completely from the work of Maureen Lewis and David Wray (*Writing Frames*, EXEL, 1996).
Writing frames	'A writing frame consists of a skeleton outline to scaffold children's

non-fiction writing. Here the pupils are supported by material which guide their thinking and writing. The skeleton framework consist of differing key words or phrases, according to the particular generic form. The template of starters, connectives and sentence modifiers which constitute a writing frame gives children a structure within which they can concentrate on communitcating what they want to say, rather that getting lost in the form. However, by using the form children become increasingly familiar with it.' (Lewis and Wray, 1995:1)

Within non-fiction writing Lewis and Wray identify six main genres:

1   Recount
2   Report
3   Explanation
4   Persuasion
5   Discussion
6   Procedural

The first five are directly germane to history, the sixth deals with organizing scientific experimental activity. Lewis and Wray draw on the same theories as the NPHP in terms of co-operative learning in suggesting a best way of using writing frames:

- Teacher exposition, modelling and demonstration
  Giving an example or examples, and working through it with the class
- Joint Activity, where the teacher works with individuals and groups on their writing
- Scaffolded Activity. Here the pupils share ideas and build upon each others perceptions
- Independent Activity. This can follow on from 2 or 3, or be a completely independent, self generated and controlled piece of writing.

Using the frames, we need to take care. Remember to start with discussion and teacher demonstration of the frame's use. Then move to the next stages of joint construction, with the resolution being the child's own writing using the frame. Not all children in a class will be able to use a writing frame. The frame should only be used when there is a clear need, a purpose. It must be made clear to the class that the frame is a draft, used in the expressive stage of writing.

Frames are only one of the many ways we encourage and support writing. Frames take many shapes and forms. They are not rigid structures. The frames given below are only examples of an infinite possible number.

Using frames in history writing

In detail, how can we relate five of these genres to children writing history?

Recount A recount retells 'events with the purpose of either informing or entertaining the audience.' (Lewis and Wray, 1995:12) It deals with three stages – what was known at the start, new knowledge and what is known at the end. A recount usually consists of:

- A scene setting opening (orientation)
  'I went on a trip to Totnes Castle.'
- A recount of the event as they occurred (events)
  'The first thing we saw was the stone fort on top of the mound. We ran up the hill as if we were attacking it.'
- A closing statement (reorientation)
  'When we left the castle I knew how the Saxons must have felt when Judhael ordered them to build his Motte and Bailey castle.'

Within this pattern a frame can cover a single or two elements, thus a sequence frame simply records the steps in acquiring new knowledge, without involving a reaction to existing understanding. Recount Frames are useful in providing the pupils with a framework upon which to build, both in terms of adding ideas and information, and resolving issues in their minds through assimilating the new and the old knowledge. The can take a number of forms (see page 106):
– prior knowledge + reaction
– prior knowledge + revision of what has been learned
– prior knowledge + reaction to what has been learned (on a visit)
– sequential
– enumeration, listing of what has been learned
– enumeration, listing of what has been learned (on a visit)

Report A report is written to describe the way things are. Reports can describe a range of natural, cultural or social phenomena. Reports usually have three elements:

- A opening, defining statement in general terms
- A fuller listing of what is being reported on
- A detailed description of the phenomenon

Comparing and contrasting is a skill that be developed for more complex reports. These are sophisticated forms of writing, and the children will need to go through a process of organizing their ideas, using a grid like the one shown on page 107.

Explanation Historical writing is largely about explanation. Explanation covers issues of causation, consequence and of interpretation. It deals with key questions such as why, what and how. An explanation is a general statement to introduce the topic followewy a series of logical steps to explain how and why something occurs. Explanation frames take a number of forms.On page 108 is an example.

Persuasion Role play in the form of drama, gaming, simulation and expressive movement plays a central part in our teaching. A persuasion writing frame is specifically tailored to pupils' needs if we as them to argue a point of view. The persuasion frame consists of:

– an opening statement often in the form of a position/preview
– the arguments often in the form of point + elaboration
– a summary and restatement of the opening position (page 109)

Discussion Discussion and debate are central to children's learning of history. They play a key part in historical investigations. How can children present their findings and conclusions? Discussion frames can be ordered as below:

– a statement of the issue +preview of the main arguments
– arguments for + supporting evidence
– arguments against + supporting evidence
– recommendations given as a summary and conclusion

This form can be applied easily to activities such as the child's suitcase (page 154).

Conclusion

Writing frames can come in many shapes, sizes and forms. Soon you will develop your own to take account of both the context in which you are teaching and the different genres of historical writing.

Reflection Using writing frames
- Consider carefull each writing frame in turn, and how you would adapt it to your own teaching.
- When next asking children to write, develop your own writing frame to help the pupils or
- Take any one of the genre listed on page 103 and produce a writing frame for it.

RECOUNT

Although I already knew that

I have learnt some new facts. I learnt that

I also learnt that

Another fact I learnt

However the most interesting thing I learnt was

(LEWIS and WRAY, EXEL)

REPORT

Although   and   are both
they are different in many ways.

The   has   whilst   has

they are also different in that

Another way they in which they differ is

Finally

(LEWIS and WRAY, EXEL)

107

EXPLANATION

There are differing explanations as to why (how, what when etc)

One explanation is that

The evidence for this is

An alternative explanation is

This explanation is based on

Of the alternative explanations I think the most likely is

(LEWIS and WRAY, EXEL)

PERSUASION

Although not every body would agree, I want to argue that

I have several reasons for arguing for this point of view. My first reason is

A further reason is

Furthermore

Therefore, although some people might argue that

I think I have shown that

(LEWIS and WRAY, EXEL)

DISCUSSION

Some people think that

because

They argue that

Another group who agree with this point of view are
They say that

On the other hand   disagree with
the idea that
They claim that

They also say

My opinion is

because

(LEWIS and WRAY, EXEL)

10 Learning About Time

We all know that the phrase 'having time on our hands' means more than wearing a wristwatch. In the modern world we are constantly reminded of when to do things, and organize our lives accordingly. We take the measurement of time and the tyranny of the timetable for granted. In the study of history, time is central, being one of its nine structural concepts examined earlier.

How can we develop our understanding of time and teach its elements: chronology, sequencing, temporal relationship of events to each other and the related concepts of change, continuity, cause and consequence? The section below introduces the topic, dealing with the concept of time and how it might affect thinking about how we teach.

Teaching time

History is about time, it subsists in time, time is the medium by which it happens. No one can deny the importance of time in teaching history, yet it is probably the one element that causes more dispute than any other.

The meaning of time

There is time we can understand and time we can't. You may say to me '400 years ago' until you are blue in the face and although I can do calculations with it I can never comprehend it. Sometimes I try ridiculous enterprises with children – saying seven times my age would be nearly it – but in truth we are no nearer comprehending the figure than before.

Equally phrases like 'The seventeenth century' or 'The Middle Ages' or 'The Victorians' cannot be comprehended in any real terms at all. I can mark them by dates, I can count the number of years, but in truth I know nothing of their time.

What we do know a little about are minutes, hours, days, weeks, possibly years. Yet we must remember that our knowledge of these is not the same as children's. A year goes by pretty fast for me, where for a child it is an age. So we must be careful. Looking at specifics, we can begin to comprehend. For example, Mary Queen of Scots was in prison for nearly 18 years (no wonder she was so foolish with the plotters). It took Elizabeth three months in the end to decide to execute her (what a long time that must have seemed to her counsellors). They set up the execution in three days (such speed). They gave her twelve hours' notice (I am beginning to comprehend more). They delayed by two hours (two agonizingly long hours). Her mouth moved as if with speech for fifteen minutes after the decapitation (horror upon horror). Her son took twenty-six years to raise her tomb (the swine). This is what I mean by understanding real time, and the more we use real time in our teaching the deeper the understanding will be.

Dates and duration Wherever we are in our study of history we need dates to establish the dimensions of what we are doing. We need to engage in calculations of duration and to observe the process of sequence so that we are able to make some judgements on how and why the events happened. The dates are the fixed points around which we may weave our understanding of motivation, cause and consequence.

A further question about time might be about the stages of development of a process. Did the 'factory system' spring up suddenly or did it come surprisingly slowly? How long before an invention takes off? Above all, however, we must ask questions about the meaning of time for the people in the period. We think of a holiday as maybe as much as a fortnight – in the eighteenth century a visit to a country house might have lasted three months. Would that have been as boring for them as it might seem to us or was it for them just right?

Time is not like an ever-flowing stream, but is more complex. It is not just clock time, it is time perceived, time lost, time wasted, it is being in time, and some moments are timeless. It is the great issue of history and must be always discussed.

A sense of period The idea of a sense of period seems to me to be much more attractive and possible than the blind chronological approach, and it has more authentic quality about it – it feels much more like doing history.

Thus we must ask children who are studying a period, whatever its designation or duration, to grow more and more aware about the context of that period. Above all we must get children to understand that what they are studying is not now, that it is *then*, that it had its own standards, values and morals and that its difference from us is not a cause of mirth or derogation or even astonishment – we must start to value the period in its own terms, for what it was. To respect difference is one of the greatest educational goals we can have, and here we are on to something of real value for children growing up. As we teach children to enthuse about a period rather than merely sit in judgement upon it we are getting closer and closer to the business of doing history. This does not mean that we need to abandon judgement, it means that we have to learn how to judge a period on its own terms.

Seeing the context Thus when a group of 9 and 10 year olds had heard a story about a chimney sweep and his child employees, they asked to interview him and I took the seat. They were cross about my cruelty, about my carelessness and about the conditions that made this happen, and I let them spend a fair amount of time pelting me with their abuse. But then I began to show them how, if I didn't employ the boys they would probably die and their families suffer. If I didn't employ the boys the chimneys couldn't be swept and whole families would die of suffocation or conflagration. I had a part to play in the system as it was, and I was not to blame for that system. I felt unjustifiably abused.

It was undoubtedly hard for the children to accept this, and to accommodate to it, but learning is hard and we do need to work at understanding – a sense of period requires acceptance at a very high intellectual level. To be able to look at the Elizabethan age and see how the pirates fitted, how the ridiculous play-acting of the Virgin Queen fitted, how plague, pox and scurvy fitted with Shakespeare, this takes effort, but it leads to understanding; it is the stuff of doing history.

Reflection Thinking about teaching time
- Read the section Teaching time
- Discuss the ways or list how it suggests you might teach about time
- Compare this with how you teach chronology, sequencing and the relationship of events to each other in time.
- How might its content influence your teaching about time ?

The measuring of time is a peculiarly human phenomenon. All of the ways in which we think about and use time were something which man invented and developed. Different cultures take different starting points and use different conventions for measuring the passage of time. For example, our system of seconds, minutes and hours is based on an Assyrian mathematical system, that uses base 60 instead of our counting system that adopts base 10. Similarly Celtic, Roman, Saxon and Norse factors shape our calendar, determining the names of the days of the week and the months.

Dates

The notion of time is deceptively simple. Dates are the most common way of encountering the use of time in history. Simply, dates are a way of organizing items of information in relation to each other and a prescribed point in time. When we produce a table of dates on a subject we are producing a statement about the past through making a connection between events and indicating their relationships.

Children's thinking and time

Some understanding of how children handle time and chronology in history might help. If they can't handle the terminology and concepts involved, there is not much point in teaching them. Happily research findings suggest that children's understanding of time can develop through it being taught consciously. Ideas about time and their application can both be taught and reinforced through constant acquaintance, repetition and reinforcement. So, there is sense in adopting teaching strategies that stress the time factor.

Teaching about time

In teaching history we can consciously develop children's awareness of and understanding of time. We take the presence of clocks and time conventions for granted. Yet all are human inventions and constructs.

Reflection Wait a minute

Thinking about time

- List all the terms you can think of that we use to measure time, such as year, month, day, hour, minute.
- How would you use such terms to plan out the key activities in a year, such as when to collect in the rents on Lady Day (the day of Christ's conception) and to celebrate Easter and Christmas?
- You can make up a short story of less than 100 words incorporating the maximum number of terms, but not using numbers.

Measuring time

As noted, we take our watches and clocks for granted. How many ways can you think of about how we, and people in the past, measured time?

How many kinds of time measuring devices can you make using the materials below?

jug of water	A hundred foot high	300 feet of strong
large plastic	bell tower	string
containers	eggs	rubber bands
small plastic	a long thin stick	plasticene
containers	wax	large candles
string	small lollipop sticks	ruler
paper clips	matches	10 kilo weight
scissors	sun, moon, stars,	tides a dozen fresh
tiny birthday cake	large nail	
candles	marker pens	

If working in groups, judge which group produced the best clocks using items from the list.
Using the clocks the children have invented, ask them to solve the following problems. As a prehistoric tribe, how would you plan when it was time to
– soft boil the king's breakfast egg,
– plant crops,
– celebrate the midwinter solstice,
– carry out religious festivals to make the crops grow?

Sequencing

Work on time constantly involves putting events into the order in which they occurred. Typically we give our children chronological puzzles to solve, presenting them with two or three objects to put into chronological order. They handle and discuss them, and then say in what order in time they occurred. Similarly the pupils work in groups to sequence a set of cut-up pictures that describe the farming year or the process of making bread from planting grain to eating the loaf. The pupils have to place the pictures in order, stick them on sheets of paper and write a commentary underneath. Clearly such sequencing is central to historical study. It creates order out of chaos, creating a concrete, tangible process that involves the children in physically manipulating time and seeing the relative relationship between events.

This is a particularly useful approach to the teaching of farming, be it in the Saxon, medieval, Tudor, Victorian or modern periods. When teaching medieval farming, we seized on the idea of Dr Who and his time ship, the Tardis. The Tardis lands in a village where the pupils find pictures of scenes of the farming year, taken from a medieval calendar. We gave the pupils, working in pairs or threes, these illustrations as a set of separate pictures in an envelope. The number of pictures in the envelope varied according to the ability level of the pairs or groups. We had found that more able children could handle a number of pictures, the less able, two or three. An extract from our lesson plan shows the idea in action:

The farming year lesson

Resources needed:
- cut up pictures of the farming year in envelopes. These can be a modern drawing or a cut-up photocopy of a medieval calendar (see Illustration 14).
- A timeline of a year, showing the months and seasons.

The Teaching:
- Split into pairs or threes. Each pair or three gets an envelope with the pictures in it.
- Sorting into sequence. Put the pictures in the envelope into order.
- Sort them out along the timeline.
- Produce a title and captions for the pictures to put into a book on the history of farming.

Chronology – relationships

Where we select from a variety of events and incidents, we produce a chronology. A chronology provides a simple, point by point guide to the past. In a chronology we establish relationships in time between what we consider to be significant events, selected from the plethora of information available. Chronology provides the backbone of the historical narrative; without it we are left with an amorphous mass of unstructured information.

Timelines and retrographs

In the classroom timelines and retrographs are a major medium for isolating and handling chronology. They can be a powerful way of bringing home the relationship between events. Timelines look forward from a point, retrographs look back. Both can help children develop a sense of order, story and narrative, the spine of history.

Timelines are marvellous for getting children to come to grips with

Illustration 14   *The medieval farming year*

the past in a concrete way. A timeline can emphasize and highlight the relationships between events. A piece of string or cord with clothes pegs can be used to make a class timeline. On the timeline we hang information about key events. It gives a clear visual idea of the passage of time, and how things function in sequence. The timeline is a powerful medium for almost all topics. It can be used to sort out time in all its contexts, from a few minutes to a millenium. Thus we use timelines to illuminate brief events such as the launch of Yuri Gagarin into space as well as the span of time of a period or dynasty. In the Yuri Gagarin case, we took a newspaper account of his launch listing the times, and turned this into a clock face. For periods of a few years we have used timelines and retrographs for the personal histories of pupils, mounting dated photographs and documents for individual children in sequence.

Reflection Making day timelines

Resources needed: Egg-shape day templates, large piece of paper for mounting the day timelines, marker pens, gluesticks.

- Introduction: You will have to produce a retrograph or timeline in the form of an egg diagram of a day in your life – within the last week, or an exciting day you can remember.
- Note that you will have to think of how to split it up. Into day / night? Using the hours? Activities?
- Produce the diagram – of a day in your own life.
- Character in history: Take the role of a character in the past and produce an egg timeline for that person.
- Tree diagram: Where there are historical families or groups which can be organized as a tree, stick the timeline on the tree.
- A historical situation: work out who might have been present. Choose two or more of the characters. Produce egg day timelines for each of them for the day.
- Compare the timelines you have produced.
- Mount them on card as a wall display.

Making retrographs

There is a powerful argument that to get children to produce lists of dates, timecharts and timelines is misleading, simply because we don't think in that way. In our own lives we don't start from a previous point and work forward, we start from now and look backwards. In other words we treat time retrospectively. An alternative but complementary approach to timelines is to do this with children through retrographs. A retrograph is a back to front timeline. We can create all timelines in this way.

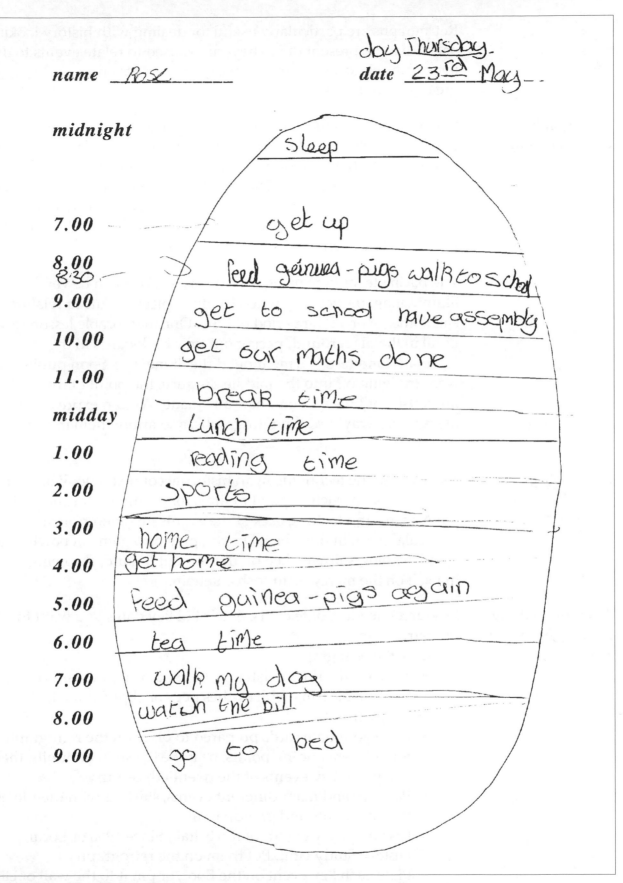

name _Rose_

Thursday
day Thursday
date 23rd May

midnight

sleep

7.00 — get up

8.00
8.30 — feed guinea-pigs walk to school

9.00 get to school have assembly

10.00 get our maths done

11.00 break time

midday lunch time

1.00 reading time

2.00 sports

3.00 home time

4.00 get home

5.00 feed guinea-pigs again

6.00 tea time

7.00 walk my dog

8.00 watch the bill

9.00 go to bed

Illustration 15   *Egg timeline*

119

Retrographs are particularly useful for dealing with history looking back from the present day. They can be used to relate events to the lives of the children, their parents, grandparents and great-grandparents.

Retrographs – teaching strategies

One way of livening up the approach is to get the children to pace out the retrograph and hang events from a timeline. We chalk the retrograph on the floor or use a timeline of string , using clothes pegs to hang information. The retrograph has on it the hours, days, weeks, months, years, decades or centuries as appropriate. The pupils have to pace back in time from a given point and clip to the timeline a key event they have been given.

The pacing technique using children as markers can be very illuminating, particularly when trying to place events in relation to each other over a long period of time. One memorable lesson saw us all in the playground, pacing out time backwards to the Norman Conquest. We mentioned the Stone Age. Soon pupils were trudging off into the middle distance, the point of the immensity of time was emphatically made. We can express our ideas in this way through retrographs, and apply them in our teaching.

You can use the technique in an historical context to look back at events from a particular point in time, for example, starting with the Armada and looking back at the events involved from a particular point in time, be it Drake's playing a game of bowls or a Spanish sailor, shipwrecked on the coast of Ireland, throwing himself on the mercy of an Irish chieftain.

A lesson making twentieth century retrographs

Resources needed: date cards, or a list of key dates you want for the retrograph.
Creating the retrograph
- Mark on the floor a dateline, or use a wall pinboard or a timeline of string with clothes pegs or clips from which to hang cards.
- Have your date cards prepared to place on the retrograph for different ending points, be it the life span of pupils, their parents or key events of the twentieth century.
- Pace out and mark different events, starting with their lives, that of parents and grandparents.
- Decide on key events of the Britain Since 1930 or Local History Study Unit. Put them on the retrograph.
- Place each key event on the floor, or pin it to the wall or clip it on to the string timeline working back from the present.

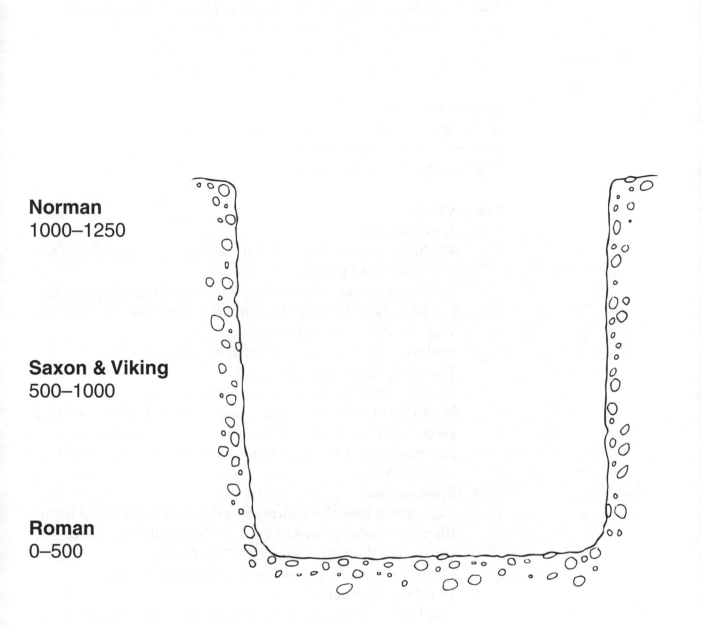

Norman
1000–1250

Saxon & Viking
500–1000

Roman
0–500

Illustration 16   *A time pit*

| **An archaeological cross-section** | Timelines and retrographs can take many forms. A recent idea, now well established in our repertoire, is the archaeological dig. The aim of the activity is to develop an idea of chronology and period, with some feel for change through time through examining the sources. In your teaching you can produce your own archaeological cards for the topic you are studying. |

Resources needed:
small pieces of card, glue, scissors, pens and pencils
archaeology information cards
large sheets of cartridge paper with the timeline pit on it.

The teaching:

1 **Introduction**
   We have to try and organize the information found on a site into some kind of order.
   To help us we have created a pit (inverted bell shape) with the periods on the outside, Roman, Saxon, Viking, Norman, with the dates down the side.

2 **Split** the class into pairs or small groups of 3-4.

3 **Handling the information cards.**
   Each group takes a small pile of the information cards, and is told that they have to draw what is described on a small piece of card with a brief label of what it is and its date or period and stick the description card on the cross section in the right place.

4 **Presentation**
   Each group uses the information which it has derived from their information cards to work out what life was like on the site during the period which the dig covers.
   Each group presents its ideas in a hot seat session.

5 **Display – Synthesis.**
   Display the diagrams, and each person in the class then works out from the evidence how life changed through time.

| **Timelines and a History Study Unit** | A timeline can help pupils come to grips with a History Study Unit. It is a marvellous way of creating an overview. We use our topic books and other resources as the basis for the pupils' research. |

| **Teaching about change, continuity, progress and regression** | If history is about one thing, it is about change. When we begin to fire questions about any topic a central issue is what changed and to what extent, what caused change to occur, what were the relative importance of the factors that determined change and what stayed the same. For example, preparing to teach the Britain |

since 1930 HSU, immediately the eye fixes on all the elements directly involving change:

- the ways in which people were affected by the Second World War and changes in technology and transport
- changes in the role of men and women
- changes in employment, automation

Reflection **Using a timeline to make sense of an HSU**

- Take the next HSU and break it down into the topics or events suggested in the exemplary section. Link each of these to a date or dates.
- Topic cards
  Make out a separate blank card for each of the dates, giving only the date and/or title.
  Give each pupil or pair of pupils a blank card.
  Ask them to think of a question or questions they would like to ask about the topic.
- Research the card and complete it.
  Each pupil chooses a topic book or source to match the card's title and their questions.
  They then research the topic and produce a card to present their ideas.
- Creating the timeline
  In turn they put the cards on the timeline and tell the class about each one.

The concepts of change, continuity, progress and regress are at the same time difficult to grasp and central to the teaching of history. Children can develop an understanding of these concepts through constantly using them in their historical education. How can we get our pupils to develop an understanding of change using ideas for teaching time?

The comparative approach

A key element is the comparative one, looking at how and why things have changed through time. This requires the pupils to build up their conceptual understanding. You can start with the simplest of frameworks, using terms such as new and old. We were working on housing and took this approach. We wanted our Year 3 and 4 pupils to think of sequencing and date order. The key idea was to get them to work from the perspective of an architect designing a modern house along the lines of the period chosen.

The idea can be elaborated to take in almost anything, particularly if you cast the pupils as designers of working models.

Reflection Historical architect

Resources needed: a selection of books with pictures of houses and house ads from a newspaper.

The task: to design a model period house incorporating all of the main features of the particular style.

- Ask the pupils to choose one of these headings for kinds of houses, or decide on their own: new, quite old, old, very old or Medieval, Tudor, Stuart, Georgian, Victorian, 1930s, Modern
- Put it on top of a sheet of paper.
- Use books and advertisements to find houses which fall into the different categories.
- Draw a picture of a house which shows the features of the category. Give the picture a title and caption.
- Discuss what are the features of the houses in different periods and why they have changed over time, and why they have stayed the same.
- Comment on what the pictures tell us about:
  the people who designed and built the houses,
  what it might have been like to have lived in them when they were built and what the houses tell us about the society that produced them.

Comparing pictures and objects

Another approach to change is to compare single pictures of scenes and tease out what are the differences and why change has occurred. When we were teaching Study Unit Britain Since 1930 with our Year 3 and 4 class we had two photographs, one of a harvest scene with a tractor, binder and threshing machine and another of a modern combine harvester. Sticking the two pictures to face each other on sheets of A3 paper and then using them as the basis for class discussion was most fruitful. The same idea was developed during our study of Victorian farming, taking a scene of a Victorian farm and comparing it with a modern one. The lesson went as follows:

1 The farming year – discussion
- What kinds of animals might the villagers have had ?
- Look at the picture of the modern farm scene.
- Study the model animals.

- Now discuss what they might have been like in the old village.
- Draw what they might have been like.
  Each person in the group draws one animal or bird, cow, goat, horse, chicken, sheep.

2 The fields
- Work out the problems farmers would have faced in growing their crops.
- Look at the modern grain. And then say what it might have been like in the early 19th century.
- Draw ears of grain.

3 Making things better
- Each person or group comes up with ideas of how to make things better.
- Each person or group in turn comes to the front and presents his or her idea on how to improve things.

4 Picture study
- Compare the photograph, of a modern farming scene and models, of modern farm birds and animals with the scene of earlier equipment.
- Discuss why and how things have changed.

Conclusion

Unfortunately you cannot say that you have a blinding headache every time a colleague suggests teaching about time. In this chapter we have explored the whole thorny issue of the meaning of time, of chronology, sequence and time as a referencing point. Either overtly or subliminally in almost every lesson time intrudes on our consciousness. The extent of this engagement can vary from a few seconds to the organizing of our teaching around time-based activity, such as sorting out the farming year, producing a timeline or retrograph of an incident or a character's life. Through such activities over a programme of study, pupils should develop an extensive and well-grounded understanding of the concepts involved and their application.

11 The Visual Image

A picture is worth a thousand words. Pictures come in many forms, shapes and sizes, from aboriginal art and cave paintings, to computer produced images. To us all pictures are fair game, none more so than photographs like Illustration 17. Pictures do not have to be contemporary. We can even use Asterix and Walt Disney cartoons as they convey interpretations of a topic and period. One of us built a whole course on the Romans around Asterix!

Reflection **Interpreting a picture**

Study Illustration 17 of the Jarrow March in 1936. What questions would you ask your pupils about it? Photocopy the picture and write your questions around the picture.

Illustration 17   *The Jarrow March*

Using pictures with children

Children grow up surrounded by pictures – moving pictures on the TV, still advertisements on hoardings, pictures in newspapers and magazines and comic books. 'The media' are ever present, and so we assume that our children are visually literate – wise eyed. When we see them flicking through books 'looking at the pictures' we assume they are taking the easy option, doing something they all can do. Yet when you question children about what they have seen they often enough are unable either to remember what they have seen or to comment on it. The images have passed by, passed on, have never been held still for long enough to take a concentrated, analytical and critical view. We need to teach visual skills to our children, and to do that we must start using pictures in a special way – not as illustrations to our text, but as sources in their own right. We must also give children reasons for looking, and ways of looking.

Sometimes I will choose a picture that is hard to see – small, dim, dirty, one which you really have to screw up your eyes to see. In such circumstances I might give special permission: 'If you think you can see something no one else has yet seen, you can come out to the front to examine the picture closely.' I might also have a magnifying glass which I am willing to loan to someone who might just find something new – a magnifying glass confers expertise on the user; you become Sherlock Holmes at once.

The Flemish bicycle

I have on occasions been thoroughly mean and only allowed the children a fast glimpse of the picture, to force them to look hard and quickly. I recall the first time I used this technique, with a small leaf from a 15th century Flemish book of hours. I said to the children that as it was a kind of magic to see what someone saw 500 years ago, we would look at it in a magic way – just glimpsing it. After I had flashed the picture, at great speed, they all told me what they had seen – loads of things – sheep, washing on a line, birds – children have good eyes. But one small girl proclaimed she had seen a bicycle. This caused a great hubbub as most of the children had at least a rough idea of the impossibility of this.

So I said that it was just possible that some medieval Fleming had invented a bicycle and that it hadn't caught on, and it had to be re-invented later. So for the time being we would have another brief glimpse, but this time the task would be harder: you had to confirm what you had seen, see what someone else had seen, see something new and look for the bicycle. They saw lots more, and this time thirteen saw the bicycle. I was baffled and had to discard the device and say 'show me' – there at the top of the picture, in a cartouche no bigger than a little finger nail, roughly sketched in grey were the two spoked wheels of the chariot of the sun.

Entering a picture Once one has children wanting to look, one must turn to devices for helping them enter the picture and explore. Usually the picture will be too intense, too demanding, too alien for the children to be able to make their own entry, so the teacher must help. Very simple things work wonders – 'How many men and how many women can you see?' As we count the different jewels on Queen Elizabeth's dress we are scanning the surface of the picture, we are usefully active, and we are already beginning to think – if only to say 'Does she wear these every day?' The questions that arise from the preliminary scan of the whole surface of the picture are often the way in to the next layer of investigation.

Another approach is to bring a picture alive by asking the children to supply additional 'before' and 'after' pictures. I often use an old engraving of 'When did you last see your father?' for this, and, like so many of the Victorian narrative pictures it turns into a film quite easily.

One entry point to a picture was given to me by God one day when I had been hired to make a film on using difficult manuscripts with clever sixth formers. I prepared sheaves of documents on the life of Strafford, and at the last minute thrust in a slide of the Petworth Van Dyke portrait. On the day all was ready when the wrong children arrived – a group of disaffected sixteen year olds who were very cross at having missed their lunch sweltering in the Tube en route to me.

They really couldn't read, I was sweetly assured by the accompanying teacher, and to this day I am looking for the person who gave her instructions on whom to bring. So I put the slide on and asked them 'Could you trust this man?' – a question God popped into my mind at that moment because He was sorry for me. The children argued and peered, argued some more, asked me to tell them about the man, (and to a child when I got to the point of Charles signing the death warrant, they chorused 'the bastard') then they argued some more, and looked and looked, and finally begged to take the documents away, confident they would find people to read them.

Then and now comparisons

The key question at the next stage, after we have reported on 'What is there?' in a picture is to ask 'What is the difference between then and now?' Now this is not an invitation to scorn the past and praise the present: the best breakdown for 'what's the difference' questions is to say 'What do they have which we lack, what do we have that they lacked, what do we share?' An enormous amount of list-making will now ensue and soon they will begin to dance under headings – headings are ideas, and here we are closer to the heart of understanding, of reading the picture.

Who made the picture?

Our final explorations must be of the vision of the artist or photographer who created the picture. Why was the subject posed that way, dressed that way, set against such a background? What is the message of the picture, what is the artist trying to tell us? Why does he/she see the world in this way, so different, perhaps, from the way we see it? What does all this tell us about them in their time, and the ways they thought? Can we step back into their shoes for a moment and see just the possibility of a different vision?

Interpreting pictures

Children work on pictorial sources to develop their knowledge and understanding of a topic. Prints, photographs, cartoons and paintings are windows into the past. They provide an insight into both the mind of the artist and also evidence about the situation the picture shows. No doubt you already use pictures widely in your teaching of history. Have you ever thought about what is involved when your pupils work on such pictures? How do their activities tie into your, the History National Curriculum's and professional historians' views on pictorial evidence?

Typical of such pictures is Illustration 17. We often mount such pictures in the middle of a page, allowing the pupils to write their questions around the edges. In using pictures like this pupils pass through eight stages :
1 Scanning
2 Observing and focusing
3 Questioning, a continuous process
4 Entering into the picture to understand what the scene might have meant to the people who were alive then
5 Using other sources to find out about the scene
6 The recording of findings and perceptions
7 Hypothesizing, speculating, interpreting, synthesizing
8 The presentation of views

<table>
<tr>
<td>

Reflection Extending ideas about pictures
- List the possible approaches explained above for using pictures.
- Compare these with your original questions you listed for Illustration 17. Which are the same and which different.

</td>
</tr>
</table>

Learning activities and pupil tasks

The NPHP believes that children construct their own view of the past from a variety of perspectives. To do this they need to engage in meaningful activities. How can we get children to use a picture to develop their historical understanding? The teacher has to provide the information and support that pupils need to understand the pictorial source.

Pictures can take many forms. We will study four types: pictures of an object or objects; portraits – drawn, painted, sculpted or photographed; artists' reconstructions of historical scenes; and photographs. In teaching with pictures we often combine two or more of these elements, plus others that are relevant such as engravings, pencil drawings and landscape paintings.

<table>
<tr>
<td>

Reflection: The Sutton Hoo postcard

After reading **Buried treasure**! below, attempt to list the strategies the teacher employed in getting the children to develop their understanding of the topic from studying the pictures. Think about:

–questions asked.

–the use of imagination.

–observation.

–resolution of the children's thinking, the activity involved.

</td>
</tr>
</table>

The topic explored in the account below was the Anglo-Saxons; the specific subject the Sutton Hoo ship burial. The ship's burial mound contained a king's ransom in gold and jewellery. Indeed, it contained the worldly and spiritul goods needed for his voyage into the next world – be it pagan or Christian.

Buried treasure!

Students having stolen all my slides of Sutton Hoo, I stalked in to the British Museum to buy some more, to find to my horror that as part of their economy drive they were no longer selling slides. All of my time as a teacher trainer I have told students never to wave nasty little postcards at children, because if they did not go to see the object themselves, then the children deserved a decent reproduction. Now the BM offered me four exceptionally nasty little postcards.

In one way this did us a good service (although my rage against the British Museum is undiminished) in that it took our sights off resources and pushed us to think about the teaching and about the questions which are at the heart of the matter. So we began with another story – the story of Mrs Pretty and how her Egyptian holiday that switched her on to thinking about buried treasure closer to home. In fact the discovery of Sutton Hoo is a wonderful story in its own right and the children were entranced and amused by it. The worried archaeologist on his bike, the four top men in the business, excavating away like fury against the clock that pointed towards September 1939, the packing of the finds in wet moss (to be watered throughout the war) awaiting another resurrection in 1946. To be fair to the museum all these details may be found in their excellent and inexpensive booklet on Sutton Hoo. By this stage the children were fascinated and desperately wanted to see some stuff, so we just focused on the 32cm-long belt buckle. They automatically began measuring it with their hands in the air – huge! 412 grammes – we weighed out the equivalent in paper and held the pile reverentially – pure gold! We thought of the £5000 worth of gold alone it represented – what could we buy with that – a car maybe? When the children learned of Mrs. Pretty's generosity in presenting the lot to the nation they were as moved as I was.

Illustration 18   *The Sutton Hoo belt buckle*

Examining the finds   We gave each group a postcard of a find – belt buckle, helmet, shoulder straps, purse lid. We asked them to examine them with care (would that I had had the sense to bring magnifying glasses, which are not only useful in such an exercise but add status to the operation) and to write down the skills the people had who made them. Soon we had a huge list of skills. We looked back over the list and asked whether they could now tell us something about the wealth and power of these people. They could indeed – another long list of ideas. The list is given here in the order in which the children presented it.

moulding	mixing colours
using strength	measuring accurately
working in glass	making chains
mining metals	working with metals
intricate, detailed work	using gold
using fine tools for cutting	bending wood
weaving patterns	making nails

Finally we asked them to consider again what made people put such treasures down in the ground. The range of thought about the burial of treasure was astonishing: some thought it was for a journey; some said it was out of pride – their king should appear good when he got to heaven, some thought they might have feared the return of the king, either as a ghost or in some reincarnation to punish them for keeping his things; others thought it was just out of very real respect for a great man – there were many more ideas. By the end of session two these children were beginning to think something like archaeologists and historians.

Using portraits: a classroom example

A teacher on a recent inservice course, Zara, used a portrait of Queen Elizabeth in teaching her Year 3 and 4 class. An account of her teaching describes the strategies employed:

Zara had been on a Montacute House course on portraits. A lecturer from the National Portrait Gallery had taught her a great deal about imagery. Analysis of portraits of Henry VIII had been a vehicle for developing an understanding of the king, how his portrayal changed through time and his relationship to his courtiers. Could she do the same with Queen Elizabeth?

Zara's approach was adapted from our inservice session, using an Elizabethan portrait, developing teaching strategies based upon the portrait.

To make the connection between themselves and Elizabeth's portraits, the pupils were asked to say what they would want a

Ilustration 19   *The Armada portrait of Elizabeth I*

photograph of themselves to show. They then related these ideas to
the Tudor pictures. The class looked at different portraits of
Elizabeth, trying to work out what messages the pictures conveyed
through the face, clothes, symbols of office – crown, orb, sceptre –
body language, props. They worked on how things could be added
to the picture to build up the image, how the picture was created.
To help them they looked at other sources. The class then pooled
their ideas.

The children were introduced to the idea of 'pouncing' to produce
a template for copying portraits. Using pictures from magazines,
they were able to work on outlines of faces, picking out the jaw
lines, hair, jewellery. The class was set the task of creating a portrait
of Queen Elizabeth. The task was split up between them – the
result was displayed at the inservice day. How can we get inside a
portrait to unlock its messages?

The lesson plan below is based on teaching a Year 5/6 class using
the Armada portrait of Queen Elizabeth and a modern cartoon of
faces. We had previously taught a lesson on political power,

133

looking at who is in charge of whom inside the children's homes, in the classroom and at school. We had drawn up sets of rules and argued fiercely about the kind of political system we would like. Our lesson plan, modified in the light of experience, reads as below.

The Queen Elizabeth portrait lesson plan

1 Ways of thinking about portraits

Discuss these five elements involved in creating a portrait

- the face
- body language
- dress
- props and setting
- the relationship between the artist and the client, that is, the wishes of the client and the artist's role.

Are there any other elements ? We can now work on these five dimensions, relating the first four to the final one.

2 Portraits as carriers of messages: the face

- Split into pairs. If you are working on your own, use a mirror. Write down a particular mood which you would like to adopt.
- See how well it ties into one of the moods illustrated on the cartoon of faces.
- One of you now poses in the mood you have chosen while your partner draws a portrait of your face.
- When finished, swap roles.
- Discuss how well the portrait has captured the mood you had adopted.
- Pooling ideas. The group can discuss the portraits of all the members.
- Rogues gallery. Stick the portraits on a large piece of card/paper and present them as a Wanted, Dead or Alive! poster.

3 Body language

A second way of sending messages is through body language.

- Talk about body language.
- In your pairs or threes demonstrate feelings like love and anger to the rest of the group.
- The rest of the group has to guess what messages the body language is trying to impart.

4 Dress messages

Now look at clothes as a way of passing messages.

- Members of the group can come to the front and the rest of

Illustration 20   *Portrait of Henry VIII*

Reflection Teaching with a portrait
Study a famous portrait of Henry VIII. Plan out a lesson or series of lessons in relation to it, taking into account the ideas already presented.

the group can discuss the message which their clothes are trying to impart.

5 **Supporting props and context**
- Discuss the role of supporting props and context. If you were going to have a photographer to do a family portrait, what setting would you have for it?

6 **Studying a portrait**
- What idea does Elizabeth want you to have of her from her portrait?
- Draw up a list of all the things that you can see in the picture, and questions you would like answered.
- Discuss how the five elements involved in creating a portrait had influenced this picture.

7 **Questions**
- How would you find the answers to the questions you asked about the portrait?

Using artists' reconstructions: The pre-modern village:

An artist's reconstruction can provide a valuable way of getting children involved in a topic. There are thousands of marvellous pictures for you to use. Pictures which reflect a particular time and point of view can be equally valuable, whether a Victorian painting of the murder of the Princes in the Tower or a 1930s Errol Flynn epic of Viking lives and loves. As part of a Local History Unit, we wanted to develop in the children of a Year 3/4 class an understanding of what a village was like and how its economy might have worked. The medium was to place the children in the position of time travellers who land in a pre-modern village, explore it and report back to the rest of the crew. The approach works equally well with any village society before the Victorian period.

This was the first of a pair of linked lessons. In the second we staged a market. Pupils were cast in the roles of traders, buying and selling goods they needed. This simulation explored ideas of how a village economy might have worked.

Learning objectives
- To develop an understanding of how a pre-modern village worked as an integrated economy.
- To relate this to the topic of food.

Resources
- Drawing of the village – an artist's reconstruction
- Sheet of what the village produces.

The teaching   Your spaceship, the Tardis, has landed in the village.

1 The Tardis lands in the village
- Your time machine has landed in a medieval village – the one shown on the picture.
- The machine has landed in the village square, near the well. Put a finger on the well. What have you spotted on the way down and what can you see out of the window on landing?

2 Studying the picture of the medieval village
- You are going to be explorers, and you are going to find out what you can about the village.
- Jot down three things you can see for an 'I spy with my little eye' game.
- Use the 'I spy' session to draw up a list of things in the village.

Looking at the artists reconstruction we gave them, this is the list our pupils came up with:

Things seen (facts)
the mill is old
there is no clock
the village is small
there is a well
cows and horses are used for ploughing and transport
the people took fire wood from the wood
animal muck was used on the fields
each person owned some strips
the mill has no sail
some people carry things in bundles on their shoulders

You can now think of questions you would like to ask about the village. These were some that our pupils came up with.

Questions
How many rooms were there in the village ?
How many animals did they have?
How old is the manor house?
How many people are there in the mill?

Village economy	Raw materials ➡ Use						
Open fields	Grain, *vegetables*						
	Rabbits: meats		fur		boots, gloves		
Common land	Cattle: *beef*	*milk*	*butter*	*cheese*	*horn*	*hides*	boots, gloves	*tallow*
	Sheep: *wool*	*milk*	*mutton*	*cloth*			
	Pig:	*pork and bacon*	*fat*	*wax*			
	Chickens: *meat*		*eggs*	*feathers*	*mattresses, pillows*		
Soil	Iron ore: *iron pots tools*						
	Tin: *weapons, tools*						
	Lead						
	Peat: *fuel*						
Woodland	Timber: *fuel fencing building charcoal*						
	Berries: *food jam*						
	Roots: *hurdles medicine*						
	Acorns: *forage for pigs*						
	Bees: *honey candles wax*						
Rivers	Fish						
	Power for mill: *grinding corn*						
	Washing						

Illustration 21 Medieval village chart of goods

Where did the priest live?
How old is the village?
Why are the roads so big?
Is the well a wishing well?
How big is the village?
Why fences around the houses?

- You are now ready to be a history detective studying the village.

3 Briefing – the economy sheet and picture
- Study the village economy sheet.
- Using it and the picture you can work out what might be going in different parts of the village.
- For example, what would be grown in the meadow? what would the peasants use the wood for ?

4 Briefing – village characters
You can now bring the picture to life through thinking about some characters who lived in the village. The following people lived in the village. What might they tell you about their lives?
- Rainald the Lord and Eleanor his wife, plus kids. Rainald owns the village. The villagers farm their land in return for working on Rainald's land or strips.
- Odo the bailiff (or reeve) helps run things for Rainald and Eleanor. Odo lives in the manor house.
- Orderic the priest
- In the village there are 11 peasant families, one family to each hut.

(This gives us 14 families in all, so with a class of 30 pupils, about two pupils to a family)

5 The investigation – the history detectives
You can now switch into explorer mode, setting yourselves up as investigators. To find out about the village you will visit the different parts. For teaching purposes, we split the kids up into seven teams, each exploring an area of the picture:
- The West Field and the wood
- The Watermill
- The meadow and pasture
- The church and vicar's hut
- The manor house where the lord lives
- The villagers' huts
- Hedge Field and the East Field

When teaching, we cut the picture up into seven pieces, with a piece for each group.

6 The explorers' questions

Exploring is one thing, but you should have some idea of what you are looking for. Here are some questions and ideas – the first is important in that we want to involve all of the senses.

- What do we see, hear, smell, feel ?
- Whom do we meet ?
- What questions will we ask ?
- Who might you meet ?
- What might they say ?

Now you can go exploring.

7 Report back

When teaching, we use the hot seat technique. A person is placed in the hot seat and then quizzed. In turn each of the seven groups chooses a member to sit in the hot seat, a special chair, usually the teacher's. They report on what they have found out and then answer questions.

Using photographs Photos are one of the most common and accessible sources. Two elements are involved in working on photographs: the intentions of the photographer, and the behaviour of the photographed. Both of these elements vary according to the particular context in which the photograph occurs. Photographs are, perhaps, the most immediate and intimate of all evidence that we have available. In teaching Local History, the Victorians and Britain Since 1930s we are literally buried under a mountain of photographic evidence.

Another wonderful source is an aerial photograph. It immediately provides a focus for working with other sources from the past, such as maps and plans, photographs of the school and its surrounding and memories of local people. With a photograph the children are literally then and there, they are looking down the same lens that froze the reality for ever. As the starting point for an enquiry, photographs immediately grasp the attention.

When we were teaching about the Victorian seaside we found a local tourist guide for 1901. Using its photographs and three further contrasting photographs of the Victorian seaside, we were able to move our children around the room, from table to table, studying a different photograph at each. Circulation was not random, for they had to use the photographs to plan out a day at

Illustration 22 *Children in a trench*

the seaside. Then, when they had visited the resort, they would use a photograph as the basis of a postcard to send home.

Mining a photograph

Almost more than any other source photographs provide an incentive to dig, to burrow, to stretch, to tease out, to investigate and follow up random leads. Our use of the photo of children looking out of the trench was typical. We mounted it on a sheet of A4 with lovely wide borders. It was our first lesson with Year 5 and 6 children on the Britain Since 1930 Study Unit. We handed out the photo. The lesson went as follows. We told the children:

- To look at the picture and get a clear impression of what it was about and then to focus on small parts of it.
- To write any questions and any statements that they could make about the photo, statements of fact, around the edge.

We gathered the children around the blackboard and held a question, answer and discussion session in which we chalked up their questions on the board. The questions rained thick and fast, and served to focus the discussion:

English or Germans?   In or out of the shelter?
Why trenches?   Why squashed?
When did they see it?   Is it a play?
Where are they?   What was it like?

141

Could be grown ups now?   Why looking up?
Hot or cold?   Why looking in different
What year?   places?
Why no adults?   Can you tell if happy?
What age?   Smiling?
What around them?   How would they get the
Could be aeroplanes   picture?
What are they sitting on?   Who took it ?
Abandoned by parents?
Christians or Jews?
Why would the picture be taken if there was danger?

Then we explored the idea of the role of the photographer in charge of taking the picture, and reasons why the picture should take that form. Why was the picture taken and published? The class was told of censorship and government control of the press. From this arose hypotheses that the government published the picture because it wanted people to join the forces, to get them to protect our children, to warn people to get their children into safety. The final part of the discussion led on to the idea of the photograph being propaganda – one pupil even suggested 'Is it a fake ?'

This was a driving piece of teaching and learning, in which the whole class was fully engaged, paying attention and involved. Pupils were massively on task, and there was good matching of task to abilities.

Reflection **Brainstorming ideas for using a photograph**
- Copy a photograph you are thinking of using with your pupils
- Work through **Using pictures : a quick fifty** thinking about how you would use the ideas with photographs.
- Jot down on the margins of your photograph how you would use it, or any new ways of teaching with it.
- Use these ideas as the basis for planning a lesson.

Using pictures : a quick fifty

1 Walk through all or part of a picture, describing the scene.
2 Say what you can see, hear, smell, touch, taste.
3 Identify characters and talk to them.
4 What was going on before?
5 What was going on afterwards?
6 What is going on in part of the picture?

Illustration 23   *Town and Eton College boys outside Lords Cricket Ground in London*

7   What might be happening outside the frame – top, bottom, left and right sides?

8   Colour the picture in, researching the context to produce an accurate representation of the original.

9   Trace over an outline to get main features, labelling them.

10   Provide a title and a caption.

11   Produce titles and captions from different points of view.

12   Discuss what one or more pictures tell you about a topic.

13   Add pieces of information that you have ready about the picture. Ask the class after each new piece is added to tell you about the picture in its new context.

14   What might have been the use of an object or thing in a picture, for example a boat?

15   How was an artefact made, be it dress, boat, building, landscape?

16   Why was it made?

17   Who might have made it, for whom?

18 Draw up a history of the thing or things shown, from its or their origin up to the time the picture was made.

19 Compare two pictures of the same scene drawn at different times. Look at their origins, and suggest reasons why they differ.

20 Identify the story in a picture, for example, a well known biblical scene. Tell the story.

21 Suggest what was going on in the mind of an artist when he or she created a picture.

22 On what evidence might the picture be based?

23 Using a photograph of a scene, draw a plan of what the site might have been like and label it.

24 Complete a picture where only a fragment has survived, for example, of a mosaic.

25 Give a list of objects and ask how many can be recognised in a picture.

26 Carry on a story from the viewpoint of people in the picture.

27 Use a set of pictures to create a story.

28 Compare pictures to show how things have changed through time.

29 List differences between pictures and their similarities.

30 How much trust can we place on the picture or pictures? What is the point of view from which it was created? Who influenced the form it takes, the artist or the commissioner of the picture?

32 What one thing in the picture interests you?

33 Who do you like in the picture?

34 How might a person in the picture have spent the day up to the time of the picture?

35 Let's play a game. You have one minute to look at the picture. It will then be hidden and you have to make a list of things it shows. The longest list wins.

36 What impression does the picture give you as a whole?

37 With a series of pictures, or a picture cut up into pieces, focus in on one picture or piece. Tell us about it.

38 Focus in on a minute detail of the picture, even using a magnifying glass. Tell us about it.

39 What do the signs and symbols in the picture tell us?

40 Is there anything odd about the picture?

41 In groups split the characters in a picture up among you. Act out the scene, and what might have happened next.

42 Put pictures into a sequence.

43 Draw a similar scene to the picture, carrying on the story.

44 Interview a character in the picture, one pupil taking the role of the character, the others doing the questioning.

45 Give pupils the roles of characters outside the picture. For example, with a portrait, ask how members of the family might have felt about the picture of their mother and father. How might others have felt, for example their best friend and most deadly enemy?

46 If you were selling the picture, how would you get somebody to buy it?

47 Take a picture of an object. Draw or describe how you might improve it.

48 What do things in the picture tell us about the period, for example, clothes, travel, weapons, raw materials, crafts, skills, attitudes?

49 How was the picture made? What are its raw materials?

50 How might the picture have been changed through time, for example, through restoration, it being varnished, part of it missing, such as panels of a triptych.

Children creating pictures

Pupils can either interpret or create pictures. Creatively, children can present their knowledge and understanding pictorially. Here the pupil translates and represents ideas encountered in spoken, musical, written, enactive and dramatic media into visual images. Such images can take many forms, such as cartoons, collages, sketches, drawings, paintings, diagrams, illustrated plans and maps. Frequently when we tell a story, describe a scene or read a document we ask the children to produce a quick sketch of what we have told them. Alternatively, we fold a piece of A4 paper in four, six or eight and use the spaces to draw a cartoon sequence of the tale.

The creation of a picture forces pupils to have a perspective upon the past, to see it through the eyes of the artist or photographer. For pictures to be historical they must be based upon the historical record, the sources that the pupil has used. Pictorial representation crucially provides less literate pupils with a medium in which they can successfully demonstrate what they know.

12 Objects

Objects or artefacts are a central feature of our teaching. Objects are a powerful, tangible means of approaching people in the past. They carry with them ideas, associations and messages about the people who made, owned and used them, and the environment from which they came. Illustration 24 shows one of my favourite teaching objects, a small pebble. I sit the students in a circle and they pass the stone from hand to hand, adding an idea to it. Step by step I introduce information about it, how I found it at Maiden Castle, the great Iron-Age fort near Dorchester, where it came from originally (Chesil Beach near Portland), what it might have been used for (it was a sling-shot), what climactic event it might have been engaged in (the Romans stormed Maiden Castle during Vespasian's campaign of conquest) and what has happened to it since. Using the information and ideas gained each child then has to tell a story about the stone.

Illustration 24   *Pebble from Maiden Castle*

Reflection How do you use objects ?
- Think of how you have used objects in your history teaching in the past year
- Read Using historical objects.
- How does it suggest that you might use objects?
- Compare its approach with your own.
- For each of its teaching ideas suggest a possible application in your own teaching. Make out a list to show this.

Using historical objects	I was talking about this subject with a young teacher the other day when she closed the discussion with the statement 'It's all right for you, you're old, your house is full of old things – how do I get them?' Alas – I had to agree with her, and so we must first consider the matter of gathering materials.
Museums and loan services	Most museums have loan services for schools and often these provide objects of almost frighteningly good quality – one unpacks them thinking, should they really be loaning such stuff out to me? What's nice about museum loans also is that they come with details attached; one is not left speechless by an object which looks, quite frankly, like nothing on earth.
Objects for the classroom	But you don't need wondrous material for what you are going to do, nice as it is to have. Very ordinary objects from the past can yield wondrous results with children – a Victorian coin, an old school ink bottle, a button. Any junk shop will provide you with a small museum of bits and pieces for a tiny investment. What you need to do is to consider the use of the objects in the classroom. How about an old razor strop? Not very enticing, but as an example of difference between then and modern dad's electric razors, really very useful. And a bottle with an advertising slogan on it – how different from today.
	Another way of collecting artefacts, especially from the recent past, is to ask parents to loan objects for school use. This is especially fruitful for Britain Since 1930. I remember asking some Year 4 children to steal the most embarrassing photograph they could find at home of their parents. We got Hell's Angels, hippies at pop festivals, even a local bank manager with shoulder length hair smoking something which did not look like a Players No. 6! Although not strictly artefacts, the information we got from these was immense. As well as being huge fun, it showed the children that the past was something that was alive, was full of people enjoying themselves, was a time similar to our own, with human aspirations, failings and successes. The children copied their photo as a large blow-up and we displayed them on A3 paper with the caption 'Those were the days!' Open evening that term was a lot of fun! You can find lots, if you look, and every school should be busy building its own economical but substantial and useful museum.
Presenting objects to children	One of the first things to think about is how you present the objects to the children, and as any good businessman will tell you, packaging is all important. I have posted objects to school,

shrouded in layer upon layer of packing, tightly tied and sealed with sealing wax – because the harder you make it to get at the object the more you invest it with speciality. I sometimes pack objects in an old lawyer's tin box with a rather a wonky key – it takes ages and great care to get it open and that itself is useful.

Another feature of presentation with small objects is to keep them hidden in your pocket or your hand for long enough to build up excitement, to make the children want to look. As the children begin to look at old objects they will need to consider with you what it is we are doing when we cherish things from the past – after all they are second-hand, used, scratched, faded, dirty, out-of-date, and to children who long for new things the respect we pay to the old is quite strange. So we will need to think about our values, about rarity, about difference, about the evidence objects can yield up about the past.

Practical archaeology

Maybe we will need to spend some time thinking about how things survive, and how they are found – some practical archaeology is always useful. A box with a glazed side, with layers of different coloured soils, and grassed over at the top, with various objects hidden in different layers is worth making, and actually worth digging out, mapping each find in three dimensions, and thinking about what its position has to tell us. The preparation of this is a perfect task to give any student attached to your school.

The idea of a museum

Similarly it is important to investigate the notion of museum with children. Some will have visited museums, some will not, but all will need to think about museum practice. What are the rules for handling and taking care of rare objects from the past? How do we catalogue them, how do we arrange and display them, how do we explain them to our visitors? The best way to deal with all of these issues is to make your own classroom museum to which you will invite visitors. (See Illustration 25, the Class Museum form.)

Looking closely – storytelling

Getting children to look closely at an object that may at first appear not very enticing can be difficult – and they won't just look because we urge them to do so; we need to find ways of conquering inattention, of building concentration and application. I remember, for example, being asked to work with some stone age flints by the local museum service because they were 'boring' to children. So I told the children the story of a tribe which had been led by an old chieftain who had a magic stone, but alas he died

Class Museum

Name of object ....

....

....

Who might have owned it when new ....

....

....

The owner might have used it for ....

....

....

A picture of it being used

Overleaf *The object's story since its left its first owner*

Illustration 25 *Class Museum form*

before being able to tell the tribe which of the many stones it was. The children looked with great care at each stone, and soon, when I had given them pencils and paper to record what they saw, began to report that they had been chipped, that the flaking had been purposeful, and we began to consider what each had been for. When they had decided what each object had been for, and which they thought had been the magic stone, we put it to the test. I told them more news of the tribe – sad news, a drought, no food, disaster. I went to each child and said what was now wrong – this one couldn't speak any more, this one couldn't walk. Then I said when all were asleep the chief would touch them with the magic stone and we would see when they awoke whether it worked. When dawn came I said good morning to the girl who could no longer speak and she croaked back to me 'Good morning'. I asked the boy who couldn't walk to come to the mouth of our cave to see the rain falling and the reindeer returning, and, stumbling, he came. The stone was true magic!

Drawing

Close and careful drawing is an invaluable tool in slowing down the pace of looking so that children get a chance of really seeing what is there. I often use an old gas tap that was torn from a college building, and given me by the caretaker, who knew about old things, and was willing to forego the swap value, which was then about 50p. I think I should pay him many pounds for the value I have had out of it. Again I ask children to make a drawing of it while they consider a question: what difference did the introduction of gas make to a household? After twenty minutes quiet drawing and conversation, it was easy to fill a huge blackboard with evidence of change – huge changes like the lengthening of the day, the convenience of instant light and heat, down to the changes that meant you could now see the dust in the corners of the room, and would have to do something about it. My gas tap is one of the best ways of achieving understanding that I know, and similar things would do equally well – an old radio, for example, or a steam iron in comparison to a flat iron.

Bringing objects to life

I think the great thing with objects is to attempt in some way to give them life again, to put them into a context of a living, continuing story. I have a small reproduction of an ivory plaque showing the nativity, dated circa 1400. It cost little enough, but like the gas tap, it has paid dividends. It clearly has been ripped from another plaque, the hinge marks show, so that once it was a diptych or a triptych. At the top two rough holes have been bored, as if to turn it into something to hang round your neck. I just ask the children to work with me on recreating the history of this object, and the stories begin to roll, but all are based on careful observation.

Detectives at work

How best can we introduce to pupils the idea of working from objects ? How can we introduce a sense of wonder and mystery, of finding out, of unlocking the meaning of the past?

A powerful medium is to take 'the historian as a detective' metaphor and apply it to ourselves and the class. There are many ways of doing this; below we explore some of them. The suitcase idea needs preparation, but a list of its contents or a picture of them is a poor substitute to either making up a packed suitcase yourself or getting a parent to do it. Pocket detective is the same idea and literally requires no preparation! It is a marvellous way of starting off a course with a group of children. The pupils can investigate the person sitting next to them on the basis of the information they discover from examining their personal effects. Usually this is what they will have in their bags or pockets. The idea is that the pupil has been killed or knocked down, or even gassed unconscious by a friendly ET type alien, and the police are trying to find out what they can about them. Use the idea of being unconscious if death is too emotive. We have used this strategy on numerous occasions – it has never failed us.

With younger children we can introduce the detective activity through telling the story of the Princess and the Pea, the point being that the pea is an artefact, an object, that has its historical meaning from the story of its past. Reading the tale to one of our daughters at bedtime sparked off the idea when at the end the book told us that the pea survived as an exhibit in a museum case! In the classroom telling the Princess and the Pea story was a deliberate attempt to get children to see that the significance of an object comes from the part that it plays in people's lives.

Detectives lesson plan

The **Learning Objectives** of this activity are
 1 To get the children to think about artefacts and see that each object will have a story from when it was made until today. The focus should be the object being used for its original purpose.
 2 To encourage the children to work together to think about the objects.

The activity includes these **teaching approaches**: storytelling, handling artefacts and detective work through investigating sources

Resources needed:
- The Princess and the Pea story
- The objects
- Template for the children's own picture / representation of the objects
- A children's doll, preferably Victorian in type
- Pupils' bags, contents of their pockets (for accident)
- An Accident Report Form
- Suitcase full of child's things, if possible, those of a child who is the same age as the children you teach.

The activities – there are three of these, numbers two and three link in to the first.

1 The Princess and the Pea Take the story of The Princess and the Pea to the point at its end where the pea was put into a museum. The pea had been placed under a huge pile of feather mattresses in order to find out if the young lady sleeping on it was a princess. If she woke up in the morning black and blue it proved that she was. Anyway, that is what she told the young prince's mum at breakfast. The pea ended its days in a glass case instead of on the end of a fork. Produce a diagram, using Illustration 25, Class Museum form with a label and a brief story or caption for the pea. Move on to the examination of objects, using either the pocket detective or the suitcase approach.

2 Pocket Detective Split the pupils up into pairs – there may be one threesome
Set the scene – there has been an accident. Tell the children that their partner is either dead or unconscious.
Empty bags or pockets and put things in a neat pile in front of them. Remove all objects which are either embarrassing or incriminating.
Give out the Accident Report Form (Illustration 26)
Each child changes places with his/her partner (far easier than moving piles of goodies)
Draw up a list of the things found.
Write out the list on the Accident Report Form.
Report back. Go round the group getting them to tell you about what their partner is like on the basis of the things that you have found.
They can be as imaginative as they like! The only constraint is **that**

Accident report form

Date ....

Surname ....

First names ....

Age ....

Address ....

....

....

List of objects/things

....

....

....

....

....

....

....

Report on what the person was like

....

....

....

....

....

....

....

Overleaf *Drawing of the person*

Illustration 26   Accident Report form

the stories must be linked to the evidence.
Resolution – the completion of the Accident Report Form.

3 The Suitcase The suitcase contains the evidence about a person. It can be made up and presented in a number of ways. In this case we can say the suitcase has been found and been handed into the police.

History detective results and follow up

As the history detective we have to ask some questions, and use the clues to answer them

- The questions Put the closed suitcase in front of the group. In pairs you have to come up with questions.
- **The investigation** How do we go about the investigation ? How do we organize it ?
- **The handling of the clues** Split the clues in the suitcase up on tables, the children can then circulate investigating them.
- **Discussing, reporting back** Each pair can take one of the clues or a set of clues and say what they tell us. This can focus in on your original list of questions.
- **The story** Having been through the clues, work on a story about the person.

Follow-up There are many follow-up activities possible. Here are a few we have tried:

- Ask the children to bring a bag of objects of their own, which would tell a stranger all about them.
- The school is to bury a time capsule. What will they choose to put in it? (Not the headteacher!)
- Britain Since 1930 – The class are to be evacuated away from their homes. Each child is allowed to take a small bag with them. What will they take and why?
- Creative stuff – Design five objects an alien would bring with him from his home planet to help him survive.
- Take a well-known book character, Pooh Bear, Alice, Batman, what might you expect to find in their suitcases? For younger children the teacher could list the contents for several characters and then ask the children to work out whom each object belongs to.

Handling objects

There are many approaches to squeezing objects for the information they contain about people in the past, (see **Seventy-five ways of Using Objects** at the end of this chapter). Pupils can be a marvellous source of objects. For example, during teaching the Britain Since 1930 HSU our Year 3 and 4 pupils filled our classroom museum with a range of objects, including a chain with a hook on it, fossils, an electric bell for a shop, an advert for toothpaste, a very rusty sickle and a photograph album with detachable photographs. Pupils can investigate and focus on any such object or objects. It helps if each can have a magnifying glass. Our procedure is to get the children to: sit in a circle, take an object and pass it round, each add one new observation about the object, and then pass it on, and one tell a story based on the object. Often we put up 'buzz' words on the blackboard as both a stimulus and an *aide mémoire*. The activity can be built up through feeding in information, as with the pebble from Maiden Castle.

Questioning : a doll

We place questioning at the heart of our teaching. Pupil questions can help focus an enquiry. In our teaching of The Victorians HSU we had a large Victorian doll. The teaching went as follows:

- We put the doll on a chair so all the pupils could see it.
- Questions. On a slip of paper each pupil wrote down questions that they wanted to ask about the doll. The pupils in pairs or threes talked about these questions before jotting down their ideas.
- We then went around the pairs, writing the questions up on the board. Those who were unable to write gave oral questions. Our list ran:

Is it Victorian?	What colour hair?
What is its hair made of?	Where is it from?

The body in the bog: *Peter Marsh*

In 1884 a farmer digging on Lindow Moss found a human body in the ground. At first he thought it was the remains of someone who had been murdered recently, so he called the police.

The police arrived and soon realised that this was no ordinary body. The police called in archaeologists from Manchester University and they began to work out what happened to the man they nicknamed Peter Marsh.

Some of the Facts:

1. The body has been carbon-dated to the second half of the first century, between AD50 and AD100.

2. The Celts believed that the number 3 was a holy number and therefore very special.

3. Peter Marsh was not tied up, nor did he appear to have struggled in any way.

4. He had three largish holes on his head, certainly caused by blows to the head. These do not look as if they would have killed him.

5. He had a garotte still tied around his neck. This had three knots on it and had been tied so tight it had broken his neck.

6. He had a gash in the side of his neck about 5cm long, but very deep. It went directly into the jugular vein, the main carrier of blood to the brain.

7. The hands and arms of Pete Marsh were soft and smooth, with no scars or cuts.

8. The Celts had 3 really important gods: Taranis the Thunder God: Esus, the Lord and Master Teutates, the god of the tribe. All expected sacrifices at certain times of the year.

9. The remains of a burnt cake-like bannock was found in the stomach of Peter Marsh.

10. The god Taranis expected his sacrifices to be burnt.

11. The god Esus expected his sacrifices to be hanged and to have their throats cut.

12. The god Teutates would accept a sacrifice, if the person was drowned or put into water.

Illustration 27 The Peter Marsh Story

Is it hungry?
Who made the doll?
Does it have a wig?
What is it made of?
Who made the clothes?
How heavy is it?

How much did it cost?
Whose is it?
Does it walk?
Does it talk?
Does it wet itself?

Circle work

We then passed the doll around so that each child had a good look at it. In turn each said one thing that they noticed about the doll. We put up a list of ideas and thoughts on the board. Having studied the doll intensively, we focused on the first question, 'Is it Victorian'? We asked the class, 'how would you find out'? Again, we fielded the answers which included:

- Look in a Flambards catalogue
- Take it to a museum
- Take it to an antiques shop
- Look in books

A group of objects

How can we use a group of objects? We drew an outline of a group of objects on sheets of paper and numbered the outlines. The teaching strategy was: to put the objects on display on different tables. The pupils circulated around the room in pairs, investigating the objects. They chose one object, and filled in a museum form for it. We asked them the sources they would use to find out about the objects, and what they might tell them. We then used the sources available to investigate the objects. In one lesson we used a collection of Victorian farm objects that had been in the teacher's family for ninety years. We found a picture of a Victorian kitchen, and got the pupils to spot the objects from our collection in use. It was a tremendous matching activity, in which the objects sprang to life in front of their eyes.

Classroom archaeology

Archaeology is a major source of objects. Involving the pupils in learning about the past from the perspective of the archaeologist is a well tried and tested approach. But, how can you get the children involved in an archaeological dig if you can't bring in a load of remains, bury them in sawdust, peat or sand and dig away with plastic teaspoons? Simulated archaeology is the next best thing. It always generates intense interest and enthusiasm.

In simulated classroom archaeology we give pupils a blank grid, usually A3 size. They then have to 'dig up' each of the squares, either in a given or a random order. As the teacher we give them pictures of what they have dug up to stick in the relevant square.

The Dig

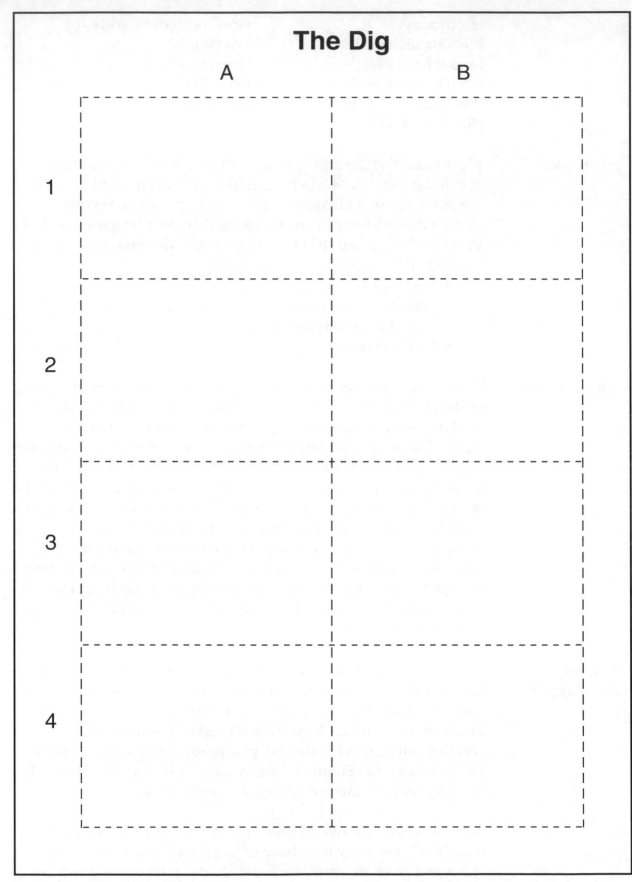

Illustration 28   *Archaeology grid*

Classroom Archaeology–*Instructions*

You have a grid marked from A1 to B2–eight squares in total.

In each square you will find some objects, these are in the envelopes. **One** person from each group takes **one** envelope and takes it backto the group. Tip out the contents. Piece together the parts to make the object. Please note that there may be more than one object in the envelope. When you have worked out what the object(s) look like draw them in your book. **One** person should draw them in the correct square on the master sheet.

Within your group you should try to answer these questions for each object.

1. What is it?
2. What is it made of?
3. How did it get into the ground?
4. What was it used for?
5. Does it tell us anything about the site as a whole?
6. Is anything missing?
7. How oldis it?

You should try to think of some extra questions of your own.

Repeat this until all 8 squares are finished. Then try and work out how **all** the objects gotb to be where they were found. Is anything missing.

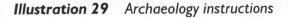

Illustration 29   *Archaeology instructions*

We adopted this technique in our teaching of Ancient Greece. Uppermost was an attempt to get to the human beings behind the evidence, with each piece of evidence telling us something about the Ancient Greeks. We used the following resources:

- blank archaeology sheets
- cut-out pieces for each square, in envelopes
- follow up materials, topic books on Ancient Greece and pictures.
- instructions given the children.

Our **Learning Objectives** were:

- To introduce the idea of the archaeologist at work
- To present resource material in an interesting way
- To develop pupils' deductive and imaginative skills in handling evidence
- To teach them about Ancient Greek civilization
- To teach them about the evidence upon which we base our understanding of Ancient Greece

The lesson plan

Our lesson plan is below. We have modified it in the light of experience.

1 Introduction

Through a series of questions we introduce the idea of archaeological evidence and how the archaeologists go about their work. What do we call a person who digs up things in the ground to find out about the past? How does the archaeologist record what he or she finds? Explain the use of a grid to record finds. If we are carrying out a dig, what questions do we need to ask to start our investigation?

2 Digging: starting

Hand out the grid sheet, one for each person or pair/three. Say that we are going to dig up each square, that is the eight squares on the grid, A1-D1, A2-D2. Put down on it what we dig up. Glue our finds to it. Make notes of what we think as we go along.

3 Choosing and discussing

Choice – the group can decide which square it wants to dig. As each square is dug up discuss it, and what you think the clue suggests. Continue digging until all eight squares are dug up. One square can contain part of an object, which can lead into a separate exercise.

4 Research

Use the books to find any other evidence which tells us more about what the dig has revealed.

5 Story Time
Each child thinks up a story about the site. Each tells their story to the rest of the group. Sum it up on the board in a single phrase/sentence. Choose the story or stories you like best.

Objects and society We can use a single object to work out what it tells us about the society that produced and used it. Thus with out Year 3 pupils, in an archaeological simulation on the great Saxon burial ship with its royal treasure found at Sutton Hoo, we gave them a picture of the remains of a harp or lyre found in the burial. On the board we put a set of headings for them to think about; Raw materials, Tools, Who made it?, How was it made?, Who owned it?, What was it used for?

Soon the board filled up with ideas. Quickly by inference, the children created a mental picture of the Saxon king and his court. In turn, you can take any other artefact identified in this exercise, and apply the same idea to it.

Surface archaeology This is an interesting and exciting way of getting involved in handling the kinds of remains which archaeologists deal with. It is also genuinely academic as it is a standard archaeological technique. The resources you need are small plastic bags. Use one to pick things up with, another to collect them. You will also need an area to walk over; a park or playing field is okay, but a ploughed field is much better.

The activity The goals are to acquaint children with the kind of evidence which can be discovered on the surface of the ground, to raise problems of evidence and how we handle it.

1 Introduction
Say that we are going to function as archaeologists, discovering evidence about the past through doing some surface archaeology.

2 The survey
Each of you takes a couple of polythene bags. Line up across the area to be searched, or stake out squares to explore inside. Pick up all the objects you can find.

3 Recording
Record your finds – list them and guess what they are. Use

them to work out what they tell us about the people who lived there. Look at the nature of the evidence, how it has survived, what trust we can place in it.

A word of warning. When we did this activity with our Year 3/4 class, we collected evidence from an area in the school grounds full of rich and varied remains. Later an indignant deputation of pupils from another form confronted us with the accusation that we had destroyed their experiment to discover the different rates of decay of objects left in the open …

Seventy-five Ways of Using Objects

1   What questions do we want to ask about it? Pool the questions
2   Who made it?
3   Who might have owned it when new?
4   How was it made?
5   What colour is it?
6   Is it complete?
7   Who made these things?
8   Is it man or machine made, or a combination of both?
9   Is it decorated, and if so, how?
10 What ideas influenced its design?
11 What ideas influenced its decoration?
12 Do you like how it looks? If so, why?
13 Do you dislike its looks? If so, why?
14 Where was it used?
15 When was it used?
16 What tools, machines materials and processes were used to make it?
17 What was it made from?
18 Draw up a table to show how it was designed and the steps in its making
19 What were the raw materials, tools and machines to make it made from?
20 Who made them and how?
21 What does this tell us about the society that produced the original object?
22 What might it have been used for?
23 Who used it?
24 Why did they use it?
25 Has its use changed?
26 Has it changed in any way since being made?
27 Is it brand new or worn? If worn, how and why?
28 What difference did it make to the lives of the owners?
29 Compare and discuss an object and how it is being used in a picture which depicts it.
30 Recreate the history of the object.
31 Brainstorm as many possible uses for the object as possible when it was made.
32 Tell a story of a day in the life of the object when it was in use.
33 Where could we find out about it?
34 List the sources and say what they might tell us.
35 Pass the object from hand to hand, with a new observation from each person about the object.
36 Provide information or sources for pupils to research the object.
37 Describe the object in detail.
38 Handle it. Say what it feels like: heavy, light, rough, smooth, comfortable.
39 How much is it worth to you, to a museum, to its present owner?
40 How much was it worth to its original owner?
41 What did it mean to its owner, how did he or she value it?
42 Draw it and label the drawing.
43 Draw and label it as if it was a museum exhibit or in a catalogue.
44 Draw a picture of it in use.
45 Put an object on display. Sit the pupils around it. they have to sketch it,

and label their sketch. Then display the drawings of the object, and discuss what the different drawings tell us.

46 Tell the story of it from when it had stopped being used to it ending up in a museum.

47 Ask the class to closely observe an object. Remove it, and ask them to draw
it or describe it from memory.

48 Use a magnifying glass to study it.

49 Draw an object from memory.

50 Put objects on separate tables, on numbered pieces of card with their outline. Pupils circulate around the clues, observing each one.

51 They write a catalogue card for an object or objects. This is read out to see which object the other pupils think it describes.

52 A pupil is placed on a table, lying down. Pretend s/he is dead. Ask what would survive – and what the objects would tell us about him or her.

53 Draw an object on large scale to show all its details.

54 Wrap it up and seal it, to make its unwrapping a mysterious activity.

55 Hide it in a box, carefully empty the box to reveal the object.

56 Hide it in a room, so pupils have to discover it.

57 Bury it so it has to be dug up, as if the pupils were archaeologists.

58 Create a classroom archaeological dig.

59 Create a suitcase of objects for the class to investigate as detectives.

60 Put the object into a feely bag, pass it round and ask for ideas about it.

61 Make a collection of objects. Take them one by one out of the bag. Build up ideas about the whole set through the process of investigation.

62 Tell the class a story about the object that brings it to life.

63 Take a broken object, place in a box, and get the pupils to piece it together.

64 Make up a series of broken boxes of different objects about the same topic. Get the pupils to work on these object to recreate them. Then pool ideas about the society they are from.

65 Take a broken object, some of it missing, get the pupils to draw the missing pieces to recreate the object as if it was new.

66 Make an object and use it, based on the remains you have or picture of them.

67 Involve the class in surface archaeology.

68 Take two sets of the same objects that will perish. Show them the class. Bury one set for a week and dig it up. Compare the two sets.

69 Pass a clean, white ironed handkerchief around the class from hand to hand. Then see how it has changed.

70 Pass an old plate around the class. Tell them how valuable it is. Then drop it.

71 Give pupils a group of objects and ask them to organise them as a museum display.

72 Give pupils a group of objects and ask them to work out how to get children to learn about them in an interesting and rewarding way.

73 Get the pupils to bring in objects. They create a classroom museum.

74 Give the pupil an object that other children do not see. The pupils then have to ask questions to guess what it is.

75 Give the pupil an object. The pupil has to make accurate statements about the object. The others have to guess what it is on the basis of the evidence. As a game, with a number of objects, the winner is the person who makes the most statements before the object's identity is guessed.

13   Maps and Plans

The Year 3 child pharaoh lies on the table, while the teacher carries out the embalming ceremony. The scene switches to a Year 5/6 lesson where the pupils are planning out an Elizabethan court masque. In another class Snoopy and the Red Baron meet Yuri Gagarin. At every point in our teaching of history our children have to deal with the physical location of people, be it the tomb of a pharaoh, the court of Queen Elizabeth or Yuri Gagarin's space ship. Continually through contextual clues pupils build up an awareness of place. This we can actively develop through stressing how people in the past fitted in to and related to their surroundings. Maps and plans are our main medium.

Reflection **Thinking about maps and children**
- Jot down the ways in which you use maps and plans in your teaching.
- Read **Maps and children**
- Add any new ideas you might use in the future.

Maps and children   Many people think of geography and history as closely allied subjects, whereas in fact geography fits better with science and history with English. But that doesn't mean that historians don't use geography, or that geographers don't use history. We need to make constant use of maps and must pay visits to as many sites as we can.

First of all we need to use maps as reference sources. That means we need to have good, adult atlases available in the classroom in the first place. Often you can get these cheaply from a book club, rather than paying the full price, but read the small print before you sign up!

You need to consult maps in many different styles. How far is it from York to Rome? How far was it when Constantine made the journey? (He did it, with his army, in two weeks when he made his bid for the Roman Empire.) What sort of barriers did he meet with

– which part of the journey took longest? It is worthwhile spending a fair amount of time on these consultations, and the teacher needs to be there to guide the children in using the map. Sometimes it is worthwhile making an OHP transparency of a map so that everyone can follow. A mileometer is useful, although, like a lot of small items of educational equipment, they tend to walk unless you keep an eagle eye on them.

Some raised contour maps exist, but they are quite expensive and often too small for whole class use, so train everyone to understand contours so that they can read a map in three dimensions. Take account of climate as well, because if you are following a crusader army it is vital to know where the desert patches are, and how long the agony might last.

A problem (especially if you are following the tracks of an explorer) is that modern maps show everything in our own terms – it's all a bit like an AA book. We need to create maps with the unknown bits (for example, Australia) excluded. This is a good task for children, and if they can use squaring-up to enlarge a map to a really big size they can take a boat or a fleet and track its journey day by day until they literally run into Terra Incognita.

Maps are a wonderful way of exploring the size of past empires. I will say to children that they are the Emperor in Rome and there is a failure of the Nile, problems with the grapes in Spain, Germans plodding westwards to the borders, and a nasty outbreak of Picts. They must use the map to help them to deploy their finite resources to cope with these many problems. As they work out their plans they begin to see just what a huge undertaking it all was.

Maps and change

Maps are also a splendid resource for teaching about change. Just five maps of your area, spread over maybe 100 years, will make the basis of some excellent work in which the children can spot when buildings disappear, or change their use or name and when new buildings appear. It is amazing how much change there is in any built-up area over a short period of time, and there is usually some major change going on at any given time.

As part of this exploration of change, we can access another valuable source, the trades directory. The local collection in your nearest big library will undoubtedly hold a substantial collection of these, some going back 200 years. Using these you can rebuild a street in, say 1870 and see what it looked like then. If you add the census records (which your county record office will have on microfilm, and which can easily be photocopied for you) you can go behind the front doors and meet the families who lived there.

If you want to go back much further, look at the fascinating English Place Name Society volume for your area. It is amazing what you can find out from these. For example, Pucklechurch in Gloucestershire was named for Puck (the Devil) who had temporarily taken over the church. It happened quite regularly in the Middle Ages – and if you require proof go to Lincoln Cathedral to see the Imp, turned to stone by St Hugh.

A sense of place

The National Curriculum History Orders require children to develop as full an understanding of historical situations as possible, central to which is physical location. Once historically and geographically in situ, be it globally, nationally, regionally or locally, the class can get inside the minds of the historical characters concerned. An understanding of place means children have to create maps, either in their minds, on paper or as models.

What is a map or a plan? It is a 'model' of a reality, that extracts specific elements and represents them symbolically in forms such as lines, icons and shading. Different maps of the same area will show different things; one map might be of military campaigns, another of population movements. Maps contains inter-related symbols, the meaning of which is shown by the key. This definition raises three linked issues:

1 How can we come to grips with the thought processes involved in mapping and planning?
2 What was life like in a world in which maps and plans did not exist, or in which they were of an extremely primitive kind?
3 How can maps and plans foster children's historical understanding?

Mental maps and mapping

Subconsciously we continually create mental maps. Textual spatial clues are woven into the fabric of history books. They enable us to develop mental maps, they play a vital role in physically locating human activity in the past.

In dealing with place it is important to give the pupils some feeling of what might have been going on inside the minds of early explorers and travellers. A simple question is how did people find their way around in a world without maps? A crucial point is that, in order to undertake journeys, early travellers had to have some idea of the relationships between places and what they were like. We have some marvellous evidence about this. The most spectacular set of sailing instructions can be found in Homer's Odyssey, while from a later period we have Viking accounts of Wulfstan's voyage. His account gives an insight into how a Viking merchant planned a journey.

Wulfstan's Voyage

Wulfstan said that he travelled from Hedeby to Trusc in seven days, sailing both day and night. Wendland was on his starboard, and on the portside were Langeland, Laaland Falstar and Skaanen—lands all belonging to Denmark. Then Bornholm was on the portside. The people who live on this island have their own king. Then they passed Blenkinge, More, Oeland and Gothland, all of which belong to Sweden. Wendland was always on the starboard, until they reached the mouth of the River Vistula. The Vistula is a mighty river which separates Whitland and Wendland. Whitland belongs to the Estonians. The River Vistula flows out of Wendland and into the Frisches Haff, which is at least fifteen miles wide. At the same time the River Elbing flows from the south east into the Frisches Haff. It flows from Estonia, From the lake on which Truso stands. The two rivers merge in the Frisches Haff, and flow into the sea.

What does it suggest to you about early travel ? How might you use the account with your own pupils? To highlight the problems of travel in a pre-map age and the creation of maps we set our pupils the problem of describing how they get to school. Hopefully it also illuminates the thinking revealed in sources like the Odyssey and 13B. Insight into the processes involved in creating maps is important in both analysing their value as sources and understanding the mentalities of those who commissioned, created and used the maps.

We also cast each pupil in the role of an explorer and discoverer. We taught such a lesson to our Year 3/4 pupils to introduce a topic on Tudor explorers and discoverers. Our aim was for the pupils to think about the concepts of exploration and discovery.

Making sense of early maps

A map or plan is constructed from the particular perspective of its maker. It is a statement of his or her intentions and perceptions of

Going to school

First I get up. Then I get dressed. After that I go down stairs for my breakfast. The I get my Things ready for school.

First I go out the gate. Then Then cross our road walk straight on until yo get to a little road. Turn up and cross that road, there is a road going of that. Go straight along until you get to the end. Cross over another road and go straight along that road. Then turn the corner. Go straight up to the bus stop. Then cross. turn to the left and go on through Lebraham close. Walk through a gate and up some steps and you will be at my school.

Illustration 31   *A pupil narrative of a journey to school*

the intended audience. As such, maps and plans are important in their own right as evidence about the past.

How can we get pupils to make sense of early maps?
In our work on a non-European civilization and contact between the Old and New World, we wanted our pupils to acquire an idea of early views of the world, focusing on the medieval Mappa Mundi in Hereford Cathedral. We began our teaching by telling the pupils that they had volunteered to go on a voyage with Christopher Columbus and that we thought that they were crazy. Our next step was to introduce the class to some evidence from the period. The Mappa Mundi provides an insight into how medieval people viewed the world they lived in. We asked our pupils to create their own medieval world map, using the outline provided. The pupils were asked to undertake the following tasks:

Create a medieval world map:
1 Animals
- Read through the descriptions of the animals.
- What do you think they are?

2 Storytelling
- Discuss how did these descriptions might have come about.
- Take a common animal such as a dog, and then describe its features in an exaggerated way.
- If working with a partner or in a small group, the next person repeats the story, exaggerating the features you described, adding new ones, and so on.

3 Drawing animals/people
- Draw one or more of the Mappa Mundi creatures.
- When everyone has drawn an animal you can swap them around to try and guess what they are.
- Get your animals back and then make a label to go with each one.
- Stick your animals on the side of the map, with a line to show where they are from.

4 Comparisons
- Compare the pupils' maps with the original.
- What does this tell us about the medieval view of the world?

Working on maps Maps come in many forms, shapes and sizes. Three of the most easily available map sources are atlases, ordnance survey and town plans. Street plans are provided in trade directories like the Yellow Pages or by estate agents.

Using an atlas   We can take maps from atlases to provide insights into the past. Maps are puzzles for the pupils to decode. Place-names, be they Celtic, Roman, Anglo-Saxon, Norman or from the Middle Ages and modern periods, provide insights into how society developed. Thus when working on the Romans we took our road atlas as the basis for developing an understanding of the pattern of Roman settlement. The problem was to provide an activity that would enable our children to appreciate the Romans' pattern of conquest and settlement Our **learning objectives** were:

1   To develop an understanding of the extent of Roman colonization and settlement.
2   To involve pupils in working on a modern map as a source for developing historical understanding.
3   To promote both enquiry and cooperative group work, associated with the skills of observation, analysis and deduction.

We took several A3 photocopies (one for each group of four pupils) of a modern road map of England and Wales amended to include Hadrian's wall. We cut each photocopy into four pieces. Our other resources were:

- A blank outline map of England and Wales.
- A plain piece of A3 paper.
- Outline map of Roman Britain showing the settlement pattern and the roads.

The lesson   Our teaching went as follows:
1 Introduction
   Take a piece of the cut up map of England and Wales.
   Use the endings of town names as clues to Roman settlement:
   ter, ster = fort.
   Thus Chester and Exeter could be Roman towns.
2 Place names research
   Search on each piece of map for what might be Roman towns, that is, ending in 'ster' or 'ter'.
   Ring any places that you think are Roman
   Repeat this for the other three pieces of the map.
   Then, piece the map together.
   Glue the pieces on to the A3 sheet of plain paper.
3 Planning a Roman road system
   Put onto the blank map the places that you identified as being

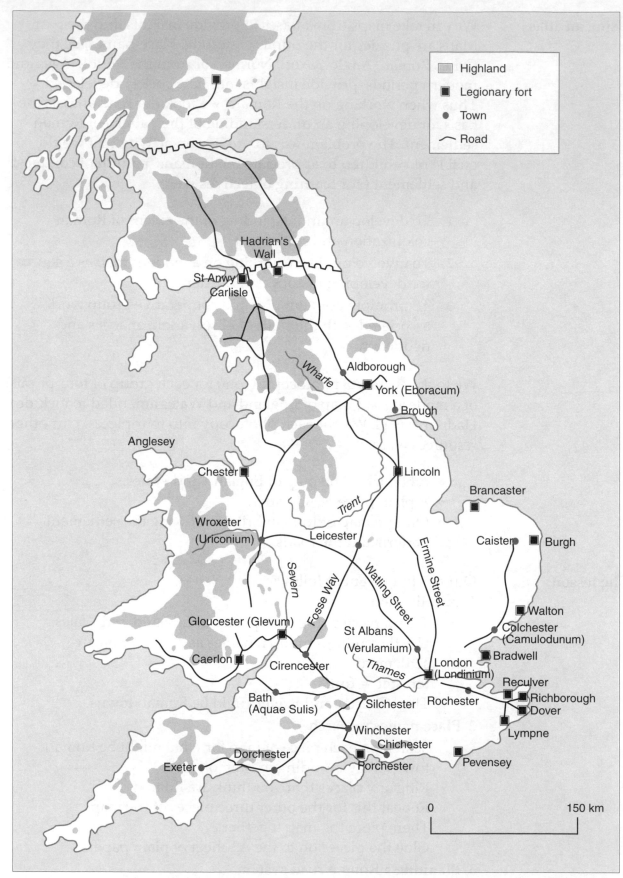

Illustration 32 *A Map of Roman England*

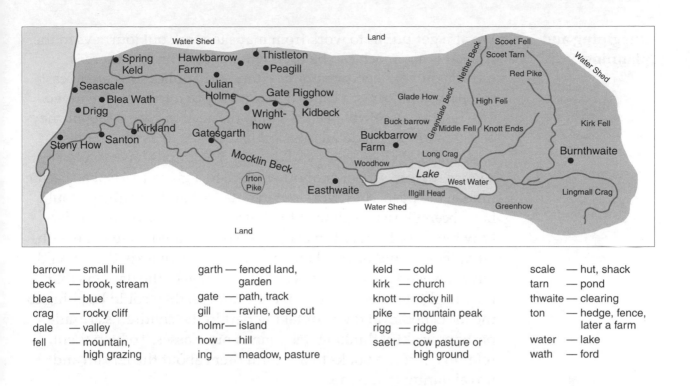

barrow	— small hill	garth	— fenced land, garden	keld	— cold	scale	— hut, shack

barrow — small hill
beck — brook, stream
blea — blue
crag — rocky cliff
dale — valley
fell — mountain, high grazing

garth — fenced land, garden
gate — path, track
gill — ravine, deep cut
holmr — island
how — hill
ing — meadow, pasture

keld — cold
kirk — church
knott — rocky hill
pike — mountain peak
rigg — ridge
saetr — cow pasture or high ground

scale — hut, shack
tarn — pond
thwaite — clearing
ton — hedge, fence, later a farm
water — lake
wath — ford

Illustration 33 *Place name derivation*

Roman, plus London, the capital of Roman Britain.
Produce your own road and settlement map of what
Roman England and Wales might have been like,
following these rules:
  a Roads are straight
  b Roads radiate out from London. Put these in first to the
     nearest towns.
  c Roads link up all the towns
     The pattern will look a little like a spider's web

4 Comparative work
Compare your map with a map of the actual Roman settlement and
road pattern.

5 Source limitations
Discuss the possible limitations of modern maps for teaching
settlement through the use of place-name evidence.

We apply the same idea with local place names.

Imagining and planning	We also get pupils to work from maps to work out journeys in the past. This approach can be used whenever in history there is movement between two points. Standard applications are to cast the class as pilgrims, a campaigning army or a tribe on the move. The resource you will need is a map of the area where the journey occurs, showing in detail physical features such as rivers, hills, mountains, ravines, lakes and deserts. The pupils have to plan out a journey from school or another place to a given place at a specific time in the past. They work out in detail what the country would have been like at the time of the journey, the state of the roads, how they would have travelled, who they would have gone with, what they would have taken with them, how quickly they would have travelled, where they would have stayed, the dangers that they might have encountered. For example, they could be going to the local medieval town, or taking part in the children's crusade, perhaps wishful thinking for some of our classes. To help them, refer to reference books that inform them about the terrain and travel during that period.

The idea is infinitely adaptable, for it can be applied to walking down a street and exploring a house or a room, providing there is sufficient detail for the pupils to recreate in their minds what the situation was like. It came to our rescue in teaching about Kennedy's assassination: an artist's aerial view of the area enabled the pupils in the role of would be assassins to plan out how they would have gone about killing the president.

Creating board games	Another approach to developing historical understanding is to use a map as the basis for pupils to produce their own board games. We have used this approach extensively in our teaching of the HSUs. In our Ancient Greece HSU we built the major part of the course around the pupils creating board games.
Ordnance Survey	The Ordnance Survey provides a most marvellous source for investigating any locality. Maps go back 150 years, and come in all shapes and sizes, 6, 25 and 50 inches to the miles. At Midhurst we seized on maps as a way of introducing Year 6 children to the study of history.

The children we taught were two Year Six groups who had just started at Midhurst Intermediate School in West Sussex. Sue and Sandy wanted their children to have some time to settle down, and in the first instance they hoped to lead them gently towards the subject through work on family history and on the nature of maps and plans. For example, Sue had a useful time with her children looking at a rough plan of a shop she remembered from her childhood. The different goods were coded on the plan and this gave the children a chance to find their way around such material and to meditate on the enormous changes that have overtaken shops in the last two decades.

Kim Leslie, the archive education officer at West Sussex County Record Office, provided us with a substantial pack of documents. The pack included five maps of the area of the school taking us back over a century; census records; parish records; materials about Cowdray, the local 'big house'; and materials about the former workhouse, whose building survives about a quarter of a mile from the school. Sue and Sandy chose to start with the maps.

Looking for changes

I began by talking with them about my journey to school. I had been coming for twenty years or so and there were some things that were always there, and some which had changed quite a bit. Houses had been altered, rebuilt or freshly built. Some now looked as though they had been there for ages, but I knew they were newer than they looked. Other changes had happened – names, for example. I was stopped in a traffic jam in Midhurst (nothing new there) and I looked over to a pub I once knew as 'The Three Horseshoes', and now it was 'The Silver Horseshoe'. Just down the road was the new mini-roundabout we all remembered causing such traffic problems while it was being built earlier that year. And beside it was the old mill – there had been a mill in Midhurst on that site since Domesday times. We calculated how long that was. There was both stability and change.

The children threw in ideas – one said his house was 400 years old, and we worked out that Queen Elizabeth was on the throne then, but it was at a time of change between Tudors and Stuarts.

Wheelbarrow Castle?

So we looked at our first map – a mere 39 years old. The children quickly saw that the strange name of the piece of ground on which their school was built – Wheelbarrow Castle – was there, but no school. We brooded about the name – I told them it wasn't in the Place Name Society book, and that it baffled everyone. Their guess was as good as any. Perhaps, they said, it was a castle that looked like a wheelbarrow. Or it belonged to a family called Wheelbarrow or they used wheelbarrows to tip boiling oil over the battlements. Perhaps, I said it was a jokey name for the local tip, where people took their rubbish in wheelbarrows. Maybe, said the children, but it could also be that they invented the wheelbarrow here – perhaps a Mr. Wheelbarrow invented it, like the Earl of Sandwich.

The observer may feel that I have let the children diverge from the point here – we *should* be looking at the map. But maps are hard to look at, and after their first victory of seeing something there, they need a pause to relish their success and build their confidence. They need also to begin to learn to speculate – because they will find very little information that doesn't raise its own questions.

So we got back to the map and looked for more detail. There seemed like some entry to Wheelbarrow Castle, maybe steps. Perhaps these had always been there or perhaps it was the beginning of the development of the school site. The allotments at the back were still here. A lot of houses didn't show on this map – not yet built? Farms are shown that now are houses – how did that come about? We had to play with these questions time and again, for the children were mastering the notion that there is a difference between then and now, and that then (on the map) there were things that haven't survived and there weren't things that are there now (and so must have been built in between). These are quite complex ideas about time, as well as complex problems of map reading and recording.

Forward in time

So next I asked the children to draw two columns on a sheet of paper and mark it '1954'. At the head of the first column they should put 'There' (that is, things we know now that were there then) and at the head of the second 'Not There' (that is, things we have now, but were not there then and therefore had to have been built between 1954 and now). I asked them to put three items in each column. To specify a precise, small number is always good, especially at this stage: it suggests a finite, do-able task, but it also offers a chance to congratulate everybody on achieving it, and getting quick finishers to go on and do twelve entries.

We found that one a snip, so we went back to 1938, which I said was a most important year because it was the year of my birth. Next year world war broke out. The children were impressed!

So, lots of recognizable things, but some differences. There was Dodsley Farm and Budgenor Lodge, the allotments and, hello, what are these, – the words 'Council Cottages'. The children wondered whether they had Council Houses then. I said we should find out, but where were the cottages – the map bore no evidence of buildings at all. So what does this mean? The children were foxed for a while, and then saw that these were planned. Were they there now? No. What is the explanation? Bombed in the war? Good idea but I didn't think too many bombs dropped round here. Slowly they began to see a picture – Council Cottages planned, war came, no supplies, money or men, never got built.

Hooking that chain of thought out of the children took some time, and clearly the ablest were doing most of the work, but because all the children were sitting together doing the same task, the idea of reasoning out explanations was beginning to take. No time spent on such reasoning at this stage is wasted – it may seem slow but it is immensely worth while.

The children added to their charts and we hurtled back to 1910 – a map with a different scale. The children found it hard to get used to it – 'The church has disappeared' – is that likely, we know the church is immensely old, way off our time scale? Slowly they saw – yes, it's off the edge of the map, it is the scale that is foxing us again. Phew! It's all right – but for a moment we thought we had lost the church!

Name changes

Then someone noticed something odd – there was Budgenor Lodge all right, but on this map it was called the Midhurst Union Workhouse. We puzzled over this name change, and I promised we would return to it. But now we had to think about how to record all this stuff. A bit of a problem, but timelines solve most things. So we worked out how to display the intervals between the maps on the edge of a piece of paper, and we would draw lines for various things on the paper itself – going all through (like the name Wheelbarrow Castle) or changing (like the workhouse) or beginning (like the golf course), or ending, like Dodsley Farm or beginning and ending (like the Council Cottages).

What a complex task I left with them – and I did not expect them to do it right first time – that wasn't the point. You don't drive competently on your first driving lesson. They were practising recording change in relation to time.

Street maps

Street plans of towns and cities are both extremely common and easily accessible. A powerful teaching idea is to transform information from a relatively inaccessible form into one which is easier to understand. Our final use of maps in this section reflects this, taking a 19th century trade directory and transferring what it can tell us about the size, shape and road pattern of the town onto a modern street map. A student developed the idea. The lesson was taught to a combined Year 3/4 class of mixed gender, age and ability. The lesson's **learning objectives** were to develop:

- an understanding of how the town had grown;
- an understanding of the present; and
- map handling skills.

The **resources** used were:

- Directory planning sheet, Illustration 34.
- 1857 Billings Directory, on A3 size paper.
- Modern street map of Crediton, cut up so that only a few street names were on any one piece.
- Coloured pencils.

Teaching history using directories

1 Introduction

The aim is to introduce the children to the idea of trade directories and local maps in a natural way.

- Ask the children to shut their eyes and think of one thing they would really like to have or need for going on holiday.
- Ask them to fill in the top line of the Directory Planning Sheet.
- On the blackboard list the things in alphabetical order.
- Talk about where they would buy their item. How do we know where to go? Do they know the address ?
- If they haven't got the address, how would they find it ? Guide the questioning around to the idea of Yellow Pages.
- What do we have if we collect in their slips in alphabetical order? We have created a trade directory !

2 The modern town and trade directory

- Tear up a trade directory to give each child a page with their kind of shop on.
- They can then look up shops where they can buy their goods.
- They can write in the address of their shop on their slips

3 Back in time

Tell the class that we want to look at how big Crediton was 140 years ago. The only clue we have is the document we are going to give them. The directory looks formidable, but it isn't really.

- Hand out the directory. Ask the pupils if they know what the document is.
- Ask them to look at it and find any one name, word, or number that they can read.

DIRECTORY FORMS   Photocopy and cut up

Thing you want to buy

Kind of shop

Where you would buy it [street name and town]

Thing you want to buy

Kind of shop

Where you would buy it [street name and town]

Thing you want to buy

Kind of shop

Where you would buy it [street name and town]

Illustration 34   *Directory planning sheet slips*

- Pool ideas, let the discussion take its natural course.
- Focus on addresses / street names.
- Perhaps put up a whole list of street names on the board, again in alphabetical order.

4 Mapping the 1857 town

- Extract street names from the directory and colour them in on your modern map.
- Discuss what conclusions we can draw from the coloured map about what the town was like and how and why it has changed.

Plans

So far we have looked at maps and mapping on an international, national and local level. Now we focus on plans and planning. Crucial is the transformation of sources from one form into another that deepens children's understanding. Written sources present a particular challenge. The key is to turn material presented in one medium into another, moving from an abstract, symbolic representation into one which is concrete and visual. At its simplest we can ask our children to look at a picture and draw and label an outline plan of it. The children's work should be based on research using available sources. These can range from a copy of an original picture or document to a set of topic books.

How have we taken written information and created plans from it? An example that explores the idea is The Victorian Nursery. The Victorian Nursery provided us with the opportunity to take a diary page, extract its information (Illustration 35), and turn its contents into a plan of a nursery. We cut the list up into sentences. Each pupil was given a sentence, and had to draw a picture of the particular toy, using topic books to find out what they might have been like.

Planning spaces – buildings

A basic adaptable idea we use is to present children with the problem of how, given an overall purpose, they would utilise particular spaces. Purposes can range from a palace to a pauper's hovel. The exercise requires a blank sheet of paper, pencils and nothing else. The next step is for the children to use their plans to make sense of the plan of a similar building. The simple exercise of giving children an outline and cut outs of the contents is also an extremely effective way of using plans. The approach works for all ages and abilities. In our teaching of KS1 pupils we used the technique to help make sense of a plan of Knossos.

October

Monday 14	Extract listing some of Roy's and Maud's toys	Sentences
	Roy has a bank of England pencil and so has Maud. Both of them has got a little Indian rubber.	1
	Roy has got a lot of pens Maud has only got a few.	2
	Maud has got from twenty five to thirty dolls and Roy has got nearly twenty boxes of soldiers with three hundred and thirty soldiers	3
	Maud has got a lovely theatre. Roy has a fly that flys along.	4
	Maud has a large dolls house. Roy has pair of horses you can drive.	5
	Maud and Roy has a nice pair of reins.	6
	Maud has nine or ten doll sets of chairs and tables and Roy has nine or ten boxes of bricks.	7
	Roy is fonder of soldiers, little fish to swim, precious stones, coins and puppys that go along.	8
	Maud is fonder of dolls and chiner tea sets	10
	Roy and Maud have three pence a week.	12

Illustration 35 *Information gleaned from a Victorian children's diary*

14 Storytelling

Story is central to history and its teaching. The stuff of history is human endeavour and achievement, the weaving together of a thousand and one tales. In society the storyteller has always had a major role in providing a sense of perspective and belonging in terms of the past in its often mythic state. We remember the Greeks for the Iliad and the Odyssey, the Anglo-Saxons for Beowulf and the Vikings for Njal's Saga. Narrative history has always been a major attraction, be it Gibbon, Macaulay, Arthur Bryant or Schama. In the twentieth century the moving image has taken its place alongside the written word. Hollywood fortunes rose on the back of historical storytelling, and any glance at a week's television programmes will reveal that history storytelling is at the core of our entertainment.

Reading and telling stories

Yet, within the classroom a sadly and sorely neglected art is that of the storyteller who through story brings the past to life. Immediately we must distinguish between reading and telling stories. While **all** of you **read** children stories, how often do you gather the children around and enchant them with a story that **you tell**? The storyteller tends to carry with him or her the aura of the magician. Teachers, perched like sparrows around the back of a classroom where a storyteller grips the pupils with his tales, invariably comment in the debriefing session, 'Ooh, ah, wonderful, but it just shows me how inadequate I am'.

However, storytelling is a teaching technique the same as any other. We can unpack its elements and put them together for us all to use in our own teaching. As with all teaching approaches, as my teacher of Ancient Greek hopefully stated, although clearly in abject despair, *'pathemata mathemata'* (experience teaches). The best way to integrate storytelling into your teaching repertoire is where and when appropriate to tell elements of a story, such as describing a character or a scene or a problem facing an historical character.

How can you produce and tell a story such as **The King's Feather**, a story a teacher created and told after attending our course on storytelling?

The King's Feather Introduction (*Pose a problem plus use a simple prop that you can hide to create tension*)
Hide a feather behind your back. Ask the children to guess what you have hidden. Show the children the feather. Explain that this is a special feather, and that it came from a royal bird, and that you'll tell them the story of the boy who owns it.

(*Set the scene – Tudor England at the time of Henry VIII*)
Thomas a young lad, son of a blacksmith, often helps his father at the forge. He handles the horses, taking care of them, especially any nervous animal.

(*Describe the houses, village set up, type of villagers' clothes*)
Although he enjoys helping his father, he doesn't wish to become a blacksmith. Thomas longs to see other places outside the village, and listens with interest to tales told by travellers as their horses are shod. He loves to wander on his own, watching wild life in the forest, whenever he has free time. One day he sees a group of riders. One of the men draws his attention. He is very imposing – richly dressed.

(*Describe the characters – Henry VIII and their 'props', the clothes of men and ladies – hunting dress. Set the scene – describe the situation*)
The courtiers are hunting with falcons. The boy is enchanted watching the birds fly off. He hides and after watching for some time, realizes by their conversation that the man he had admired was none other than his King – Henry VIII.

(*Outline the problem that is at the centre of the story*)
As the riders move on, he reluctantly leaves and returns to the village. On the grass he finds a feather dropped by one of the falcons. He treasures this. Now his days are filled with dreams. He longs to be able to handle the falcons, in the way he admired his King doing. However, time goes by, and the reality is his work at his father's forge.

(*The solution to the problem*)
One day Thomas has some time for himself. He wanders into the forest, searching for wood to make himself a bow. Suddenly he is startled. As he comes into a clearing, he sees a horse rearing up and its rider in danger of being thrown. Regardless of his own safety,

he grabs the horse's bridle, calming the horse as it struggles. Eventually he has the horse under control. To his amazement, Thomas realizes the rider is the same man that he had watched handle the falcon – his King! His horse had been startled and had bolted.

The King is joined by his followers, who had been riding hard, trying to catch up with their sovereign. They admire the boy's courage and skill, and the King offers him a gift as a reward. Thomas asks if his gift might be the chance to train the hawks with the King's falconer. His wish is granted and he goes to work at the court. His dreams have come true.

Reflection Looking at storytelling
- Read the story of **The King's Feather**
- How do you think the storyteller created his story?
  Consider
  - problems to solve
  - characters and descriptions of them
  - the actions of people in the story
  - the historical scene
  - the solution to the problem

The teacher as storyteller

Teachers and parents often read their children history stories, and I hasten at the start to say there's nothing wrong with that. Great writers put it better than we can, superb illustrators add a new dimension of reality and above all things, it is good for adults to show children their respect for books, their love of and need for books, if children are themselves to develop these qualities.

But in here I am referring to told stories, inventions, creations, productions of the moment, made for the very children sitting listening now. It is this quality of a personal gift about told stories that makes them so important, but even that cannot totally explain the almost weird concentration children will give to told stories. In years of watching classrooms where heads are nodding, inattention growing, I have always noticed that catch when the teacher simply uses the story voice and narrates, heads pop up and everyone listens. We are programmed to listen to stories, it is an instinct deep down. We know that this is how we learn about other people, and, such is our curious nature, we know also that learning about other people is fascinating, distracting, deeply pleasurable.

In history there has been for many years a move against narrative. History is all about explanation, the teachers say (what else is story trying to do?). Story manipulates the past, makes people believe that it really was like that (is the historian to spend all his time shrugging his shoulders and muttering 'I just don't know'?). Story suggests that people in the past were ultimately like people in the present and that we can learn from them.

What is story for in the history classroom?

The conveying of information Perhaps surprisingly, I would put first the conveying of information, ideas and technical language. There are three ways of experiencing the past. You may be there and look and sense in a very direct way, you may read an intellectual definition, such as a textbook account, or you may be taken in the imagination. Strangely enough the last may be the most powerful, and in a story complex issues, ideas, attitudes, values, events, even machines can make some kind of explained sense that the listener may quickly understand. It is amazing how quickly and easily the transition is made, as, for example, after a story about the birth of a Victorian warship, a six year old was heard to ask his teacher for the spelling of 'commissioning', an event that for the moment quite flustered the teacher.

The creation of context Because things are met in context, they are understood, and secondly it is the creation of context that is important to stress. Making stories for children illustrates for them the process of history, that speculative thinking that tries to stand things up and say was it like this, does this sound right, or is this version better? It also models for the children the need to come to such a conclusion, that history is a making process, that it requires a product.

Wonder Thirdly, of course, it is to serve the need for wonder, to act as ancient seers did to provide for the people a vision that they might lose themselves in and admire open-mouthed. Wonder is not passive and mindless, however, (even though storytelling looks as though it is all teacher action and no child participation) for in it the child is exercising the faculty of imagination.

Story – relating the past to the present Story does start to relate past to present, not in a direct way (Napoleon had a bad time in Moscow, memo – never invade Russia) but in that allusive manner whereby we pick up echoes of our own condition in the strangest places. Thus, in a powerful story I use about a Victorian chimney sweep whose dad comes back from the Crimean war to rescue him, there is a lot to be learned about chimney sweeps, but there is also something to learn about dads who go away, and something to be hoped for about dad coming back. Not all stories have happy endings, but all stories about the human condition should leave us with constructive knowledge and thoughts about ourselves.

How are stories made?

I can only describe my own process here, and it is hard, because like every artistic experience, one wishes to keep it magical and intuitive. First, let us get rid of the febrile notion that story-making consists of 'plotting'. If a story has a plot it is too complicated to tell. It must have instead great simplicity, and consist of one or two characters, one or two situations, a problem and a conclusion. And it is the problem you must look for first. That is often hard to find, particularly because it rarely lies plumb centre of the subject of the story.

Let me try to illustrate my meaning: I had recently to do a story for some young children about the birth of agricultural trades unions. Now I don't want to discriminate in history; I do find most subjects interesting myself, but when faced with this one my heart did sink a little. But I then reviewed the literature, looking for the point where my children could latch in, and after quite a bit of reading I found that many farmers owned the village shop and paid their labourers in cheques to be cashed there, thus making a double profit.

Now this is quite a complicated idea (especially as the children were aged from five to eleven) but children are massively moved by unfairness. If I could get them to understand this in the story they could well understand why a small ploughboy might lead his first strike, and end up a union officer speaking to meetings thousands-strong. Strangely enough that was one of the best stories I have created in the past few years, because its bait, its problem, was set with the children in mind.

The second point I would make is that most of story consists in description, in the thickening of the texture of the central problem by describing the people and the environment. This is why I never write stories down, but rather rehearse them in my head, as a film maker might do. You must see and hear and smell and touch and even taste the story on behalf of the children before you may tell it. What is it like to go out ploughing for the first time when you are very small, it is cold and early, you are hungry and anxious? I must see the child, be the child for the children. Once I have seen it, once I have been there, I know it. I can tell the story, I don't need to write it down, I just run the film in my head again.

How are stories told?

Many teachers resist storytelling by saying 'I am not a natural actor', and I say back that all teachers are actors every minute they are in the classroom. All we are doing when we tell stories is turning up the volume of our normal behaviour. It feels strange at first, and teachers, with their secret fear of children's laughter, worry whether they will look a goof. I have learned that the bigger fool I look the more power I have, so I don't worry, nor must you. And children love story so much they are very gracious and will allow you fluffs and mistakes and nonsenses so long only as you will keep on going. Eye to eye contact is so powerful that we occasionally have to turn away! But it is a two-way system that we cannot do without. In the first place our eyes convey twice as much meaning as our mouths do – think how hard it must be to be blind. But also we receive back information: children's eyes tell us everything: where they are excited, where they are disgusted, where they are lost, where they are enthralled, where they are bored. Children's eyes say 'More of that, please', or 'No more of that, please', and if we can learn to follow those messages then the story begins to tailor itself to the audience.

We must use gesture and movement. This is hard, too, as we are trained by our culture to be still and restrained, but without gesture a story will be overfilled with words. To look up with an astonished face will convey the height of the wall to be scaled far better than a million words. To point the winding road to the castle summons up the picture quickly. To place the imaginary crown slowly upon one's head says it all – says far more than fooling around with tinselled paper trumpery. We must think out these movements as we create the story, and as the moment comes incorporate them as if a stage direction had told us to.

And we must move – the worst thing is to get stuck in a chair, imprisoned by a half moon of seated children. To be able to walk about helps us create an environment – this is where the prison door is, this is where the gaoler goes to eat his bread and cheese. It helps us pace the story by taking it for a walk, occasionally, and that can help the teacher too. Whenever I am a bit lost as to where to go next I will take the story for a walk – up the winding staircase or up and down the corridor, or to the pig sty or wherever, and on that walk I decide what to do next.

Above all, the story, if it is to work at its best, must speak as if it were happening now, and the characters must talk out of it as if this were them speaking those words for the very first time. A good story is not a recollection, it is an event, and so there is no room for 'he saids' and 'she saids', the people must speak and for that they must have voices. A simple stereotype kit for starters will often go a long way – a noisy king, a feckless rural peasant, an upper class plotter. Often, of course, in the heat of the moment one forgets which character one gave the Irish accent to, but the children don't mind – it is the voices that count, they love to feel they are there, listening to it all happening.

Planning and telling stories

To turn yourself from a reader to a teller of stories means engagement with the specific teaching approach and strategies described. In telling a story there are five phases you should think through.

1   What is the story about? What is the story for?
2   The shape of the story – the problem and its solution
3   Building descriptions of characters, situation and scenes
4   Working on voices, gestures and movement
5   Telling the story

This is really quite simple and easy to do.

Phase One – the history involved

What is the story going to be about? Which bit of history do you want to illuminate through narrative? What simple or complex intermeshed body of information and ideas do you want to get the pupils to grapple with through the clarifying medium of story? Remember, the point of story in history is to make accessible an aspect of the past that otherwise might be denied the children.

Reflection Choosing a story – sketching the outline

- Think of a topic in your last or current HSU suitable for storytelling.
- Decide what your story will be about.
- List the main points of information that you want the story to deal with.

Phase Two – the shape of the story

Stories do not need to be of Agatha Christie complexity. They should be clear, simple and have an easy-to-copy form. A story does not have to be long. It can last for a very short period of time. Often in our teaching we interject a story as a brief two to three minute interlude. The main thing is to decide on its shape and form. At each point the problem the characters in the story face gives it its dynamic dimension. The story can be told in terms of the problem alone, with the teacher taking a role and asking the children to respond to the problem posed. The problem and its solution need to be placed in their narrative context, the events that give the story its shape. A story can be made up from a sequence of problems and their solutions.

Reflection Turning topics into stories
- Having a chosen topic, identify a problem and its solution around which to build a story.
- What events led up to the problem?
- What form does the problem take?
- How is the problem solved?

Phase Three – building descriptions

A story will be about people in the past, the situations they faced, why and how they behaved and what were the consequences of their thoughts and actions. When you tell a story you have to flesh out the characters, both the main and subsidiary ones. So, you will have to do some work on finding out about them. What did they look like? What were their bodies like? How did they walk, talk and gesture? Were there any striking features? What did they wear to give messages about them? What kind of characters were they? What were their personalities? How did they behave?

Equally important is painting the historical picture so as to take children back in time. What was the situation that faced the characters? Visually, what was the scene like? What would you see, hear, smell, taste, feel if you were there at the time?

Lesson on the story of the *Mary Rose*

One of our teachers told the story of the *Mary Rose*. The scene unfolded in front of the children's eyes.

Setting – Portsmouth Harbour, July 1545.
Reason for the harbour activity – to prepare the fleet of sailing ships to fight against the French, with their fleet consisting mainly of rowing galleys. Description of crews loading the boats on the quayside – noises, smells. The food stowed on board to show the rations that a sailor in those times could expect. The amusements – backgammon, dice, books, musical instruments. On to the *Mary Rose* built in 1509/1510 with its 90 heavy cannon, guns, medical

supplies and navigational instruments. Final boarding of all the soldiers with their armour, making about 700 men on board altogether. Moving on to Henry VIII proudly standing at Southsea Castle watching his ships sail out of the harbour.

Activity on board – sailors carrying out various jobs, soldiers getting armour on ready for battle, opening of gun ports, man in crow's nest looking for French fleet. Hauling on the ropes to hoist the sails as the wind starts to rise, only to find that they have erected too many too quickly, as well as turning the ship round too sharply. Panic on board as the ship heels over and water pours in through open gun ports. Soldiers struggling out of their armour, sailors running round decks.

The scene can be made to come to life. The pupils can *be* there.

Resourcing stories

Primary school information and topic books are packed with relevant information. Excellent also are picture books based on academic historians' findings. Using them you literally come face-to-face with the past.

Reflection Building up the story

Take the outline plan of your story with its information, its problem and solution, and think about :
- The situation, e.g. scenery, rooms, furniture, pictures, decorations, sounds, smells, tastes, animals.
- Find out what you can about the situation which the characters will face, and build the description into your story.
- The characters involved, that is, people, animals, monsters, mothers-in-law, etc.
- Take your story's characters, and build up ideas about what the person, animals, etc. will be like, using books to research them where possible.
- Think about ways in which your characters might behave in role and their body language.

Phase Four – voices, gestures and movements

You need to think of children's attention spans, and how you can break the story up through the use of voice, gesture and movement during its telling. Pupils love a vital, active approach, lots of voice projection and movement. Consider carefully how you will speak, move and act while telling your story. You should work on the voices you will use. Think of how your characters will actually speak, the language they will use, what they will say. Modulate the voice and volume. Shout the commands, be hysterical, whisper as you die! The worst thing is to get stuck in a chair, so:

- Walk about to create an environment.
- Move around the room, for example often looking for people or things, fighting a battle, climbing the rigging and keeping watch from the crows nest. Go on, try it!
- It is vital to act, to take on the persona of the person. Use your body to represent the roles of the people concerned, be it love or war!

Phase Five – telling the story

And now for the easy bit! In telling the story it is important to make sure that you have created a situation in which you have access to all the children. Eye contact is essential. To achieve this gather the children around you, have them sitting comfortably. Make sure that they are ease, and that the atmosphere is relaxed and purposeful before you begin.

If you have made a set of notes to follow, read these through carefully before you begin. Then turn them over! Make sure you have a clear idea in your mind of the sequence of the story, the problem and its solution, the characters and the situation, how you will speak, move, gesture and act.

The story will develop its own momentum. Freshness and spontaneity are essential. As the story unfolds, make sure that you remember to use your voice to represent your characters, to move and to act.

Follow up storytelling

Sometimes teachers feel rather baffled about what to do after telling a good story. Things can fall flat after the story has been told if all you say to the children is 'Draw me a picture of the bit you enjoyed most'.

We have frequently followed up a story in one of the following ways:

1   Get the children to look through a prepared picture bank for illustrations for the told story. These could be correctly sequenced with narrative sentences linking the illustrations.
2   Offer the class the opportunity to question one of the

characters in the story (the teacher taking the character role). The class are given some time to prepare question which the teacher then answers in role – quite a challenge if they select the villain!

3   With a popular story the children may have heard before ask the class if they know the story and if it was different in any respect from the version they'd just heard. How was it different? And the big question 'Why'?

4   Look for other versions of the story.

5   Imagine you're one of the story characters. How would you tell the same story?

6   With older children you could use timecharts to get the children to examine the pace of the story, something we have often done with, for example, the story of the Spanish Armada viewed from the various positions of Queen Elizabeth, Philip of Spain, Drake and a Spanish sailor. This has proved an excellent way of examining different perceptions of the passing of time.

The final word   This comes from one of our teachers, writing to us about her experience of telling a story for the first time: 'All in all it was a great success and I must do it on a regular basis and encourage others'.

15 Drama

There is a threefold relevance in history: it must excite and entice children and be theirs, it must be true and honour the past, it must leave you understanding yourself and the present a lot better. If that triangle is held tight, then good history learning is in place. Drama is one way of grasping the triangle.

Reflection: Drama in the classroom
- Read through **Working through drama**.
- Consider the two main reasons it suggests for using drama.
- Then review your teaching of the History National Curriculum to see if you have been, no matter how unwittingly, engaged in dramatic activities with your pupils.

Working through drama

Drama puts the fear of God into some teachers. Some, jolly sensible souls, just don't feel dramatic, fear wearing feathered hats and using funny voices; others know, deep in their hearts, that plays always lead to trouble, sword fights getting out of hand, etc; others wonder whether it isn't all just 'playing about', wasting time that should be spent on proper work; others still consider that the past is no place for the imagination, you can't go 'making up' history.

I feel a deep sympathy for all of these points of view, yet I use drama a lot, for two very specific purposes, which I consider valid as historical thinking in themselves. First we need from time to time to concentrate our understanding on specific moments in the past when there is a great richness of texture to the events and a special quality of feeling that something important is happening. To understand such moments one must climb inside them, try them on, use whatever parallels and analogies one has to hand to bid for a feeling – an understanding of what was going on, a properly disciplined imaginative recreation. Second (but not wholly separated from the first purpose) there are some questions one has to ask about the past that require a broad band of speculation for them to work effectively. Such big questions may only be responded to by looking at a full range of possible answers, from the plain daft to the very sensible. Often enough, such speculation leads one to reconsider one's judgements about the daftness of some ideas, and it is through this route that re-evaluations and revisions enter historical thinking.

To illustrate the second purpose of drama let me describe the introduction to a piece of work I completed recently with some eleven year olds. We had read some excerpts from a Viking poem and from the Anglo-Saxon poem, the Battle of Maldon. The children quickly isolated many qualities that differentiated these two peoples and explained their hostility to one another. I explained that we had a great deal of evidence from the past to illustrate their hostility to one another, but what we lacked was any real notion of how these two alien peoples came to settle down in one country and live peaceably alongside one another. This is a real historical question, I explained, I really did not know the answer but was intrigued to explore it. To do so we would need a wide range of possible explanations and then to judge which ones struck us as being likely, a word I spent some time considering with them. Likelihood was really the historian's chief tool of judgement, but he could not exercise it without the speculation that produced the material on which to judge.

There are a hundred and one ways to do drama – any drama teacher will tell you that my ways are cramped and uncreative and that there are better ways to do it. The important thing is to try, at first something very simple, contained and controlled, and not to expect too much – you will be surprised and not a little delighted to find what you get. Why not talk to the specialist in English or drama in your school today about a joint enterprise?'

Planning to use drama in teaching history

As noted, drama can play a spontaneous part in lessons, be a focal element in part of the course or play the central role in the whole teaching of an HSU. Each use of drama is based upon a common pattern that reflects the following factors :

- **The course** Drama should be an integral element in the overall pattern of teaching. Drama enables the pupils to develop an understanding of a specific historical situation and the circumstances that people in it faced. Situations are infinitely varied, from manning a Viking boat to spending a day in a Victorian classroom.
- **The context** The information has to be rich enough to enable

the pupils to take on the role or roles of an historical character or characters, be they a Viking child on a voyage of adventure or children experiencing a day of Victorian schooling.

- **The problem** In their historical roles the pupils have to deal with a problem or problems, be it sailing the boat or coping with mastering copperplate script.
- **The changing situation** Having solved one problem the pupils can continue the drama through having to deal with new difficulties and challenges in a changing scenario.

For any drama session, what do you have to do to get ready? What does drama involve? What steps can you take to have a successful teaching experience using drama?

Step 1 – Be clear in your own mind about the purposes for which you are using a drama strategy. For example:

- are you wishing to concentrate the pupils' attention on certain specific moments of an historical situation?
- or, are there some big questions relating to an event from the past that require a broad band of speculation by the class in order to determine the most likely course of events?
- or, are you wanting to use drama to feed in information in an interesting way?
- or, are you wanting to introduce a new topic and wish to discover through drama just where your pupils stand in their understanding of how people from the past may have behaved?
- or, you may have another purpose for deciding to use drama.

Step 2 – The situation, the historical context. Remember that drama functions best within a specific historical context made up from three strands:

- roles or identity of a person or group of people involved in a situation;
- a specific place and time when things occurred;
- a focus or issue that concerned the person or group of people.

It is not necessary that all three strands are developed at the same time. In fact it is better to start with one of the strands and bring in the other two as the drama develops.

Step 3 – Choosing an approach. There is a range of drama strategies that we use all the time. The important point is to select a strategy with which you feel confident. For example, the collective making of a map by the teacher and class provides a 'safe' way of edging into drama work.

a   **Teacher in role**. It should be understood that this is not about the teacher turning into an actor! It simply requires the teacher to take on the point of view of someone else. The power of teacher in role lies in:
- being able to feed pupils information about the historical situation under consideration; and
- helping the class gain confidence in taking on a role themselves.

b   **Hot-seating**. Using this technique the teacher or pupils can question or interview someone who remains in character. Initially, it might be the teacher who keeps the role of an historical character such as a medieval knight. The pupils question the teacher who responds in his or her historical role. After a while a pupil or pupils take over the hot seat. They take on historical roles and respond to questions as characters from the past.

c   **Making maps or plans**. This is a collective activity in which the class make decisions about a place or building in which the drama will take place. Some years ago I did a topic on 18th century enclosure which started with the class collectively making a plan of a village community and then deciding which part of the village they lived in. This is a useful device for gradually moving the pupils into role.

d   **Still image**. Using this technique groups of pupils using their own bodies attempts to freeze a moment in time, an idea or theme. This can be a very useful device for studying a painting or portrait. Get a group of pupils to take up the positions of people in the picture and then gradually bring the picture to life. Still imaging is a major technique in its own right, the subject of Chapter 17.

e   **Active image** Pupils use their own bodies to bring to life a particular historical situation through reproducing the actions of the historical characters. Thus we worked out and drew on the playground an outline of a Viking ship. The pupils manned and rowed it, faced storms and enemy attacks and pondered on the problems of living on board for days at a time.

f   **Forum theatre**. A situation chosen by the teacher or group is enacted by a pair of pupils or small group whilst the rest of the class observe. Both the actors and observers have the right to stop the action and to give directions or advice. Observers may step in and take over roles or add to them. This is a useful method for helping pupils explore an historical situation based on documents or story as the observers use the evidence to check the actors' actions.

g   **Overheard conversations**. Conversations that add tension or information to a situation, but which should not have been heard. In conversation we are able to feed in information about the period which the class can overhear.

h   **Meetings**. The class gather together within a piece of drama to hear new information, plan action, make collective decisions. The teacher in role is needed to help neutrally chair such meetings, but not to take away from the pupils in role their opportunities for making decisions.

Step 4 – Planning classroom drama. Taking any of these approaches, how can you implement them?

1   **Goals** First make clear in your own mind what sort of historical learning you hope to achieve through using drama. What do you want the pupils to know and understand as a result of the activity ?

2   **Resources** What, if any, will you use? Often an historical resource, such as a story, document, picture or artefact provides a good starting focus for a piece of drama.

3   **Starting** Decide whether it will be best to start by:
   • developing roles for the pupils; or
   • developing ideas about the place and time where the action will take place; or
   • developing an issue or area of concern.

4   **Roles** Will you be taking a role – for example, using teacher in role – and what sort of role will it be? It does not need to be the leader. Often the teacher in role who has a problem but does not know what to do offers a very successful way of drawing in the interest and ideas of the class.

5   **Sources and roles** If you decide to take a role will any resource be useful in helping to establish your role, for example, a letter, a written message, a poster, a map or an object? A ring may be used to denote a higher authority than that of the role taken by the teacher and suggest, 'I am simply acting under the authority of the king who has given me this ring'.

6   **Starting the drama** How will you start the drama?
   • by directly involving the whole class?

- by using a group of pupils?
- by using an individual pupil whom you may have briefed beforehand?

7 **Drama in the lesson** Do you envisage the drama as a small part of one lesson or as something that will develop over a longer period of time?

8 **Drama and historical knowledge** Will the drama be building upon previous historical knowledge the class have already acquired? Or are you using drama to open up a new topic?

9 **Imagination and historical accuracy** How will you keep a balance between the lively imagination of the pupils and the historical accuracy of the period, a balance between fantasy and research? The apparent tension between the two can provide an exciting stimulus to learning about the past.

10 **Drama in the classroom** Drama does not need to be done in a hall. By simply rearranging some of the tables and chairs you can provide a suitable space for the drama. The important point is to ensure everyone can see and that there is space for some movement. Props are not necessary, but if you do use them keep them simple and basic.

11 **Preparing the pupils** With a class unused to learning through drama it is wise to allow some pupils simply to be an audience to the action and to structure in some opportunities for drawing them in during discussion afterwards. There are many roles an audience can be given, from simply commenting upon some of the issues raised by the drama (not on the acting ability of other pupils) to the making of records or documents relating to the drama. You might also try to structure in some roles that do not require any speaking or acting.

12 **Follow-up** After a piece of drama you will probably want to spend time with the class discussing some of the issues raised, followed by some research into history or some writing based on an aspect of the drama. This might be done as a group activity or individually. We find it best to sandwich drama activity between other sorts of work so that a balance can be kept between drama and research.

Developing a dramatic idea

Consider one area of history in your school where you might most appropriately introduce some drama, either to deepen understanding or to introduce speculation. You might, for example, take the topic 'How different were the Romans from us, and how similar?' and set up a time machine to visit a Roman encampment on the wall. You would need some thinking time to consider how Romans might react to moderns – what things might surprise them, what might surprise us? You would need also to plan for safety and abiding by the rules – it would be just silly if the Romans simply slaughtered their visitors on arrival, for example. Finally, think out what the visitors might ask when they get there.

It won't all come spontaneously, you need time to do this planning. When you are ready you can send two members of the class in the time machine, with the rest waiting to receive them.

Reflection Thinking about Drama
- Suggest when you might have used each of approaches below in your teaching of history:
  Teacher in role
  Hot-seating
  Making maps or plans
  Still image
  Active image
  Forum theatre
  Overheard conversations
  Meetings
- Take each approach and suggest a situation where you might use it in your current or future history teaching.
- Plan out a small-scale piece of drama for your next piece of history teaching, using the guidelines above.

---

16 Simulations

Simulation is a relatively new phenomenon in the teaching of history. Following its introduction in the early 1970s, by 1990 it had developed to the point of being listed alongside other teaching approaches in both the 1991–95 History National Curriculum and its related non-statutory guidance.

Introduction

Simulation and drama are closely linked. In both drama and simulation pupils take on the role of historical characters and react to the problems they face. Simulation, like drama, brings the past to life in a way which directly engages both the emotions and the intellect of pupils. Simulations are a highly controlled, carefully structured and managed kind of drama. A simulation's structure reflects and sticks to a particular historical situation, whereas drama can develop much more spontaneously. In a simulation most parts of the activity have been pre-designed and pre-prepared rather than it all happening in the event, as with drama. The safety and security of simulations is very attractive to teachers who don't want to be too adventurous too soon. They can usually be done with everybody sitting in their own desks.

Like drama, simulation actively engages the pupils in learning. Often simulation is the most appropriate way of introducing difficult, intractable material such as diplomatic treaties and negotiations. In dealing with real live problems and their development simulations can develop a momentum and life of their own within the structure provided.

Reflection Simulation in the curriculum

When reading this chapter, note the role that simulation might play in the teaching of your next HSU, using the following headings as a guide:

- Location simulations
- discussion and negotiation simulations

Pupil understanding This develops through facing the children with real problems and the multiplicity of possible outcomes at a particular point, be it planning a Saxon burial, deciding how to fight a battle or how to decorate a church and plan the opening grand service. The pupils are forced to consider the situation, the possibilities, the way things can develop. They actually live the problems, they react to the reality as if they were there. Through argument and discussion, through being forced to reach agreement on a course or courses of action the simulation demands they study in depth, consider at length and weigh up the possibilities, the options available and potential developments. Here there is a constant thickening and enriching of the fabric of history. In the Civil War simulation detailed below, used as part of the teaching of the Local History HSU, the Year 3/4 pupils had to react to a letter from Cromwell ordering them to turn their high neo-catholic Anglican church into a bleak, whitewashed Puritan preaching hall. After Cromwell's troops had arrived and wrecked their church, the children had to write a letter to their closest friend, telling him or her what happened. Two typical letters (spelling corrected) reveal how the eight and nine year olds had entered into the spirit of the age :

Dear Amelia,

Yesterday I had a scareful letter from lots of soldiers. It said all pictures, ornaments, wall hangings have to be removed etc.

The day had to come so it came, you could hear them a mile away. They got here at last. Obviously everthing had to be removed. They searched the church. I was sure that I had left something out (luckily I did not). I was so sad and angry. When they had gone the walls were whitewashed and there were plain glass, wall tablets, book of commn prayers, table, pulpit for preaching, royal coat of arms, minister and the bible in English. When I had ? it was so dull I stopped preaching and did not believe in Jesus or God.

Love from James

Dear Vicky,

When I read the leter about the church I couldn't believe my eyes. The letter said you can't have any objects, bibles or any thing like that. It came from the Parliament.

But it was terrible to think how much work so many people had put into it [building the new church]. I felt cross, angry, unhappy but most of all how much time had been awasted.

We nearly decided to fight back but they had armour and we didn't. We got very sad with only a few things in the church. It was empty and lonely no ornaments and it looked much better with all the candles and docarations and crosses. I missed all of the things the soldiers took and wished it was all a dream but it was the church of our lives.

Love from Faye

Simulation can help recreate in children's minds almost any situation that faced people in the past, from the planning out of Tudor town houses to advising President Kennedy's security forces on how to cope with a possible threat to the President's life when he visits Dallas. It is an infinitely flexible tool and provides richness and variety to teaching. At the darkest moments it can come riding to the rescue of the hard pressed teacher: for example, how do you deal with the problem of teaching ten year olds about Cortes' negotiations with Aztec tribes? Our solution was to split the class up into five tribes subject to or facing the Aztecs, the Aztecs and the Spanish, then brief them as to their roles and situations, and involve them in negotiating agreements to cope with their joint problems.

Types of simulation What form can simulations take? They come in many shapes and sizes, from the playing of board games through to the staging of class debates on issues such as enclosing a 19th century village and international peace conferences before the outbreak of World War II. Pupils can take the role of either a single historical character, be members of a small group ranging from two to five people or parties, or belong to a larger group or groups from six to over thirty strong. The common features of simulations are:
  • a problem that the pupil[s] have to solve in the role of an historical character[s]

- sufficient information for the pupil[s] to make realistic decsions
- guidance and support in reaching a solution.

Using Simulations

Simulations are remarkably easy to use. Remember that the simplest need only last for a few minutes through giving the pupils a role, describing the situation and asking them to come up with a solution or solutions. Once you get into the habit of building simulation into your teaching you will find that it gives lessons a new dynamic, provides immense pleasure for pupils and lightens the burden of much of your teaching.

Writing your own simulation

We can break each simulation activity into three elements: the historical situation; the roles of the characters involved; and the problem they face and have to resolve.

Historical situation every simulation is based upon a detailed description of an historical situation; the place, the people, their problems, possible solutions. Where this situation is similar to others we have an analogous 'model'. In history we use such 'models' or analogies all the time. For example, when talking about Roman towns we can abstract features that they have in common, and produce a typical plan that relates to most examples. Likewise, when looking at Victorian railways, each company and the lines it built will have many common featues that can be used to create a 'model' of such a railway.

Roles identify the role or roles that you want the participants to adopt. Each role should be described in sufficient detail for the player to take realistic decisions.

Problem then provide a problem or problems for the participants to solve.

We can look in more detail at two of the main categories of simulation, planning simulations in relation to a site and discussion and negotiation games.

Location simulations

Planning simulations Asking pupils in role to take decisions in relation to a map or plan is a recurring theme in our teaching. The key idea is to try and get some idea of what might have been going on inside the minds of people in the past in relation to decisions that they took. Typical was the problem we faced when teaching a class of Year 5/6 pupils who were going on a field trip to Dartmoor to visit a Bronze Age settlement as part of the Local History HSU. It contained a village of hut circles, stone rows, an enclosure or pound for animals and a prehistoric grave or cairn. What would be the best way to bring the Bronze Age village to life? How could we best get them to make sense of the remains they would be studying? We felt that a series of simulations could be most effective. Two thoughts were uppermost in our minds in planning the teaching: the use of a village planning simulation we had used before and the 2.5" ordnance survey, with its details of ancient field patterns, settlements, burial mounds, stone circles and rows of standing stones. We had a single session of one and a half hours to get across our ideas, figure 16.1.

From the abstract to the concrete

There are numerous variations on such planning simulations. They can help us deal with abstract, difficult ideas in a concrete form. For example, we had been given the topic of religious change during the Civil War. How could we get our Year 3/4 pupils to come to grips with the problem? Why not get the class in pairs or small groups to plan out their own churches and organise the church service ? Subsequently we have adapted this particular approach to looking at religious changes in the reigns of Henry VIII, Edward VI, Mary and Elizabeth I. The approach transfers beautifully to the helter-skelter changes from Catholicism to Protestantism to Catholicism and back to Protestantism. Through a simulation pupils come to grips with key aspects of 'The break with Rome'. We taught lessons as part of our Local History HSU to a class of mixed age Year 3/4 children using the parish church. Luckily both Charles I and Cromwell had visited the town with their armies. Our specific teaching objectives were :

1   To get the children to think about why a church is planned out in a particular way.
2   To introduce the kinds of change which would happen to churches during a period of conflicting and contrasting religions, in this case the Civil War. (See Illustrations 36 and 37)

Planning spaces A very simple idea is to face pupils with the problem of planning a space *in the abstract*. Lay down the guidelines, give them blank paper and then engage them on the activity. They can be asked to plan out their ideal palace, castle, temple, ship, village, torture chamber or whatever, thinking about what the spaces would be used for and their relationship to each other. You can then compare their ideas with historical evidence, such as the plan of Knossos.

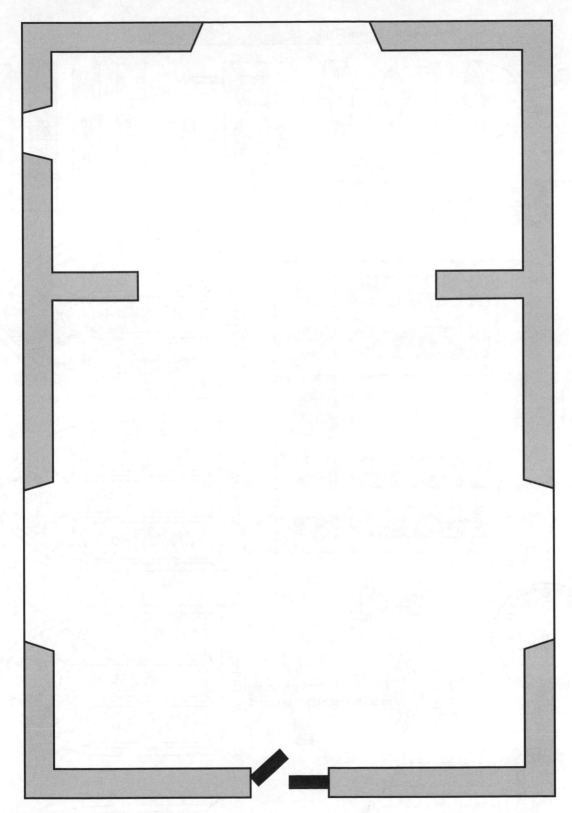

Illustration 36 *Church outline*

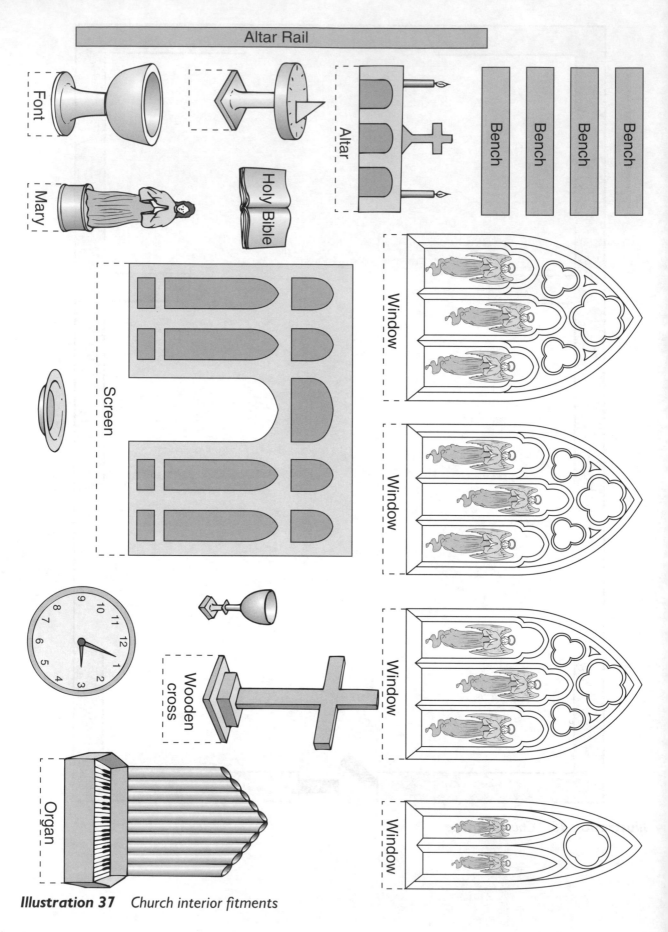

Illustration 37 *Church interior fitments*

Place-naming Another location simulation activity is place-naming. An aspect of planning and settlement is to get the pupils to work out their own names for a site. This can fit in to any exploration or discovery lessons. The simulation can include the pupils in planning out the loading of their boat, choosing a site when they land and developing their settlement. They then can decide upon place-names for the area.

Discussion and negotiation simulations

Discussion The concept of seeing how a group or society may respond to challenges it faces is central to the role of simulation in the classroom. The circumstances are universal and myriad, and can be identified in all HSUs.

Reflection Discusion and negotiation ideas
- How would you use discussion ideas in your own teaching?
- Draw up a list of when in your last History Study Unit you might have asked the pupils to consider a situation and to have come up with solutions to the problems that the characters in it faced based upon discussion and negotiation.

Negotiation plays a major role in how societies work and interact. Negotiation simulations are one of the most powerful learning methods we can use but, we suspect, one of the rarest. Below we examine a Saxon village simulation (Romans, Anglo-Saxons and Viking SU), and refer to an Aztec simulation on Cortes's conquest (Non-European Civilization HSU).

Negotiation simulations are simple to organize. There are five elements:

1 **Identify the groups** who will be reacting to a common situation. Make sure that these are as realistic as possible. There should be from three to fifteen groups.
- In the Saxon village there is a pair of pupils for each peasant family, so with a class of thirty we have fifteen families, plus a reeve and a priest (the teacher).
- Likewise in our Aztec simulation we identified seven groups: the Spanish, the Aztecs, the Princess People, the Valley People, the Pole People, the Cactus People and the Tomb People.

2 **Describe each group in enough detail** for the children to identify with both the group and individual characters and to take realistic historical decisions.

- What is the group's collective identity ? What is its thinking? What principles and policies underpin its behaviour ?
- Who are its members ? If necessary, identify the characters of individuals so that they will react differently to the common set of circumstances. '

3 What is the situation that each group faces?

What are the circumstances in which the group is interacting with others and reaching decisions ?

4 How do the groups reach their decisions and act upon them?

What are the rules for the groups' interaction? How do they reach their decisions? What happens next? This aspect of the simulation needs careful structuring.

- In the Saxon village game each group of pupils, as a family, can negotiate with another family group to try and solve the problems it faces.
- The Aztec simulation is based on the passing of messages between each group. With seven groups involved it means that at each decision point they can send up to six messages, one to each other group, and receive in turn six messages from the other groups. They can then negotiate or respond to these messages.

We frequently use this sending of messages in our teaching. It provides a tremendous dynamic to a lesson.

5 Resolution

When the simulation is over, what steps will you take to resolve the pupil's thinking? How will they reinforce their learning and reflect upon what they have been doing?

The Saxon farming year

The Saxon Farming Year game shows the process of adaptation and transferability at work. It was based squarely upon a similar simulation, The Country Life Game. The Saxon Farming Year took The Country Life Game's idea of giving each family in a village a card that tells them of the situation they face, with two major changes. The Saxon Farming Year made sure that each family had something to offer other families in the village and also that it needed something from them. Each family was given a chance card that it had to respond to. In terms of having something to offer, and requiring something, the chance cards were carefully synchronized, that is, one family's wants and surplus matches other families' surpluses and needs.

The lesson

Introduction How can we focus in on the farming year? The idea was to involve the pupils fully in the problems which Saxon farmers would face, and to do this through the medium of a simulation. The teaching ideas were:

1 The situation
- In the previous lesson we had worked on exploring the village, and looking at the village economy.
- Hand out again the picture that shows the village with its huts, church, hall, fields and common.
- We can now draw up a list of possible villagers, with the different occupations which they might have had, for example, the things which they specialized in.
- Work out a list of fifteen jobs, so that there are two villagers to each family.
- Each family decides on its family name, and puts it on a piece of paper on the desk in front of it.
- Tell them that each villager will have the same amount of land, 40 acres, and rights to the meadow.
- They will have 10 strips in each field, and will have all the other villagers as their neighbours.

2 Running the village
- The village has to take communal decisions, and to sort out disputes in the thegn's court.
- The teacher, the thegn's reeve, is in charge of the court,.

3 The farming year
- The villagers have to keep a diary of their farming year.
- There are two main seasons: winter/spring and summer/autumn .
- For each season they each get a chance card which tells them what has happened to them (Illustrations 38 and 39).

4 Negotiation
- When each family gets its chance card it can negotiate with other peasants in the village, asking for their help and support.

Your plough has broken. This means that you cannot plough your strips. Your oxen calves from last year are now ready to make up a second ploughing team.

You have lots of spare barley, oats and beans to sow in the fields this year. The sheep you have been keeping on the pasture have all died.

Your oxen are sick and cannot pull the plough.
You have had a new plough made at the smithy.

In hedge field your neighbour has let his strips get very weedy, and there are lot of thistles growing on your crop of winter wheat.
Two of your cows caught murrain, a disease. They both died

The rats have eaten all the barley, oats and beans that you have been keeping to sow in the west field.
Your sons are old enough to help you with the ploughing and sowing of your strips.

Beacause you have been ill you have been unable to keep the weeds down on your strips in the hedge field. This winter wheat is doing badly.
The village carpenter has made you a new harrow.

You have broken your leg and cannot do the ploughing and sowing this year.
Your sheep have had lots of lambs and you have some to sell.

Your harrow for breaking up the soil has broken.
Your four cows have had calves, you want to get rid of two of them.

Chance cards–*autumn*

Photocopy and cut up. Give each family one of the chance cards

Illustration 38 *Chance cards – spring*

210

You have had a bumper crop of winter wheat.
Your oats have all died because of drought.

Your sickles have all been stolen, and you are unable to do your harvesting.
One of the villagers animals has broken into west field and eaten the barley, oats and beans from three of your strips.
You have a fine crop of beans, far more than you need for the winter.

Your crop of winter wheat has not yet been harvested as you have been working on your lord's land, and you are now ill.
You have three spare sickles that you were going to use to harvest your bumper crop of winter wheat.

A gale have flattened your winter wheat, and it will mean that you are unable to do any harvesting in that field.
In the wood you have some fine young pigs which other villagers might like.

The weeds from your neighbour's land have wrecked your crop of winter wheat.
Your oats were grown in a wet part of west field, and they have done very well.

Your barley is ready for harvest, but you have gone sick.
Your crop of winter wheat is also good, although some weeds have got into it from your neighbour's strips.

You need help to plough the fallow land in East Field for the sowing of winter wheat.
Your flock of sheep has done very well on the pasture and fallow field, you have plenty of spare wool.

Your animals have broken into the west field and eaten the barley, oats and oats of some of the villagers.
Luckily you have a bumper crop of winter wheat.

Chance cards–*autumn*
Photocopy and cut up. Give each family one of the chance cards

Illustration 39 *Chance cards – autumn*

- It can send messages on the message form (Illustration 40).
- Note down what you have decided to do.
- As a village you can also meet to decide what the peasants will do about cultivating the fields.

5 The Thegn's court
- Each family can write out a claim for the thegn's court to deal with. The claim will be against other villagers.
- The claims are written on pieces of paper and given the bailiff to read out.
- The bailiff then takes cases in turn, and asks for any other evidence which other villagers might have. These are written on pieces of paper and handed in to him.

6 The diary / account
- At each point pupils should keep a detailed account of what is going on.

Conclusion

Simulation can be used, along with drama, in almost every teaching circumstance. We can even see the whole of children's historical learning as a simulation, in which we cast pupils in the role of historians and ask them to work along similar lines to real historians. Thus in our investigation of the body of Pete Marsh, we use the metaphor of the historian as detective. Through all our teaching the concept of the pupil as investigator prevails, for example, as journalist, detective, private eye or archaeologist. When studying a picture with our children, we give them magnifying glasses to pick out the detail. Which famous detective had a magnifying glass? 'Sherlock Holmes', came the reply from a number of our Year 4 children. As a way of getting inside the skins of both people in the past and of historians, simulation is an invaluable teaching tool.

MESSAGES FORM

Date .... Place ....

From ....

To ....

Message ....

....

....

....

Illustration 40 *Messages form*

17 Expressive Movement

The Christmas production was over. The stunned parents had watched a class dance the story of Anne Frank using movement to express the story without words or music. Some members of the NPHP have experimented with this form of teaching, which we have called expressive movement. This is not a perfect term, but it is about the best we can do. The method certainly has connections with both dance and drama, but we have found that the work we have done with children is quite distinct from these other disciplines – hence the term expressive movement.

In this chapter we describe two sets of lessons. Both sets involved Year 4, 5 and 6 children and were completed over a period of a few weeks.

> **Reflection: Drama and dance in the classroom**
> Before you go on to read **Expressive movement and the teaching of history**, consider the following questions:
> - Do you ever use drama in your history teaching?
> - Do you ever use dance in your history teaching?
> - If your answers to either of the above questions was 'no', can you think of a way either could be used?
> - Is there a place for individual creativity in history?
> - Do we, as teachers, wish to encourage all children to develop an identical understanding of what we teach?
> - Finally, should we know in advance how a lesson, or group of lessons, should end?

Expressive movement and the teaching of history

Should I give the children a large body of received knowledge, and turn them into junior masterminds, or is there some other kind of history which has its place within the primary curriculum? And if there is another form of history which should have a place within the primary curriculum what does it look like?

For many years the argument has continued. On the one hand are those who would view history as the story of the great and good, of Kings and Queens, of battles and court intrigue, of wars lost and won. Others, equally, see the past as the story of ordinary people, of the struggle for survival, of fate and chance.

Of course the truth lies in the middle of these two exaggerated points of view. To teach history well is to create a balance between the factual detail and the more impressionistic 'I wonder what it felt like?' approach. Here I would like to advise some caution. The empathy argument has long raged and I do not want to resurrect it here, but one has to be quite clear that there are dangers to be faced when one advocates the empathetic approach. No child, nor adult, will ever 'feel' what a person in the past felt. I will never know how Tom Paine felt the morning after he knew he should have been executed during the Terror, when the guard missed the four chalkmarks on his cell door. What I can feel is a sympathy with the situation, to discover all the necessary detail until I can, with a combination of historical knowledge and my own life experience, establish a mind picture of that historical event.

For children to do this they need considerable help. Their own life experiences are necessarily less developed, their historical knowledge less advanced than ours. And yet in a special way they have a great advantage over us. Because they do not have such a wide background of knowledge and experience children can bring to a familiar historical event a sense of excitement and wonder which we, as adults, have long since forgotten. It is this sense of wonder, excitement and thoughtfulness into which we attempt to tap through the use of expressive movement.

Dance and emotion In dance the performers attempt to convey emotion through the combination of their body movement, their relationship to other performers, and the music. It is a very simple art form, and yet one of great complexity because language is not usually involved. It operates at an almost subliminal level. Emotion and feeling are both present, but without language the communication is through gesture and movement.

Drama operates on a similar level. Through gesture, movement and language, emotions are described and demonstrated. In effective theatre the audiences identify with the situation and the characters, and experience the shown emotions for themselves. In educational drama those same emotions and experiences are explored by the children, while the need to present a performance is not usually involved.

Expressive movement seeks to combine the best elements of both disciplines. The element of performance is used to encourage an end result. While an external audience will not be involved, the children are told that they are working towards a performance, a performance in which they will all take part.

Our first illustration of using expressive movement moves the children back to one of the oldest civilisations, Sumeria.

Reflection Organizing expressive movement

By the side of each of these points, note how in the case of the Sumerian mystery the technique came to life.

1   The story – with detail for scenes in the expressive movement. Only the start of the story is told, the remainder is kept back to build up suspense.

2   The selection of a scene and breaking it down into parts.

3   The pupils work on a 'still image' of the scene, and upon the actions leading up to it.
     Time should be strictly limited.

4   The 'pictures' are presented to the class.

5   Additional pictures. Two similar pictures, one leading to the scene, one afterwards – to be done as 3.

6   Sequence. Three scenes are put together in a sequence, each scene ending in the 'still' picture.

7   Speech. A short statement is to be made at each sequence.

8   Teacher tells final part of the story.

9   Class discussion of how the work is to continue.

10   Expressive work carries on.

11   Resolution to the expressive movement.

Repeat the exercise after reading the Ghetto Diary.

A Sumerian mystery

Now for the story. I came across this in a book published in 1968 by Hans Baumann entitled *The Land of Ur*. The book itself is a fairly scholarly account of the Sumerian civilization. Somewhere in the middle he describes the discovery and subsequent interpretation of one of the royal tombs of Ur. I have no idea how accurate the interpretation is, but the evidence presented supports the interpretation and therefore is perfectly acceptable. More importantly, the story is full of the magic and mystery of the past, old gods and burial ceremonies, belief in an afterlife, and objects which mystify.

In 1927 the entrance to a tomb in the royal city of Ur was uncovered for the first time in at least 4,000 years. Beyond this entrance, among other things, were found several copper spear tips, daggers, chisels and other tools, and a set of arrows. In the centre of the grave chamber was a coffin containing the body of a man. Behind his back were many objects: bracelets, rings and amulets. Most impressive of all was a gold helmet, beaten into the form of a wig, with a knot of hair and headband clearly beaten into the golden form. Inscribed on two gold dishes and a lamp found nearby was the man's name – Mes-kalam-dug – 'Hero of the Good Land'. The inscriptions went on to state that he had found his 'eternal dwelling' inside the tomb. He was probably a high ranking prince, placed there to guard the tomb complex.

As the archaeologists went further into the tomb they uncovered more bodies. There was a total of 63 bodies altogether, but the impression was one of complete calm. In the next chamber they found the remains of five more guards. They each had copper daggers around their waists, and small clay cups by their side.

Still further into the tomb more bodies of guards were found, and then, at last, the resting place of the queen. Her name was Shub-ad, according to a lapis lazuli seal. Near her coffin were the bodies of more guards, together with the remains of several women. They had clearly been dressed in fine clothes with much gold jewellery. The remains of fine head-dresses were everywhere, while gold and silver flowers lay strewn over the floor. As in the other chambers small cups lay amongst the debris, some of clay, but here in the chamber of the queen were also gold and silver vessels of intricate design. To complete the scene should be mentioned the cockle-shells with paints of different colours dried on them, make-up for the women who were accompanying their queen on her last journey.

Despite the destruction caused by the passage of time, all was peaceful. The interpretation was simple, clear and beautiful. All had voluntarily gone to their deaths, passing from this life to the next in the certainty that they would live forever with their queen.

Teaching pause

I hope you agree that this is a lovely story, very evocative of a long past age. When told to the children it captures imaginations and is an excellent vehicle for discussion, along the lines, 'What do you think was in the cups?', 'Why were so many people buried together?' and 'Why were so many precious things buried with these people?' The empathetic/sympathetic process begins …

A living picture

The teaching exercise which follows was completed with a mixed ability, mixed-aged class drawn from Years 5 and 6. They were split into groups of 4 or 5. They were now told to go into their groups and discuss how they might have felt if they had been alive in the time of Queen Shab-ad. Had she been a good queen? What did it mean now that she was dead? The children were reminded very clearly that, like the ancient Egyptians, the Sumerians believed that their king and queen were a human embodiment of the Gods, a living connection between our world and theirs.

Children create a tableau The children were told that they had three minutes to work on a 'still picture', showing how they have reacted to the death of the queen. The time aspect is of vital importance. All through this kind of work the children are forced to work at pace, three minutes for this, two minutes for that. Never are they allowed to pause for breath. The emphasis is on action and thought, reflection and assessment. The question 'How well is this working?' is constantly present, and one of the most important tasks for the teacher is to encourage what works, and discourage what doesn't, and as with any art form, the dividing line is sometimes very fine.

The tableau After the three minutes I told the children that I wanted to see their pictures. The children took their positions and I went from group to group to see what they had come up with. Once all had shown their 'pictures', the children were told that I now wanted another two from each group, and I wanted all three joined together, so that each group would have a short sequence of movement, followed by the still pictures. Again, the children were given three minutes to do this.

Inevitably, at this point, or some other, you will get a group or individual child who will say 'I can't do this'. Obviously one needs to be sympathetic to this dilemma, but such is the activity that all children, regardless of academic or physical ability, can participate fully. The children are not performing as academic historians, or dancers or actors. They are exploring through movement and words a situation which is highly structured. All that is asked of the children is that they react in the way they feel is appropriate. They are told at the start that there is no 'right' or 'wrong' way of doing this activity. Therefore, if ideas do not come immediately, a simple word of encouragement usually is sufficient.

Adding speech Once the children had worked on their short sequence it was time to add the next element, speech. After watching each group the children were asked to sit together and for each 'still photograph' they were asked to choose one member of the group who would make one statement. Again they were given three or four minutes to decide who was to speak. Some children volunteered, others were told. It was made clear, however, that they did not need to discuss what was to be said, this was left entirely to the child concerned. They could say anything which they felt fitted.

To demonstrate the outcome of this activity let me attempt to describe the work of one of the groups, three girls and two boys. Their first position saw one girl leaning with her head on the shoulder of another. The third girl had her hands in the air and was shouting a silent scream. The two boys merely looked at one another. The girl who was supporting the other said quietly, 'I wonder if the sun will shine tomorrow.' And then they moved into their next position. And so it went on.

Additional scenes The children were given other situations to respond to. The first four situations were:
- Reacting to the death of the queen
- Preparing the tomb
- Moving the body from the palace to the tomb
- Beginning the burial ceremony

This was spread over two lessons. Some parts of the expressive sequences involved speech, others simply movement. As the work progressed it was necessary for the children to remember all that they had done previously for the smaller parts were to be joined together. Therefore it is necessary to keep returning to previous sequences. This has the effect of forcing the children to refine and improve, for since none of this is scripted in any way they are free to change and adapt to new and better ideas.

Once the burial ceremony had begun, it was time to give the children the key element of the story.

The story continued The Sumerians had possibly the most beautiful way of explaining day and night. Not for them the dull, but accurate, explanation of the earth revolving around the sun and spinning on its own axis. Their myth tells of the sun-god who shone in his radiance, celebrating each day his marriage to the earth. Each day, at the end of his journey, he was locked into a stone cell by the god of darkness, and imprisoned. Each night the sun-god slowly sawed his way through the rock with a golden saw. And each morning he celebrated his escape by filling the world again with light.

As the archaeologists went about their work in the chamber of the queen, they found things which could not be explained easily. On the inscriptions both on the walls and on some of the objects were references to the king. His name was A-bar-gi, but he was nowhere to be found. They did find the small body of a richly dressed young girl, about seven years of age. She wore a head-dress similar to that found on the queen, only it was a fraction of the size. Rings, bracelets, even a tiny gold cup, two inches tall, were all miniature versions of objects found on the queen. Might this princess have been the queen's daughter, or was she the child of one of the court?

Among the grave gifts found scattered around, one seemed to be of great significance. A small golden saw lay on the ground near the coffin of the queen. At first no one had any idea what the purpose of this was. No one is exactly sure now, either, but there is an explanation and it was discovered soon after the tomb was being cleared.

In the chamber before that of the queen were found many bodies, and the name of the king repeated many times. And yet there was no sign of any coffin or body. The archaeologist Leonard Woolley had discovered when he opened the tomb that in this chamber there was a hole in the roof just about big enough for a man to climb through. Clearly, he thought, this was where tomb robbers got in and out when robbing the tomb. Yet, once inside, the sheer amount of gold and silver suggested that the tomb, once closed, had remained untouched. If tomb robbers had visited the tomb, why had so little been taken?

The myth tells its own story. Perhaps, some years before, the king had died and had been buried in great splendour in his chamber. Some years passed, and upon the death of the queen the final preparations were complete. Either before, or more probably after, the ceremonies surrounding the entombment of the queen, a hole was made in the roof of the king's chamber and his body was taken out to complete his journey. His unification with the sun-god was complete. The king and queen reunited in the after-life, symbolising again the union between man and the Gods, the earth and the sun.

Back to the teaching The children had worked well and had, mostly, remembered their movements, expressions and speech for the first four scenes. They had taken the story forward, and as I introduced each scene they moved and performed with admirable concentration. We had reached the point where the second part of the story was told. As earlier, the children were sat in a group and they were told the myth and then the details of the discoveries in the chambers of the king and queen. A discussion followed in which the children were quick to associate the hole in the roof and the golden saw. The children were told that we now had to find a way of ending the story we were working on. What was the best way? What did we need to include?

Ending the story We had reached a point where we had the bulk of the story in place and the children were put in the position of deciding how the whole sequence should end. We had a brief discussion and then the children were sent away to work in their groups. The fifth sequence was entitled 'The closing of the tomb'. The children had to decide how to react. Were they to be guards or handmaidens, or perhaps a high priest? The resulting sequences were interesting as there was a significant number who chose to die peacefully, while a few others were more active, re-arranging objects, taking care that others were comfortably positioned, before moving off to close the doors. Each group retained a sense of unity, in that they were moving and performing as a group, while still being able to respond in the individual way they wished.

The final scene The final scene beckoned. How would the children decide to finish? The children were again given a time limit, in three minutes, they were told, they would do the final scenes. Two body pictures, with no speech, only movement. The tomb has been sealed, what will you show?

Each group, perhaps dominated by the strength of the story, or perhaps by the strength of the idea, chose to have a 'king' figure rising from the tomb, and finding the saw, then began to saw their way through imaginary bars. It became fairly obvious to me how the piece should conclude. The children were brought back together and ideas discussed.

The children and I could see that we needed to bring everyone together for the final scene. Of the several 'kings' we chose one, and then brought all the groups together. As children moved gently together, or were grouped in a sleep/death silent tableau, the king arose, searched for the golden saw, and after stretching his way upwards, and sawing through the imaginary roof, then he moved away from everyone.

Music Finally to present the piece, music was introduced. This was not intended to dominate but enhance the mood. The music was one of those 'relaxing' tapes which seem to go on forever but never do anything! It seemed just right for this work.

The performance Once the children had gone through the whole thing once they were told that we were now going to perform the complete work for the last time. Starting positions were taken, the music began, and I called the first scene, 'The queen is dead'. About three minutes later it was all over.

In total those three minutes had taken, in terms of teaching time, about two hours. So the question must be answered, was it worth it?

Conclusion

When we had finished I felt that the children needed to reflect on what they had done, and that I needed to confirm that what seemed to have worked well, had actually achieved the aims of the lesson, that is, to put the children in sympathy with a mystery of the past in such a way that they begin to understand the behaviour of the people involved. As explained in the earlier essay, the aim is not to pretend that the children will behave in the same way that the people in the past did, that is simply impossible. The aim was to put the children in such a situation that they would react in ways which are consistent with the historical information they have, while behaving and thinking in ways which are sympathetic to that situation.

Once back in the classroom I congratulated the children on the quality of their work. I asked them what they thought they had learnt. It is source of constant amazement to me how accurate even small children can be when asked this simple question. I leave the children to make their own comments:

- I learnt a lot about their religion, they thought their gods were really special.
- They must have wanted to die with the queen. I am not sure how I would have felt if that was me. I suppose it must have helped if you really believed you were going to live forever.
- I liked the way we were all working together. When I was not sure what to do I looked around and got loads of ideas.

- I still don't know what really happened. What was the saw for, and what happened to the king? I would like to find out more.
- Can we do it again tomorrow? It is better than doing real work.

Another example : The Ghetto diary

The same class were engaged on a topic on Britain Since 1930. A large part of this work had concentrated on the war period. We had looked in detail at the Blitz and also the treatment of the Jews. Although not strictly part of this study unit, it is a personal view that children, even as young as these, should learn that there was more to the Second World War than the military aspect. We therefore looked at the treatment of the Jews by the Nazi party and used as the major source material extracts from the Kovno Ghetto Diary, written between 1941 and 1943 by Avraham Tory.

I had been asked to demonstrate the techniques of creative movement at an inservice day in Bristol for teachers with my class as the 'demonstration', and it seemed a good idea to combine the work the children had done with the potential of expressive movement.

The format was to be quite similar to that described already. The children were given a short introductory story and then scene by scene built a sequence of movement and speech. Space does not allow the lesson to be described in such detail as the Sumerian work. It should be noted that teaching a class in front of approximately 30 teachers is an interesting experience. The time allowed was 90 minutes and we just about finished. Ideally what follows would cover two one hour lessons.

The story

The children sat together and we had a 'reminder' of how the Jews were treated in the cities conquered by the Germans. Details of concentration camps were not discussed since the children had little knowledge of this. They did know, however, that Jewish people were forced to wear yellow stars on their clothes if they went out, and were often subject to unprovoked attacks on the street. They also knew that many Jews were transported across Europe, often being separated from their families.

Once this background had been established the story could start. The children were asked to get into groups and were told to work out a character together. This character was to be no younger than the age of the children (a ten year-old trying to be three is always bad news!). They had to establish age, occupation etc. This only took a few minutes and I then sat the class in a circle and each child, in role, had to tell everyone who they were, what they did and were asked questions which they also had to answer in role.

Describing scenes

This complete, I gave the children the opening of the story. The year was 1941. Each group had gathered at the home of one of them for a meal. They were discussing the war and what might happen to them. The children were asked for three still scenes (tableaux). Each group then were given a few minutes to work these out. After the second performance the children were told that as the scene finished they heard on the radio that all Jews had to report to the railway station at 7.00 the next morning. Each person was allowed one small suitcase of personal belongings only. Any person not complying with this order would be either forcibly removed, or shot. The third scene should reflect the initial response to this.

The scenes of this particular expressive movement sequence ran as follows:
- The meal and the radio announcement.
- Gathering belongings together, closing the case (with speech).
- Arrival at the station. For these scenes I involved another teacher as a Nazi guard, who shouted unpleasant orders at the children as they made their pictures.
- Boarding the cattle trucks having had their suitcases taken away. Families were separated.
- The journey (with speech).
- Arrival, the gates of the truck are opened.
- Walking towards the gates of the concentration camp.

At this point we stopped. For the final presentation music was introduced. I used Taverner's 'Protecting Veil' as the background for the arrival scene. The opening few minutes of this music is evocative. As a conclusion, the children froze their final picture while John Fines read the following poem:

> Pigtail
> When all the women in the transport
> had their heads shaved
> four workmen with brooms made of birch twigs
> swept up
> and gathered up the hair

Behind clean glass
the stiff hair lies
of those suffocated in gas chambers
there are pins and side combs
in this hair

The hair is not shot through with light
is not parted by the breeze
is not touched by any hand
or rain or lips

In huge chests
clouds of dry hair
of those suffocated
and a faded plait
a pigtail with a ribbon
pulled at school
by naughty boys.

(by Tadeusz Rozewicz, translated by A. Czerniawski, from the museum at Auschwitz)

The process of this lesson was slightly artificial since the children were being watched, and they were aware of the 'performance' nature of their responses. I was also aware that we had to get to the end in the time available. The sequence was therefore rushed. To balance this out the additional two adults contributed significantly to the end product. However, the end was a moving occasion, with children and adults sharing in the sympathy and sadness of the moment.

Final words

The technique described above is one way into teaching history so that the human element is strongly present. Story sequences involving the expressive movement techniques can be developed in any of the study units present in Key Stage 2. Teachers have discovered that this kind of work needs thorough preparation to be successful, but then this is true of most good teaching.

The two stories described above are special, but then there are many hundreds which can also be special in their own way. The following subjects have all been used in the past few years for expressive movement activities:

- The Blitz
- Story of Anne Frank

- Dissolution of a monastery
- A Viking raid

The list is probably endless, for if this technique is to be of genuine value it should be fairly adaptable for different circumstances. I am certain that many, many more stories could be listed.

As a final activity, can you think of an aspect of your recent history teaching where this technique could have been of value? If not, how about one which you are planning for the future? Plan how you would develop the story, where you would expect speech and where silence. How would you want the story to end? What would you leave open-ended, what would you insist be done your way? Would you let the children work on their own ending? Would you use music, and if so, what would it be? Is there anything else you are going to need, another adult, a prop of some sort? If you can answer these questions reasonably accurately, you have just organized your first expressive movement lesson. Congratulations!

18 Using Sites and the Environment

To be taken out 'on location' is one of the most common and valuable parts of KS1 and KS2 children's educational experience. It is a way of bringing them face to face with a reality that is radically different from what they encounter inside the classroom. They can touch, feel, smell, listen and experience things in three dimensions. They can get ideas of scale and texture, of a living reality that brings to life the often inevitable two-dimensionality of the classroom. In our teaching of Victorian Britain we visited a working wool mill in the locality. How could we make this live for our children? We set them the simple task of telling them that they were apprentices, they were being taken from their homes to live and work in the mill. Some parents were delighted, they sent their darlings to school on the day as ragged children with their precious possessions done up in a bundle. Yet, how often do we find a glass barrier erected between our children and the situation in which they find themselves? Museums are often the worst offenders in this respect – the past hidden inside a case, dead, inanimate objects, removed and dehumanized. And all the kids do is gawp and move on, clutching a worksheet.

With the mountain of sites available, it surely is the simplest of things to provide an enactive learning environment for children where they can stop, question, investigate and reconstruct the past from working in detail.

Site visiting

Site visiting emphasizes this notion above all. If we are thinking of taking children to an archaeological site, a country house, castle, cathedral, gallery or any other historic feature it would be common sense to work out what children need to notice and then point these out to them in a clear, logical sequence. 'Look', we shout, 'This bit is important' we underline, 'Make a note of that', we urge, and the children do what we tell them but see nothing. It is wrong imagine that simply directing children's eyes towards what we see as important will give them our vision. All they will see is a feature that their teacher thinks important.

Engaging the children with the site

Of course there are things we want children to see, otherwise why would we take them? But we have to exercise constraint. For example I took a group of children to the gallery at Petworth, and I wanted badly to tell them things about Turner, in case they missed him. Instead I was restrained and asked the children just to look around and see what they could tell me about the collector who had filled this gallery by looking at what he had bought. Within minutes some children came rushing to me to say that they thought they had discovered his favourite painter 'Oh, who?' I said 'He's called Turner – there's four of his pictures over here', 'And another six over here,' chimed in another group. As we went from Turner to Turner and the children told me what they saw and we discussed what might have attracted the third Earl of Egremont to buy, so the children established a hold over what they had found, by exercising their own minds in their own ways over what they had discovered. They felt excited and important about what they were doing, confident and eager to go further.

What I had done was not to point to what I wanted them to see, but I had put them in the way of seeing it for themselves. Such knowledge, so gained, is memorable, impressive and personal.

Circumstances

Thus we must spend a great deal of time thinking about the circumstances in which our children will view the site to which they are being taken. It might be that we chop the subject up into bits so that the children may become specialists. Thus when I took children to see the great warship the Warrior, I made some into experts on wood, some on brass, some on iron, some on rope and so on. This gave the children status and responsibility – brass was theirs, and they would have to report about brass when they got back, so all they did in relation to their subject was important.

Scope and scale   We should never expect children to take in the whole site at one gulp – they need ways of cutting down to just what they can manage. I remember with some bitterness trips to sites where everyone had to take in everything so that towards the end I was carrying tired children and what had begun as a great adventure had turned into an endless trail.

Splitting up the task It is a good idea for different groups to complete different tasks so that some children see one part in detail, or at least to complete them in a different order. A mob of children all trying to look at one item at the same time can lead to problems and a little advanced battle-planning can ensure that this doesn't happen. Also if a group is responsible for one item on which they will have to report back to the whole class, they will look all the harder.

Splitting up the site There is a variety of ways of planning for this to happen. For example one may do a strict plan whereby one allocates to children specific jobs before going. On the other hand one can have a more open approach: I often take children to galleries and we literally race around, looking hard on the principle that something will shout out to each individual as they hare past. So when we get to the end I say 'What spoke to you, and you, and you …?' and they then go back to concentrate on what they have seen and chosen. Those who have seen nothing will have the dubious honour of undertaking the race again!

Focus   Focusing on one feature is a way of making observation possible – the vast majority of sites are simply too full of things to see for children to cope with. But children need to be given some aids to help them focus, and the best aid of all is a pencil. Now many children will cry out 'But I'm no good at drawing', and I reply that I don't want 'Art', I want them to look through the point of their pencils. As they slow their eyes down to the rate of their fingers they will begin to see things they did not first see. As they attempt to record in drawing what they have seen, so they will see more.

The camera   Sometimes there is not time to draw, or the weather makes it impossible to stand still for long. Then we can use the camera, but we ration the film, so that I say to the children, 'We can only use five shots on this trip, now look hard as we go round and decide which pictures do you think we should take and at the end we will debate and decide by vote'. No better way of 'focusing' could be imagined!

Discussion

It is important to do some discussion actually on site, so that one has the facility to go back and check. I spend a good proportion of my time on site with the children gathered, telling me what they have seen and discussing what it means. If we have questions we can go back to check, or indeed if some children have seen something really interesting that the rest of us haven't, then the children can become our guides and take us to show what they have seen. Adult guides and guards are not half so good as children in this respect. They have their agendas preset, and children don't – what they have seen for the very first time is much more exciting than the dull learned litany of old folk. And of course children's eyes are better than ours. I cannot count the times when children have seen things I have not, and never would without their sharp eyes to guide me.

The guide as a barrier

I shall never forget taking some five year olds on a visit where I had felt sure I had properly arranged for us to do our own work, but a guide was imposed upon us. Spreading his feet wide and crossing his arms he began his two hour spiel 'Paradoxical though it may seem …'

He had learned his lines and we were going to get them. Two hours later I was carrying two rather damp children as we struggled yawning and distressed back to our coach. I do not know why sites lay on such tours and insist that school visits must conform to their plans. I have seen children arriving already on the rampage, having no clear instructions from their teachers and not able to cope with what they see. I have flinched with the curators whose first duty is to protect the property. But does it need to be like this? Could we not do some things better?

Requirements for all sites

The sites one may visit vary from the large, impressive and demanding, like a great cathedral or a large museum, to the small, domestic and local like the church next door. Whatever the place it is necessary to have three things: a good understandable map, clear instructions and an angle of approach. Take the equipment you will need – not just the sick bag, but magnifying glasses, torches, binoculars, pencil sharpeners, crayons and a small step ladder. The children are often too small to see what is set out at adult level, and need some help. A cushion is always helpful if someone has to kneel in a hard place to do a sketch. And take three spare pairs of shorts for those who fall into the ornamental pond.

Planning

If one is using parents as extra helpers on a visit (and how useful they can be) it is important that they latch on to your planning and understand the documentation as well. Determine precise timings if groups are going to peel off in different directions, and allow in your schedule time for groups to move from place to place. With good military planning you can make sure that no part of the site is overcrowded at any one moment, and you should include in this planning the shop, if there is one. Children lurching round a shop for long periods are wasting time as well as money, so ration it.

Angle of approach

In terms of 'angle of approach' a certain amount of perverse psychology will be required. If you tell children not to do something, for example, they will want to do it, and this can often be quite helpful. When I take children round my local cathedral I say at the start 'Now most things in here are very old. Any fool can find old things in a cathedral. What I want you to look for is the newest thing here, so don't come rushing to me to say you have found something Roman or Medieval or Tudor, because I won't be the least impressed'. The children find the treasure hunt aspect of the task quite motivating (and I always have to check with the Cathedral works office in advance, for new things are installed in old buildings almost week by week!) but inevitably their eyes are drawn to the 'forbidden' old items – they simply cannot resist it.

Finding a reason for looking

What we are doing here is finding a reason for the children to look, a way in which they can look, can concentrate. Children left alone will simply scamper, flicking their eyes to every corner and not resting on anything. At the end of this process (which comes quite soon) they readily declare that it is 'boring' and they are right – they have seen nothing. Our job is to help them see, partly by setting tasks, partly by pacing the event right.

An open task

At times I might set a very open task. I have been known to sit down heavily and say to the children 'I am an old fat man, I can't gallop around anymore, can you find something really interesting to take me to see? Mind you, it must be interesting, because I don't want to get all out of breath going to see nothing at all'. The children find this a good task, and as I have mentioned already make excellent guides and explainers.

The value of silence I have in the course of my teaching career learned many hard things but the hardest of all has been to shut up. The instinct to lecture children is profound and we have to chain it, and to learn to listen. Recently I was in a gallery full of sculptures, mostly of nudes, with some Year 3 children and it was a matter of minutes before two of them came racing back to me with the news, 'Ere, we found something rude'. I simulated great excitement and gathered all the children to go off and look. When I got there, towed by the boys, I was most deflated 'Oh how disappointing', I cried, 'how sad, this isn't at all rude – it's just people with no clothes on. They have to be doing something for it to be rude'. The children were surprised, almost ready to argue the case (some were clearly getting geared up to ask what it was they were doing that made it rude) when I asked them to find one of the sculptures they would like to work on in detail.

Solving a puzzle

After a little argument and some voting they chose a strange piece where a naked boy lay on a nest of snakes whilst a bear licked his leg. Above, naked goddesses leaned out from heaven looking worried and doves bearing herbs in their beaks fluttered downwards. I expressed total mystification. 'Is the boy dead?' No, they thought, not quite. 'Is the bear about to eat him up?' No, it was licking snake stuff out of a wound on his leg. 'Whatever are the ladies for?' They are in heaven. 'Oh, well what are the birds for?' They are bringing medicines down to cure the boy.

Slowly – much slower than that, in fact, the children explained the story to their rather slow and stupid teacher, and as they looked for me, and as they thought about what they saw they knew more than ever I could tell them. And when they had finished telling me, I had the sense to sit quietly with them for a short time whilst they chatted on like birds in a nest and I heard one boy say 'Ain't them ladies lovely?' and a little girl replied with some feeling 'I like the boy the best'. We had moved in half an hour from 'These are rude' to 'These are lovely', but it needed that time.

Overdoing it

We all try to show our children far too much. The coach cost a lot, the planning was difficult, we've come a long way, the children will probably never see this again, so we try to do everything. But we are seeing it, sadly, through adult eyes, not through those of children who find it hard to endure. I recall taking some Year 2 children round Fishbourne Roman Palace and when we came to the end one child said to me 'When do we get to see the palace?' She had endured the strange man jabbering on about all the old stones, in the hopes that at the end what she had clearly heard would appear – a palace. What a disappointment for her, what a lesson for me.

The locality

And thinking about going places, let us turn to the use of the environment. We often think of visits and site-work in history as being to 'big' places – national museums, cathedrals, castles, country houses. These are valuable, but let us stress at first that things which are close to school can be equally valuable. A walk down a road of Edwardian speculator-built terrace houses, observing their pattern book decoration, looking at changes in style where a new builder takes over or time advances, being shocked by infill development – this can all be good work, of great value. Close observation is difficult for children, so you will need to teach them to look up and down, to see the barge-boards and the foot-scrapers and to take careful notes of their findings. Often it is valuable to pause and sketch, not just to have a record to take home (a camera will do that better for you) but to help the children look really hard. I call this 'looking through the end of a pencil', and children quickly see the point!

The parish church

A trip to a local parish church can reveal a lot. If you are doing the Tudors, for example, think what a church would have been like with a screen and rood loft, with the priest with his back to the people whispering at the altar. If you were standing in the nave you would feel that something magical was going on there, especially as you looked up and saw heaven and hell painted on either side of the chancel arch.

Now imagine the paintings whitewashed over, the screen down, the altar removed, a communion table with the priest behind facing the people, speaking the liturgy in clear loud English. Some change – a revolution rather than a reformation, and it can all be imagined with ease in any cruciform church.

Conclusion

Not all teachers will have worked their way diligently through every exercise and argument in this book, and who can blame them? It is here to offer people the chance to look hard at methodologies that might be new to them and to fly over the areas where they already feel confident. Yet the totality of our book does lead to two quite important propositions:

- **First**, that there is a great, and growing repertoire of strategies and techniques for teaching history available for use by the primary teacher, and
- **Second**, that young children can indeed take the challenge of doing real history and can do some remarkable and remarkably valuable things if their teachers give them the help they need and point them in the right directions.

Variety and more variety

Variety of methodology is such an important component of successful teaching that it cannot be stressed too much. Pupils often see themselves as the prisoners of their teachers, and indeed they are correct – children have to come to school and there work without pay while teachers have chosen to come, are paid and even grumble about their condition! Children in these circumstances have a right to be given the most interesting and delightful curriculum that we can make without damaging their chances of effective learning, and the key to this is variety.

Each of us has our special skills and of course there are things we as teachers enjoy doing. Some, for example, are a good storytellers and enjoy telling stories and children enjoy them too. But if they did no more than tell stories, by the end of a fortnight children would be casting their eyes to heaven and miming sickness at the thought of another.

The balanced curriculum

The balanced curriculum must have a balanced methodology, and this keeps both children and teachers on their toes and makes possible that deep study that we call for throughout this volume. It was interesting in the early days of the NPHP how many teachers told us that history was too difficult a subject for young children, that they lacked the experience of life which the proper study of history needed, that there was just too much of it. We consistently responded by saying 'So, children find maths and reading phenomenally difficult – do you give up on these too?'

History is hard – one child once confided to me that it quite hurt her brain. Working with documents, with ideas, struggling with evidence and trying to explain – it quite makes you sweat to think of it. But as we have shown in the book, when you put children to these fences they will try hard and often scramble over when it looks impossible.

During this project we have seen young children succeeding at all levels – Key Stage One, Key Stage Two, non-readers as well as clever ones, inner city children as well as the middle class, disadvantaged in all sorts of ways as well as the hale and successful. The common feature is summed up by one word – pride, pride in their work and their achievements. We can think of just two examples – a little girl who claimed she could not draw at all and was not fitting in at all well with her peers – in fact there were fights galore. Yet she made a picture with two friends that really worked, and when I asked her how she felt she whispered 'Very proud'. And Huseym, who had sat for two terms apparently doing nothing who, on hearing the story of Alcibiades suddenly was shaken by the gods and in two days wrote that story in 4,300 words. If he hadn't been stopped, he would be writing now. After it was typed for him and we gave him copy, he declared, 'I do feel very proud'.

Make your children face challenges, have fun in hard work, make them proud of being young historians and you will get the bonus the project has given to us as teachers – pride and delight in our children's achievements.

Further Reference

The following books are among the many available for teachers of primary history. As well as those listed, most of the pupil books published to support primary history at Key Stage One and Key Stage Two have teacher's guides. Also, a large number of specialist books exist for teachers relating to the teaching approaches highlighted in this book such as drama, expressive movement and writing.

Andreeti, K. *Teaching history from primary evidence*. London: David Fulton Publishers, 1993.

Cooper, H. *The teaching of history: implementing the National Curriculum*. London: David Fulton Publishers, 1995.

Cooper, H. *History in the early years*. London: David Fulton Publishers, 1995.

Copeland, T. *Maths and the historic environment*. London: English Heritage, 1991.

Dean, Jacqui. *Teaching history at Key Stage 2*. Cambridge: Chris Kingston Publishing, 1995.

DES. *History in the primary and secondary years – an HMI view*. London: HMSO, 1985.

DES/HMI. *The teaching and learning of history and geography aspects of primary education*. London: HMSO, 1989.

DES. *History working group, final report*. London: HMSO, 1990.

Durbin, G. *A teacher's guide to learning from objects*. London: English Heritage, 1991.

Egan, K. *Imagination in teaching and learning*. London: Routledge, 1992.

Egan, K. *Teaching as storytelling: an alternative approach to teaching and the curriculum*. 1988.

Elton, G.R. *The practice of history*. London: Collins, 1969.

Fairclough, J. and Redsell, P. *Living history: reconstructing the past with children*. London: English Heritage, 1985.

Fines, J. and Verrier, R. *The drama of history: an experiment in co-operative teaching*. 1974.

ILEA. *History in the Primary School*. London: ILEA, 1980.

Knight, P. *History at Key Stages 1 and 2*. London: Longman, 1991.

Knight, P. *Primary geography, primary history*. London: David Fulton Publishers, 1993.

Marwick, A. *The nature of history*. London: Macmillan, 1970.

Morris, S. *A teacher's guide to using portraits*. London: English Heritage, 1991.

Pownall, J. and Hutson, N. *Science and the historic environment*. London: English Heritage, 1991.

Reeve, M. *Why history?* London: Longman, 1980.

Tosh, J. *The Pursuit of history*. 1994.

West, J. *Classroom museums*. Elm Publications. 1989.

Teachers' journals: There are two specialist journals for primary history teachers, *Teaching History* and *Primary History*. The generalist journal, *Child Education*, often contains useful materials for primary history teaching.

Useful Addresses

The following addresses may be useful to teachers as sources of information, artefacts, illustrative material, advice or possibility for visits.

Articles of Antiquity
(replica artefacts)
0161-705 1878 or 0161-736 6232

The British Museum Education Service
Great Russell Street
LONDON
WC1B 3QQ

The Cabinet War Rooms
The Education Officer
Clive Steps
King Charles Street
LONDON
SW1A 2AQ
0171-222 2168

The Council for British Archaeology
The Education Officer
The King's Manor
YORK
YO1 2EP
01904-671417

English Heritage
The Education Service
Keysign House
429 Oxford street
LONDON
W1R 2HD

The Geffrye Museum
Kingsland Road
LONDON
E2 8EA
0171-739 9893

History in Evidence
(replica objects and costumes)
Unit 4
Park Road
Holmewood
CHESTERFIELD
S42 5UY

Imperial War Museum
The Education Officer
Lambeth Road
LONDON
SE1 6HZ
0171-416 5000

The Mary Rose Trust
Education Service
Porter's Lodge
Building 1/7 College Road
HM Naval Base
Portsmouth PO1 3LJ
01705-839766

Milestone Pottery
(historical pottery replicas)
Unit 234F
Redwither Industrial Complex
Wrexham Industrial Estate
WREXHAM
LL13 9UH

The National Gallery
Education Officer
Trafalgar Square
LONDON
WC2N 5BN
0171-839 3321

The National Portrait Gallery
The Education Officer
St Martin's Place
LONDON
WC2H 0HE
0171-930 1552

The National Trust
The Education Service
36 Queen Anne's Gate
LONDON
SW1H 9AS

The National Trust for Scotland
The Education Officer
5 Charlotte Square
EDINBURGH
EH2 4DU
0131-226 5922

The Tate Gallery
The Education Officer
Millbank
LONDON
SW1P 4RG
0171-821 1313

Public Record Office
Ruskin Avenue
KEW
Richmond
Surrey
TW9 4DU
0171-392 5200

The Victoria and Albert Museum
The Education Officer
Cromwell Road
LONDON
SW7 2RL
0171-938 8500

Your local telephone directories also will be a great source of local resources and advice, such as museums, local historical sites, County Record Offices or County Archives and public library local studies departments. Many towns and even small villages may have local history groups or societies.